Here is my secret,
a very simple secret:
It is only with the heart that one can see rightly;
what is essential is invisible to the eye.

Antoine De St.-Exupery

Fiction by Susan McGeown:

A Well Behaved Woman's Life

A Garden Walled Around Trilogy:
Call Me Bear
Call Me Elle
Call Me Survivor

Rosamund's Bower

Recipe for Disaster
Rules for Survival

The Butler Did It

Joining The Club

Biblical Women
and Who They Hooked Up With

The Heart of Things

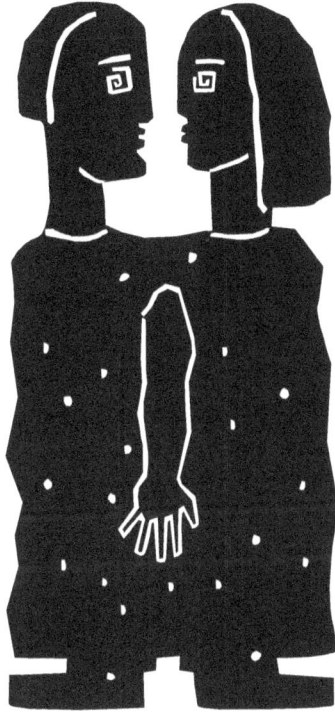

By Susan McGeown

Faith Inspired Books

Published by Faith Inspired Books
3 Kathleen Place, Bridgewater, New Jersey 08807
www.FaithInspiredBooks.com

The quoted ideas expressed in this book (but not the scripture verses) are not, in all cases, exact quotations but rather obtained from secondary sources, primarily print media. In every case, the author has made every effort to maintain the speaker's original intent. While every effort was made to ensure the accuracy of these sources, the accuracy cannot be guaranteed. For additions, deletions, corrections, or clarifications please contact Susan McGeown at the above address.

Bibliographic credit appears at the end of this work.

To Girls Important To My Heart

My daughter, Gracie
My nieces, Hannah, Maggie, and Lara
My goddaughters, Jayne-Lynn and Hannah

Table of Contents

Disclaimers and Other Stuff You Should Know

❖ The author wrote this book because upon in depth study of the following biblical women she discovered a personal change regarding herself and her perception of others. *Why not share all this good stuff?*

❖ It is the author's earnest desire that what you take away from all of this, first and foremost, is that *you* are God's. He loves *you.* He wants *you.* And the only thing that is keeping you from a personal relationship with The One True God is *you.*

❖ The author hopes that upon reading this book you might a) come to appreciate yourself and your abilities more, b) develop a clearer understanding of what God intended for you and your life, and c) hunger to learn more, grow more, and pursue more regarding God, His word, and your personal destiny.

❖ The following biblical interpretations are the expressed opinion of the author and, although arrived at through extensive research, prayer, and discussion, hold merit only with the author and those who choose to agree with her.

❖ In all cases, the author encourages you to read the biblical story *first and foremost*, as well as pray, before pursuing each chapter's study. If a Bible is unavailable to you but a computer is, www.BibleGateway.com offers numerous biblical translations (as well as languages) in which to read and study *for free.*

❖ Unless otherwise noted, any scripture quoted is from Tyndale House Publishers' *New Living Translation* Bible, the author's personal favorite.

❖ The author believes that the Bible is the true, inspired, living word of God, complete in its entirety and totally relevant to today's world. No other source is necessary to learn The Truth.

Taking it one step at a time …

A Heartfelt Introduction

Your Heart's Condition

Every relationship in your life past, present, and future is directly related to the state of your heart. That means whom you love and whom you hate, whom you are repulsed by and whom you are drawn to, whom you befriend and whom you choose to call enemy is all wrapped up with the internal, invisible, mysterious part of you. There is no exception to this rule. We call this "core" of ourselves our heart.

The state of your heart is the very essence of who you are as an individual. That means the reason people love you or hate you, seek you out or avoid you, trust or mistrust you is totally reliant on the person you project to the world. While other people's hearts and the image they project to the world are also viable factors in any relationship, if you are almost always the one who is wronged, abandoned, angered, unloved, avoided, fired, accused, or left out, then that is a pretty big personal message about you and the condition of your

> I'm just an old chunk of coal, But I'm going to be a diamond some day.
>
> Billy Joe Shaver

1

heart. Life is not about lousy coincidences or bad luck. There is no such thing.

Who you are as an individual is matchless, one of a kind. That means you're priceless. Irreplaceable. It means that all the qualities that you have inside you are all part of the precious person that you are. Do you remember the exact words to every top forties song that's ever been sung? Is it impossible for you to understand even the rudimentary concepts of basic algebra? Believe it or not: it's all necessary.

Q?

How do these italicized statements make you feel? In your opinion, are they true? Why or why not?

The unique person that you are is precisely designed and carefully and specifically created by God. Which means that the way you are is the way God wants you to be. More than that, God planned for your existence and the very person you were born to be with more precision than a rocket scientist puts into his or her life's work. Not only are all your talents and foibles accurate, they were desired and planned for to make you the person God needed you to be today.

God does not make mistakes. The very person you are as you sit and read this is exactly the person God needs you to be:

❖ The person who gets pure enjoyment from spending hours upon hours being lost in the magic of painting a picture.

❖ The person who is poetry in motion, cooking up a spur of the moment meal using just the leftovers in the family fridge.

❖ The person who can listen to a car engine and know exactly what is making that funny rattle.

❖ The person who needs only to hear a person's name once and never forgets it.

In addition, your weaknesses are the very areas in which God intends to show His greatest strengths. Your talents are the very tools with which God intends to show you your greatest joy. Your passions and loves are the directions in which God intends to lead you on this journey called life. You've got everything you need to succeed.

First Things First

Question to ask yourself before you read any further:	If everything in your life is keyed into your heart's condition, what do your life and your relationships reveal about you? What kind of shape is your heart in?
Connections:	Do any of these words apply to you: faithful, believer, self-confident, strong, trusting, honorable, reliable, joyful, or wise? Would you like them to? Wouldn't it be wonderful if, instead of aspiring to be like someone else, you liked everything about the woman that you are and wouldn't change a thing?
What the Bible says about you:	**Womb time:** Job 10:10-12, Psalm 139:13 **When your education started:** Psalm 51:5-6 **God's awareness of you:** Jeremiah 1:5a **God's protection of you:** Psalm 139:14-16 **Who designed you:** Isaiah 64:8

The Core Story

The Facts vs. The Reality

So if all of the above is true, why are people so unhappy? While we spend precious parts of our life dreaming of what we wish we could be, we miss out on the greatness of what we already are. Why do so many people feel lost? It's all about the state of our hearts. Our hearts lack faith, self-confidence, belief, trust, strength, commitment ... We might talk the talk but we don't always walk the walk. "I believe, it's just ..." "I know

> The heart has reasons that reason cannot know.
> Blaise Pascal

we're supposed to have faith, but ..." "I'm never good at ..." "I have trouble sticking to ..." More often than not we are more steadfast in our excuses as to why we can't, than why we can.

Our heart, when spoken of in the Bible, is the special thing that makes us unique and precious from *all* of God's other creations. It is from "deep in your heart" where "true knowledge exists." (Joshua 23:14)

3

According to Job, instinct comes from the mind but intuition comes from the heart. (Job 38:36) The animal world is loaded with instinctual behaviors while we human beings are pretty helpless right from the start. But this ability to be intuitive – knowing or sensing or understanding something without being able to rationally explain it all - ratchets us right up there to the top of the earthly living population. Only we have the ability to function according to our own free will. In giving us the ability to choose how we live, God gave *only us* the ability to please or disappoint Him.

Only us.

Biblical author Amos said, *"For the Lord is the one who shaped the mountains, stirs up the winds, and reveals His thoughts to mankind."* (Amos 4:13a) We're the only creatures God talks to and reveals His thoughts to. Whispers His desires and plans. Gives His instructions and commands. He does this through the inside being that we are – our hearts.

Only us.

The Inside Vs. The Outside

It's your inside person that God looks at and values. He couldn't care less about your job title, your bank account balance, or the number of wrinkles you have on your face. The Bible talks about this inside and outside concept a lot. Samuel as he searched for Israel's new king was told specifically not to judge by appearance alone. Isaiah states clearly that Christ will "not judge by appearance nor make a decision based on hearsay." (Isaiah 11:3) The truth of who you are inside is all He cares about, and it's where all of the most important things that He has given you come from. Not only does God delight in your uniqueness, He specifically desires for you to be one of a kind. He doesn't want you to be like anyone else because He already thinks you have everything you need to become the person He wants you to be.

> People judge by outward appearance, but the LORD looks at the heart.
> I Samuel 16:7b

This life we live is one gigantic testing ground where we fumble and grope to succeed. And whether we are born rich, handicapped, talented, intelligent, or disadvantaged, I firmly believe that the course of a lifetime pretty much levels the playing field for all of us. For you see, the measure of a person's true success is not determined by the world's standards but by God's. The promise of salvation through Christ is the great equalizer. Our success is not dependent on anything but the choice we make or don't make to have Him at the center of ... you guessed it ... *our heart.*

Once we choose the correct spiritual path, the different tools we have in our spiritual toolbox helps us refine the person God needs us to be. Are we using our God-given talents for Him? Are we utilizing those things that we

> **My worth to God in public is what I am in private.**
> Oswald Chambers

enjoy doing towards godly pursuits? Does the primary way that we spend our time have a God-related tone to it? Are we making God smile?

Sigh. The human race hasn't done a very good job in the listening and pleasing department. Right off the bat when the evilness of mankind got so bad "that every inclination of the thoughts of mankind's heart was only evil all the time" (Genesis 6:5) God regretted ever making mankind, saying specifically, "it broke His heart." (Genesis 6:6)

On the flip side, "heart's desires" (Job 17:11) are the most precious things we could imagine having or achieving. Only those whose hearts are "true and right" are the ones whom God shields and protects. (Psalm 7:10) Finally, a person "after God's own heart" (I Samuel 13:14) is the epitome of mankind's God directed goals.

Obviously, from the biblical perspective the heart is the definitive way to measure a person's credibility and worthiness. So, I'll ask you: How're your insides? Or, more specifically, are you a person "after God's own heart"?

Q?

What takes up the most space in your life? How can this become your strength and purpose for what God has in store for you?

The World vs. The Promise

Unfortunately, the way of this world draws us in the opposite direction from God's own heart.

In fact, despite the apparent value of our heart, we seem to spend a significant part of our life trying to mask, ignore, or downright disobey it, don't we? We are repeatedly embarrassed by personal qualities that make us unique from others. "I wish I wasn't so outspoken ..." We regularly don't value our own worth and let others redefine it to their standards. "I thought it was a good idea, but everyone else ..." We allow ourselves to become involved in situations that do not afford us the respect we deserve. "I knew it was a mistake when he invited me back to his apartment, but ..." We doubt ourselves and what we know to be right. "I know it wasn't the best thing to do, but ..."

> **The love of God pays no attention to the distinctions made by natural individuality.**
> Oswald Chambers

We ignore our heart, and in doing so we distance ourselves from God.

We ignore our heart, and in doing so we accumulate mistakes, failures, and missed opportunities that keep us from forging positively ahead into the future.

We ignore our heart, and in doing so we lose sight of the person God wants us to be.

We ignore our heart and miss joyful experiences that we are meant to have.

We ignore our heart, and in doing so do not fulfill the job that only we are capable of doing.

We ignore our heart, and end up in a place that is sad, dark, lonely, and hopeless.

Our job here on earth is to continually 'shore up' our heart: get it right, make it strong, start anew, and become improved ... GROW. The Bible addresses that, too. "Becoming a

> **God wants you beyond your resources so you have to depend on Him and His resources.**
> Rev. Dr. Todd Buurstra

new person" affords those of us with a past as bleak as a burned out forest the opportunity to get away from the smoke and ash. 2 Corinthians 5:17 states clearly, *"Anyone who belongs to Christ has become a new person. The old life is gone; a new life has begun!"*

We human beings just don't appreciate the magnitude of this promise. We repeatedly don't believe it, nor do we take advantage of it.

"My whole life is and always will be a disaster." "I've got things in my past that are too big to forget." "I've got bad luck." "I don't believe in fairy tales." "I've got issues." The first step to a changed heart is to step out on faith and believe. Eliminate "but" from your vocabulary. Give God the opportunity to show you what your life can be.

Rationalize this for me: if God is willing to forgive and forget everything bad about you and your past, why can't you? Usually it's because forgiving and forgetting involves making conscious decisions to change for the better. It means becoming proactive towards your future and taking the necessary steps to ensure your success. What you must come to understand at some point is that your refusal to let go of past disasters, making the same mistakes over and over, and failure to accept the responsibility for your life becomes your very own ... tombstone. (Sorry, but someone's got to tell you.) Aside from prayer, reading, studying and *applying* the Word of God is the single most influential way towards becoming a person after "God's own heart."

Q?

How can a weakness of yours become a strength? How can a strength become a weakness?

The Bible and You

Except for the dates, the Bible is chock full of the most private personal details of people who were just like us except for the lack of electricity and indoor plumbing. They've gone through it all and left behind a rather amazing account of how often and how gloriously they blew it. And, every now and then, how they got it right. All of their most private and personal mistakes, failures, sorrows, and bad deeds are spelled out for us in glorious black and white text to read, chuckle over, pompously shake our heads in disbelief, and ... hopefully ... learn from. Rick Warren said, "While it is wise to learn from experience, it is even wiser to learn from the experience of others." Here's a question for you: "How wise are you?"

> What lies behind us and what lies before us are tiny matters compared to what lies within us.
> Ralph Waldo Emerson

Reading the Bible is like looking into our sister's journal. It gives the opportunity to live vicariously through another person's life that is perhaps more exciting or appealing than our own. It allows us to see, up close and personal, what secrets some people have deep inside that they would *never ever* share with anyone. It permits us to see just how bad and just how good things can really be. It teaches us what should be important in our God-given life and what should be ignored.

For you see, the men and women of the Bible experienced the same things we do today: stupidity, lust, jealousy, hatred, fear, loneliness, worthlessness, sorrow and true love. They also battled with the same internal and external pressures that we struggle with: money troubles, poor self-confidence, illness, doubt, bad people who wanted to do mean things to them ... There is not one situation that we face today that someone hasn't had to deal with already in the biblical journal account. Why not take the opportunity and learn from someone else's mistakes as well as successes?

Which brings us full circle. All your relationships – *good or bad* – are a direct window into you and your heart. What do you think about that comment?

The collection of people that surround you shout loudly and clearly the condition of your heart. People are often quick to give excuses as to why that statement isn't accurate. But let's face it: the people that you are attracted to (romantically and just as friends) are specifically linked to your own individual make-up. Some people appeal, some do not, and what you are *internally* is the deciding factor.

> **May this journey bring a blessing,
> May I rise on wings of faith;
> And at the end of my heart's testing,
> With Your likeness let me wake.**
> Margaret Becker

How about this quote from the website Despair.com: "The only consistent feature of all your dissatisfying relationships is you." How terrifying is *that* quote? The first time I read it, it struck me as quite funny. But then, after its brutal frankness began to sink in, I took a big gulp and rather hesitantly began to reflect back on my rather dismal personal track record of relationships over the years.

What do people see when they look into your personality window? What do you say to others about yourself in the way you live your life? These are hard questions, whether you choose to face them or not, that in the end will be the reality of what people think of you. *You* can ignore these questions, but the impact of the answers will not go away.

The purpose of this book is to give you the opportunity to peek into some very personal diary entries and read about all the disasters that would never have been spoken about, *and maybe learn something* in the process. Give your heart a thorough examination and ...

- ❖ Apply some of the lessons.
- ❖ Do a little thoughtful introspection.
- ❖ Examine the quality of your heart.
- ❖ Realign your priorities.
- ❖ Fix what's broken.
- ❖ Strengthen what's weak.
- ❖ Find what's lost.
- ❖ Make God smile a bit.

For all of you out there ...

Each chapter of this book is going to take one biblical woman and study her heart and her resulting relationships. In addition to giving you information to help you understand the culture of the times and appreciate the story, I'll encourage you to look up some pertinent scripture about the chapter's topic and, hopefully, make you think long and hard about the person that you are versus the person you'd like to be. Maybe you will see flashes of yourself at times? Perhaps the Lord will speak to your heart as you do this study? I even give a bit of homework. The purpose of the homework is to encourage you to really pinpoint specific areas of your life that are good, bad, and

Q?

Why is it important to be able to pinpoint a moment in your life in which you were changed as a result of your relationship with God?

9

perhaps ugly so you can know where you need to focus your growth and improvement.

> **Change your attitude about prayer.**
> **It's not a spiritual wish list.**
> **It's a spiritual dialogue with your highest source of power and wisdom.**
> Sue McG

Let's start with some questions I don't ask you to write down the answers, but I would hope you could easily respond to them. And perhaps, if you can't answer these questions easily now, by the end of this study you will be able to.

❖ Can you pinpoint a moment in your life, upon making a decision to commit to Christ, that you felt new?

❖ Who is the ultimate authority in your life? Stripped down to the bare bones, whom would you risk your life with and for?

❖ What are your strengths?

❖ What are your weaknesses?

❖ What are your interests, God-given talents and abilities?

❖ What is more important to you: God's will or your will?

❖ Are good things really worth the wait?

❖ Are many of the difficulties in your life end results of choices you wish you hadn't made in the first place?

Homework ... How's your heart doing?

The life that you lead is unique to you and only you. It is as good and as bad as you choose to let it be.

> **I will give you a new heart with new and right desires and I will put a new spirit in you.**
> Ezekiel 36:26a

It begins with your heart and is directed by your strengths and your weaknesses, which *are both* God-given. You must acknowledge them and believe that they are what make you uniquely special to God.

Depending on the strength of your heart, life stresses can give you opportunities for success or failure. Are you constantly dragged down? Do you find yourself repeatedly in situations that are disastrous?

10

Depending on the strength of your heart and how you utilize your strengths and your weaknesses, you either have great joys or great sorrows. Can you delight in the wonder of your individuality? Have you made the most of who you are and embraced the things you can do and released the things you can't? Have your weaknesses become your greatest strengths?

Try filling in the worksheet on the next page. Maybe, by the time you finish the book there will be a few changes you can make, huh?

ME, MY HEART, MY LIFE

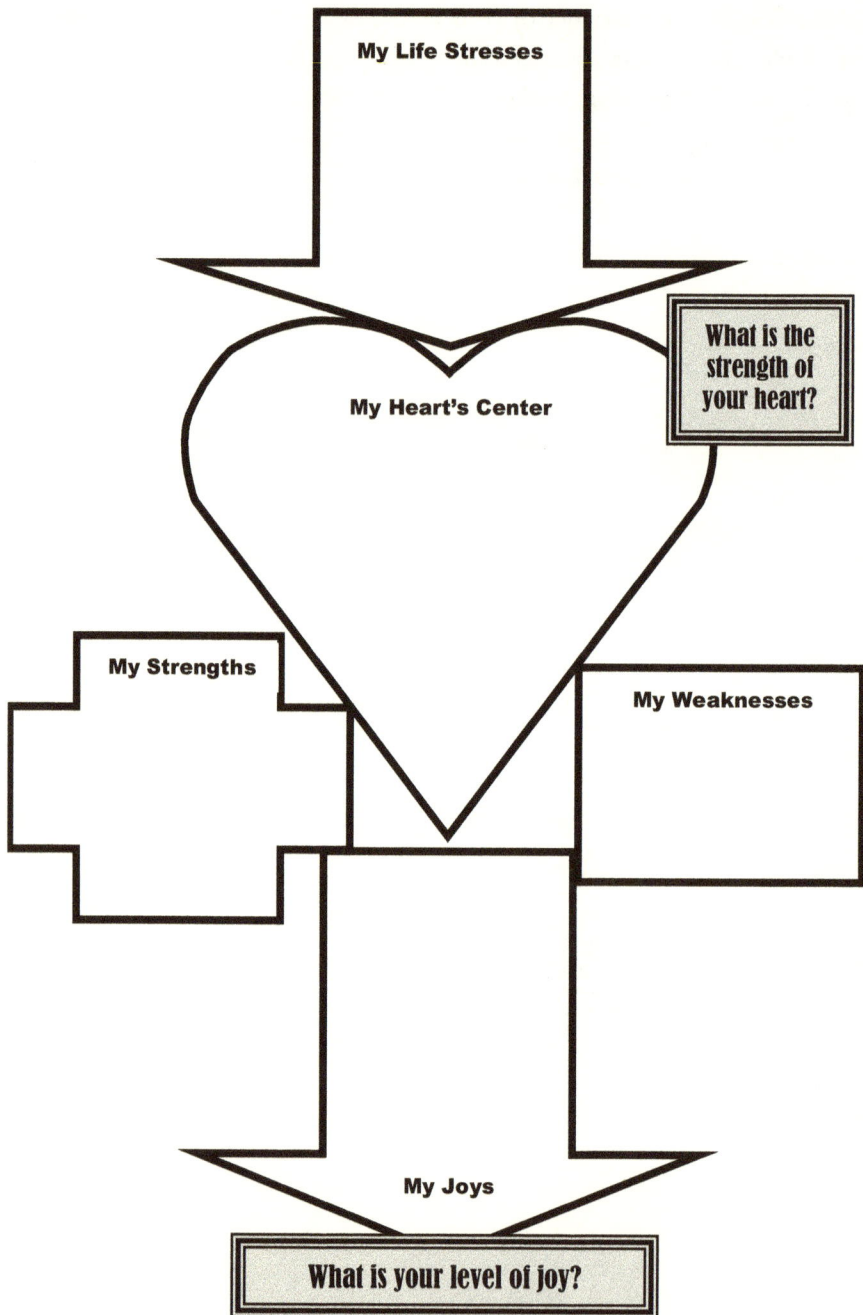

My Life Stresses

My Heart's Center

What is the strength of your heart?

My Strengths

My Weaknesses

My Joys

What is your level of joy?

Question To Discuss:

Q?

True or false:
"There is no growth without change, no change without fear or loss, and no loss without pain."
(Rick Warren)
How does your attitude towards this statement color the difficult times of your life?

Eve and The Only Guy On The Planet

A Heart of Perfection

You know Eve. The girl with the apple. The one Adam pointed to when God said, "Hey! Whose idea was it to eat the forbidden fruit?!" The person who consistently bears the brunt of the blame for the whole Garden of Eden debacle. Most famously remembered as the woman who caved when Satan decided to tempt, Eve's punishment has affected womanhood to this day: to forever bear children with intense pain and suffering, and perpetually submit to men as their masters.

> On account of [Eve] even the Son of God had to die.
> Tertullian

Salimbene, a 13th century Franciscan monk, compiled a collection of popular views of his day on women. Eve was definitely not thought of positively: "Woman was evil from the beginnings, a gate of death, a disciple of the servant, the devil's accomplice, a fount of deception, a dogstart to godly labours, rust corrupting the saints; whose perilous face hath overgrown such as had already become almost angels. Lo, woman is

14

the head of sin, a weapon of the devil, expulsion from Paradise, mother of guilt, corruption of the ancient law." Whoa. How's that for a thorough insult?

Personally, I think Eve got a bum rap. Now, don't get me wrong. I'm not here to offer excuses or place blame in another location. I simply wish that the whole person of Eve, wasn't defined by her famous moment of succumbing to temptation. (Look at it this way: How would *you* like to be remembered for your greatest personal disaster?)

The bottom line is that Eve was an ancestress of Christ. You and I can't claim that. Nor can a lot of other women. She was unique, special, and chosen. At the time when God was recounting the consequences of both Eve and Adam's poor choice, He also gave her a promise of redemption. She was the first person to be given the promise of the savior. It was *her seed* that was going to crush the head of the serpent, Satan. (Genesis 3:15)

Spend some time with me examining Eve, the person she was, and the guy she hooked up with. Take a peek into what it means to be perfect. Maybe, if we try, we'll learn something new about her and ourselves in the process. After all, haven't you always wanted to achieve perfection?

First Things First

Scripture references you should check out:	Genesis 1:26-31, Genesis 2-5
Question to ask yourself before you read any further:	What one thing would you like to change in your life that would ensure better circumstances for yourself?
What her name means:	**God-given:** "Adam" means "mankind" or "taken out of the earth" or "human being" **Adam given (while in The Garden):** "Woman" means "man-ess" or "taken out of man" **Adam given (once they are thrown out of The Garden):** "Eve" means "The Mother of All Who Have Life" or "Life-giving"

Connections:	Even though Eve was perfect, lived in paradise, and was hooked up with a heaven-made match, she had doubts about herself. Her lack of self-confidence in herself and her God-given abilities left her open for Satan's treachery, causing disaster and misery for all.
What the Bible says about being perfect:	**Regarding God and His Promises:** Psalm 18:29-31 **Regarding Perfection:** Psalm 119:96 **On Waiting For Perfection:** Ecclesiastes 11:4 **On Our Own Personal Level of Perfection and What We Should Strive For:** Matthew 5:46-48 **On Why We Cannot Judge What Is Perfect:** 1 Corinthians 13:11-12 **Advice On How To Achieve It:** Philippians 3:12-14 **Perfection On Earth:** Hebrews 9:13-15 **What It's All About:** James 1:16-18

Questions We'll Never Know The Answers To:

❖ How long were Adam and Eve in The Garden before The Fall?

❖ What was the perfect relationship like between man and woman?

❖ What was the earth like before God cursed it?

Did You Know? Interesting Biblical Facts About Eve

❖ **Equal:** God did not name Eve "Eve." Adam did that after God cast them out of The Garden. (Genesis 3:20) God named both human beings "Adam" (or, the translation, "Mankind"). (Genesis 5:2) God made no distinction between the male and female (Genesis 1:27) in His perfectly created paradise.

❖ **First:** Eve experienced everything for the very first time all on her own: childbirth (Genesis 4:1), temptation (Genesis 3:1), disobedience (Genesis 3:6), true love (Genesis 2:23-24), murder/loss of a child (Genesis 4:8), God's fury (Genesis 3:16), homelessness (Genesis 3:23) … and those are just the one's recorded in the Bible!

❖ **God's Punishment:** Genesis 3:14-19 records God's "consequences" for Adam and Eve's disobedience. The serpent was

16

cursed, forever, destined to grovel in the dust, with its ultimate punishment being defeat by the woman's offspring (Christ foretold for the first time in Genesis 3:15). For the woman, she was to have pain in childbirth and forever to be mastered by the man. (Genesis 3:16) Adam was punished to spend his entire life struggling to scratch a living from the ground to survive. And the ground itself was cursed. (Genesis 3:17-19)

❖ **Creation:** Do you find the creation story hard to swallow? Is that whole "done in six days" concept too much for you? First, you must understand that a miracle is "an event that appears inexplicable by the laws of nature." The fact that it goes beyond our comprehension is the whole purpose of a miracle. In addition we must remember two other things. First, the biblical account was not intended to be a scientific journal. Natural phenomenon's only purpose in the biblical account was for the greater glory of God's power and might. Second, "the indefinite meaning of day" (Lockyer, *Illustrated Dictionary*) causes literal objections to lose their validity. 2 Peter 3:8 states, "A day is like a thousand years to the Lord, and a thousand years is like a day." Translation: God doesn't operate within our known timeframe. Creation was a miracle we cannot explain with our scientific know-how or our limited human intellect.

The Core Story

Paradise ... Can we even begin to imagine it?

As beautiful and majestic as our world is today it cannot compare to the paradise of The Garden of Eden.

Physically, "water came up out of the ground and watered all the land ... the Lord God planted all sorts of trees in the garden – beautiful trees that produced delicious fruit ... a river flowed from the land of Eden, watering the garden ... gold was found, exceptionally pure; aromatic resin and onyx stone are also found there ... the Lord God formed from the soil every kind of animal and bird ... livestock, birds, and wild animals ..." (Genesis 2:6-20, pieces) The Garden was peaceful and lovely, filled with delicious fruit. It even smelled nice! No hurricanes or blizzards, perfect temperatures all year round. There were no thorns, no stinging bugs, no sickness or disease. Every item mankind needed to live and every condition required to make life comfortable was readily and easily available.

Man and woman did not spend their days playing and lazing in the sun. God gave them responsibilities: to multiply and fill the earth, to subdue the earth, and to be masters over the fish, birds and all animals. (Genesis 1:28) God allowed Adam to name all the animals, bringing them to him one by one. (Genesis 2:20) In doing so, Adam assumed a proprietary ownership over the creatures of The Garden just as we do when we name our pets. Mankind wasn't simply the hired help. God gave us a significant position of authority - "masters over all life." (Genesis 1:26) The required work was extensive enough that "a suitable companion" (Genesis 2:20) was required to help Adam fulfill all of the duties. These tasks required a dedicated effort to get things accomplished, otherwise the world would have gotten out of control. Mankind was originally created to be caretaker and gatherer, not farmer and hunter. Man and woman were created to work side by side, equally, sharing the load and responsibilities. Mankind would have felt a level of satisfaction of a job well done, a level of purpose for a profession tailor made for only them, and a constant level of accomplishment living within the "fruits of their labor."

Q?

If we do not desire perfection, what exactly are we seeking?

But there was more to paradise than just the physical aspect. It was a world of innocence in that there was no knowledge of pain, suffering, fear, anger, neglect, betrayal, hardship, sorrow, or hatred. Not only did these emotions not exist, but Adam and Eve *had no concept of them.* While I have never felt the pangs of starvation or the terror of rape, I am aware of the horror of such situations and live a life that is shaped by that knowledge. Adam and Eve were well and truly free. They worked for the joy of it, not because they feared homelessness and poverty. They spent time with each other, not because they feared loneliness but because the companionship was so perfect. They loved God not because they feared the consequences should they not, but because His presence was real, personal and vibrant. And they were obedient to the rules God had laid down before them, not because God had preprogrammed them to do so, but simply because they wanted to do so.

Paradise was not a life of idleness, sipping pina coladas and eating bon-bons. Paradise was a life perfectly aligned with all the things that God intended for us to have, be, and do. There were no doubts, no insecurities, and no fears. It was God's place, filled with God's creations, fulfilling God's purpose in life: His pleasure.

I'm Perfect … What is the difference between Man and beast?

Eve was the only woman who could truly say, "I wouldn't be with you if you were the only man on the planet" and really paint herself into a corner. Of course, after Eve was created, I don't think she looked at Adam and thought, "Hmmm, maybe someone nicer lives in another part of The Garden." As they were both God's first creations "in His own image" both Adam and Eve were probably the most beautiful man and woman to set foot on this planet, and were absolutely and completely delighted with each other. Think about it, for a period of time the two of them were well and truly *perfect*. And when you think about it that way, you realize that even though Adam *was* the only man on the planet, he was exactly what Eve needed. He was her personally designed, one-of-a-kind match made in heaven.

Even though Eve and Adam for a period of time were absolutely perfect, you must understand something. Adam and Eve's perfection had nothing to do with their external attributes and everything to do with whom they had allowed in the center of their hearts. For the period of time in which they allowed God and God alone to own that space they walked, talked, and communed with God, and in doing so enjoyed perfection. Being "perfect" means 'lacking nothing essential to the whole; complete of its nature or kind.' (www.freeonlinedictionary.com) Being perfect in the eyes of God meant fulfilling the ultimate purpose for which they were created.

> **Quick, name all the perfect people you know. Feel free to include yourself.**

What *was* mankind's ultimate purpose? How would you answer that question if someone posed it to you? Why did God go to all that

19

trouble to create everything in the first place? Revelations 4:11b says, *"For you created all things, and they exist because you created what you pleased."* How cool is that? God created us because it made Him happy to do so. Equate it to that bursting joy of giving birth to your child. But look closely at that verse; God created *all things* because it pleased him. So all living things on the earth were part of God's joy and design. He's the ultimate artist.

What makes human beings so exceptional, above and beyond all the other parts of God's creation, is that we're in God's image and likeness. (Genesis 1:27) *We* have the ability to know God: love Him, worship Him, serve Him, and fellowship with Him. *We* above all the rest of creation have more responsibility in that we were designed to get closer and more personal with God than anything else on this planet. While Adam and Eve walked and talked and communed with God in The Garden with no other focus than to be obedient and godly centered, they were absolutly perfect.

What's important about this level of perfection is that it was not something that God *forced* on Adam and Eve. God not only gave us the capability of getting to know Him, He gave Adam and Eve the ability to *choose* to do so. All living beings in The Garden received the preprogrammed chip that instinctually made them automatically recognize and honor God. Only mankind alone was given the ability to decide.

On the surface, Eve's relationship with Adam speaks to all those people who either a) think they themselves are perfect, or b) think the person they are interested in is absolutely perfect. In addition, Adam and Eve completely dispel any wish that many of us have that starts with, "If only ..." because their entire world was without flaw and still stuff went really, really bad. Which begs the question, "Why?" How could one perfect world plus two perfect people equal such disaster?

On first blush, of all the biblical characters, it is Eve that I have the most trouble associating with. I have no concept of what it feels like to be literally perfect, having never lived in a world towards which I was in total harmony, and having never felt I was the absolutely perfect mate for anyone. But (and this is one powerful 'but'), what I *can* associate with is the depths of her despair, the struggle with her self-doubt, and the magnitude of her failure. Talk about a reason to be depressed! When was the last time your big mistake doomed the entire future of the known world?

20

What a waste ... Why did God even bother with all this?

It really bothers me when people (once they find out I'm interested in studying the Bible) ask me the question, "Why did God bother creating Adam and Eve? If He knows everything, then He knew they were going to mess everything up, right? Why did He go to all the trouble?" Now, don't get me wrong: it's a great question. The problem is that people who ask that question have a hard time understanding what I believe to be the answer. What would you say if someone posed that question to you?

God created mankind on day six of creation (Genesis 1:26). As day seven was God's day of rest, mankind was His last and final creation. By the time God got around to creating human beings He had created all the beauty of the heavenly galaxies, all the mysteries of the ocean depths, all the magnificence of the animal kingdom, and all the glories of the world we live in. *Then* He got around to us, the epitome of all He wanted to do.

> We, your children, in your likeness, share inventive powers with you: Great Creator, still creating, show us what we yet may do.
> Catherine Cameron

The creation that would please Him the most. Only human beings were given God's likeness. The *Expository Dictionary of Bible Words* (1985) notes that "... the creation story makes it clear that the likeness-image is not of physical form: material for man's creation was taken from the earth. It is the inner nature of human beings that reflects something vital in the nature of God. Thus theologians generally agree that the likeness is rooted in all that is required to make a human being a person: in our intellectual, emotional, and moral resemblance to God, who has revealed Himself to us as a personal being. It is this likeness-image that sets human beings apart from the rest of the animal creation, and it is transmitted through the process of reproduction to succeeding generations (Genesis 5:1-3). It is this likeness-image of God that makes each human life so precious that nothing of however great value can possibly be offered in compensation for the taking of another's life (Genesis 9:5-6)."

We were the crowning glory of His creation! The only creature God created that had the ability to *choose* whether it was going to obey, love and honor the Creator. He gave us the capacity to give Him the greatest of all joys: unconditional love. And in so doing, He gave us the privilege of causing Him the greatest of sorrows: rejection and disobedience.

So why did God go to all the trouble? L-O-V-E. For God's crowning achievement of all He created here on earth, He wanted our love for Him to be freely given, just as His is to us, not instinctual or preprogrammed. Did He know that Adam and Eve were going to blow it big time in The Garden? Of course. I must conclude that the importance of our unconditional love and, consequently our obedience, will be worth it all to Him in the end.

Hi, I'm Eve … If I'm so perfect, why did I mess up?

Take a moment to think about the person that Eve was and the life that she lived. She was the most gorgeous female on earth, she'd hooked up with the perfect man, and she lived in paradise. Yet when Satan began to tempt her according to the Biblical account, she barely hesitated before doing what had been specifically forbidden: "But the Lord God gave him this warning: 'You may freely eat any fruit in the garden except fruit from the tree of the knowledge of good and evil. If you eat of its fruit, you will surely die.'" (Genesis 2:16-17)

Hmmm. Seems pretty clear to me. Except … that warning was given to Adam. It's not until four verses later in the biblical journal that God even creates Adam's companion. (Genesis 2:21) Would that have been a good enough excuse? "Well, God told Adam, but He didn't specifically tell me!" Eve said with an indignant huff. "How was I supposed to know?" It is to Eve's credit that, after the fact, she does not use this argument. And it is, perhaps, the most powerful argument as to why Adam bears equal blame when everything bad goes down. The facts are when Satan tempted, both Adam and Eve were standing side-by-side listening to the sales pitch. Eve by her actions was wrong and Adam in his silence was equally culpable.

Did Eve, in her 'clone-like' creation from Adam's rib, possess all the innate knowledge and skill that Adam was created with? Did the two of them cut a wide berth around The Tree because they both knew it was a big no-no? I suppose they could have been morbidly fascinated with the forbidden tree, always walking by it and thinking about it (just like little kids when you say, "Now don't touch this, it's breakable"). Or did they not even think twice about the only forbidden plant in their magnificent paradise? Were they too busy having fun with all they had been blessed with to give it a second thought? Maybe Satan got frustrated with the two of them and their obedience, and that's why he decided to make his famous serpentine appearance. Whatever the scenario, I am fairly certain that Eve knew not to touch or to eat from the tree. It is inconceivable to me that Adam, in his delight over the God's final creation that was "bone of [Adam's] bone and flesh of [Adam's] flesh" (Genesis 2:23), neglected to warn Eve against eating the only thing in The Garden that could cause her death.

And while we're asking questions, I'm compelled to wonder why God would warn Adam about the tree of knowledge and not about Satan? Hello? Doesn't that seem like a really big omission? "Don't go out in the open field … Oh, did I forget to mention the big, angry bull?"

My teenager has a rule that he can't go in to other people's homes unless an adult is present. Good rule, right? I haven't elaborated on all of the possible scenarios that could happen should he disobey me. Why? Well, first, *I'm the boss of him.* I don't really have to justify myself to a thirteen year old, now do I? Second, *I'm more knowledgeable and know what's wise and what's not.* I've got all kinds of experience that makes me better equipped to decide what's safe and what's not. Third, some of the scenarios are above and beyond his current level of understanding of the world and what … evilness is out there. To explain in detail what *could* happen would ratchet my son and his knowledge up to a level that I'm not ready for him to have.

But there's a last piece to the whole "here's the rule but I don't need to explain myself concept." There's a level of trust I need to establish with my son so I know what I can trust him with in the future. With bigger and more important things. And my son needs to establish a complementary relationship where he knows I'm consistent, fair, wise, and trustworthy. (*I* know I'm these things, but my son needs to have some experiences so *he* comes to know it, too.) He goes out into the big, bad world and he watches, listens, learns, and experiences what is out there. He and I grow a relationship that is rooted in trust, love, and respect. He understands that I am who I say I am and worthy of his faith. I witness his obedience and give him greater responsibilities. And in the process, he proves to himself what his strengths are, what his weaknesses are, and whom he should and shouldn't put his reliance in. Some lessons are easy and some lessons … are not.

God was doing the same thing with Adam and Eve. He put the Tree of Knowledge in The Garden and said, "Don't touch or eat from it." And while *God knew* how the whole thing was going to play out, Adam and Eve had to learn a really tough lesson.

The name "Satan" translated literally from the Hebrew means "adversary." (Christian Apologetics & Research Ministry) Given a variety of names in the Bible such as Lucifer, The Prince of Darkness, and Beelzebub, he is most commonly referred to as the devil.

Satan was at one point in his career an angel of heaven who through his own greed fell from grace with God. Some scholars attribute Ezekiel's message to the evil king of Tyre to Satan himself: "You were the perfection of wisdom and beauty. You were in Eden, the garden of God. Your clothing was adorned with every precious stone – red carnelian, chrysolite, white moonstone, beryl, onyx, jasper, sapphire, turquoise, and emerald – all beautifully crafted for you and set in the finest gold. They were given to you on the day you were created. I ordained and anointed you as the mighty angelic guardian. You had access to the holy mountain of God and walked among the stones of fire. You were blameless in all you did from the day you were created until the day evil was found in you. Your great wealth filled you with violence, and you sinned. So I banished you from the mountain of God, I expelled you, O mighty guardian, from your place among the stones of fire. Your heart was filled with pride because of all your beauty. You corrupted your wisdom for the sake of your splendor. So I threw you to the earth and exposed you to the curious gaze of kings. You defiled your sanctuaries with your many sins and your dishonest trade. So I brought fire from within you, and it consumed you. I let it burn you to ashes on the ground in the sight of all who were watching. All who knew you are appalled at your fate. You have come to a terrible end, and you are no more." (Ezekiel 28:12-19)

Interesting, huh? We must assume, as God does not create anything but good, Satan must have originally been created good but, just as mankind was allowed a choice, so too were the angels. How many times have you thought to yourself, "If only I could see with my own two eyes … (fill in the blank) … then I would believe"? For me it is mind boggling that Satan, *in the presence of God and seeing all of His majesty*, still chose to reject Him. It vividly illustrates to me the level of malevolence that we are up against in our daily lives.

Satan, at this point in the biblical journal, chooses to possess a serpent "the shrewdest of all creatures the Lord God had made." (Genesis 3:1) Shrewd means 'characterized by keen awareness, sharp intelligence, and often a sense of the practical. Disposed to artful and cunning practices; tricky.' (www.freeonlinedictionary.com) We must remember that the snakes we know *today* are not as the snake was in The Garden. After the fall, God said to the serpent, "Because you have done this, you will be punished. You are singled out from all the domestic and wild animals of the whole earth to be cursed. You will grovel in the dust as long as you live, crawling along on your belly." (Genesis 3:14) Now *that's* the way I picture a snake! But during the time in The Garden, the snake would have been the antithesis of what we know today.

> **Eve was designed for paradise. That means so are you. Can't comprehend what that means? Join the club…**
>
> *No one's ever seen or heard anything like this, Never so much as imagined anything quite like it— What God has arranged for those who love Him.*
>
> I Corinthians 2:9 MSG

Eve does not seem surprised that it speaks to her, does she? Is it conceivable that they had had conversations before? Was the serpent so clever that the ability to communicate through speech was part of its design? Had both Adam and Eve had conversations in the past with the serpent, perhaps philosophical discussions and an occasional prank now and then? When the conversation commenced between Eve and the serpent it didn't seem like anyone was surprised at the exchange.

Just what exactly was Satan's lure? What could he have said to Eve that was enough to make her risk everything? What was Satan's sales pitch that kept Adam silent and willing to risk all they currently had? Satan said to Eve, "You won't die. God knows that the moment you eat from that tree, you'll see what's really going on. You'll be just like God, knowing everything, ranging all the way from good to evil." (Genesis 3:4-5, MSG) Had the possible previous philosophical discussions between Eve and the serpent caused her to have a level of trust of the serpent's observations and conclusions? Was Satan all that more clever to entice Eve (and silent, observing Adam) with a venue that was comfortable and reliable from past experiences? Had the man and woman been careful to obey God's instructions in every way until Satan used the one area where they were the weakest: a trusted source? The Bible records Eve's thoughts as, "When the Woman saw that the tree looked like good eating and realized what she would get out of it - she'd know everything! - she took and ate the fruit." (Genesis 3:6, MSG)

Q?

Why was Eve's desire to "know everything ... good and evil" so bad?

Seems like Eve, even though she was well and truly perfect, had a few doubts about herself. Because isn't that what wanting something that you don't have is all about? Things you don't have but dream about or covet. But let's not use that word as it gets us into the whole Ten Commandments thing. Temptation – 'the desire to have or do something that you know you should avoid; the feeling that accompanies an unsatisfied state.' (www.freeonlinedictionary.com)

These desires can be as big as another job, a better home, a fancier car, more cooperative children, an attentive husband ... or as insignificant as the $100 gel tip manicure your girlfriend gets but you can't afford ... Even worse are those nonmaterial things that reflect what we perceive as lacking within ourselves and often desperately crave: beauty, intelligence, talents, or strengths. Wanting something at all costs. Needing something badly enough that you're willing to bend the rules 'just this once.' Craving things that we cannot or do not have leads us open to temptations for things we don't have and don't need – *at God's design*. The reality is anything that steers you away from God's purpose and plan is wrong.

So the perfect woman wanted more. Can you believe it? She wanted to be even better than she already was. Think about it. Eve rejected the person that God had made her to be. She decided that she would take it upon herself to improve that which was already whole and good. Whoa. *She corrected God.* That's pretty serious when you think of it that way.

Unfortunately, that is exactly where each and every one of us is *identical* to Eve. We're her twin sisters in self-doubt and low self-esteem. Because the reality is, *we* are just as perfect or just as imperfect as *we* choose to be, just as Eve was. God, you see, does not make mistakes. *He is the Rock; His deeds are perfect. Everything He does is just and fair. He is a faithful God who does no wrong; how just and upright He is!* (Deuteronomy 32:4) The person that you are, right now, is exactly the person God needs you to be to fulfill the mission that only you can complete. You see, what you must understand is that aside from the goal of your heart, you are already perfect in God's eyes.

Q?

Can you think of examples when innocence versus knowledge impacted your life?

Things We Do For … What made Adam & Eve so special?

Why do you think that Eve turned to Adam with the forbidden fruit once she'd eaten it? I don't think a lot of people realize that during Eve's entire conversation with the serpent, Adam was standing right next to her. "She also gave some to her husband, who was with her." (Genesis 3:6) Was it because Eve suddenly realized she'd screwed up big time and wanted the two of them to go down together? Maybe Adam had silently shaken his head 'no' during the entire episode, but Eve, stubborn and inherently the more evil of the two, refused his good advice? Is it possible that the two most precious examples of God's creation fell hook, line, and sinker for Satan's twisted logic? If Adam truly loved Eve (and I believe he did) and he thought she was doing something bad or dangerous, wouldn't he have stopped her? How could Adam have stood there as silently as a stone if he believed that Eve was making such a horrible, life altering decision?

No, when Eve ate the fruit and then turned to give some to Adam, I think it was something more. Was Eve eager to share something with her lover, friend, and partner? Were they so close that one rarely did something without the other? What would it be like to be completely committed to someone with *no knowledge* of heartache, betrayal or sorrow? "Adam! It's delicious! It's terrific! You've got to have some, too!" That Adam ate the fruit without hesitation tells me that he had no concern over the right or wrong of it. He'd heard the serpent speak to Eve. Why should he question or doubt her? These two human beings were completely equal. There was no mistrust or deception, no calculated manipulation or unhealthy jealousy. Their heads and hearts, up to this time, had been simultaneously focused on godly pursuits. The concept of doubt or fear just didn't exist.

I have a hard time factoring in disharmony with Adam and Eve. I suppose there was the awkward "getting to know you stage" and the "first misunderstanding" and, perhaps, the occasional "I thought you were going to do that …?" moment. But, in general, I think this was a true love match – from start to finish. They depended on each other for companionship, support, help, advice, and pleasure. Quite frankly, God joined this couple. It had to have been a true love match because *God is love. Love comes from God. Anyone who loves is a child of God and knows God. But anyone who does not love does not know God, for God is love.* (I John 4:7-8)

Don't all of us on our wedding days, have (or dream of) similar reactions of joy with each other as Adam had for Eve when he cried,

> **The things we do for love, The things we do for love …** 10cc

"Finally! Bone of my bone, flesh of my flesh! Name her Woman for she was made from Man." (Genesis 2:23-24 MSG). Or, the Sue Translation (ST), "At last! Someone who knows me inside and out! Someone who is absolutely perfect for me." Don't we all search for a love just like that? Happiness in a relationship is a perfect complement. I believe that Adam and Eve had that.

I also believe as Eve handed that fruit to Adam she genuinely wished to give him something wonderful. What about God's decree? What about her obvious blatant disobedience? The great deceiver (AKA Satan) played all the cards right. He was so clever, so insidious, that Eve never realized how he'd played her. Adam, trusting and loving, never even questioned what Eve thrust into his hand and simply ate it as instructed. Having stood beside his mate for the whole conversation with the serpent, Adam obviously was as convinced as Eve. Their resulting newfound knowledge, real and terrible and amazing, caused them to realize things about themselves and their life and their situation that must have terrified them. By the time God appeared for His daily walk in The Garden with His two most amazing creations, Adam and Eve were hiding in the bushes.

Q?

How can the desire to improve ourselves be different from the desire to learn and grow?

Do you think God asked all His questions of Adam and Eve because He didn't know the answers? "Where are you? ... Who told you you were naked? ... Did you eat from that tree I told you not to eat from? ... What is this that you've done?" (Genesis 3:9-12 MSG) Doesn't He sound like a disappointed parent dealing with a pair of disobedient children? *Maybe* God asked His questions not to find out what happened, but to hear how the two would answer.

Knowledge can be a terrible thing. It involves the loss of innocence and the understanding of the harsh realities of life. We protect our children from sexual predators, violence in the media, and drugs. And yet, when the unthinkable occurs and the knowledge breeches all of our carefully established boundaries, we cannot go back in time and replace the innocence lost. Once it is gone, it is gone forever. We know that today and God knew it back then. The event that He knew was coming - the loss of companionship with His precious creation - had happened. Now the damage control needed to be done. Stipulations and new rules needed to be written. New policies and accommodations made. Childhood innocence was forever vanished.

Despite all that love and perfection.

The Defining Moment ... How can we survive tragedy?

Have you ever made a choice that resulted in joblessness, homelessness, and the complete destruction of everything you considered familiar? That is what Adam and Eve faced as they were forced by God to leave The Garden. Standing outside The Garden's entrance, wearing clothes of animal skins, the realization of the consequences of their choice would have been crushing. Turning back to look at the entrance to The Garden they would have seen "mighty angelic beings" stationed as guards to keep them from ever returning. (Genesis 3:24) No second chances here.

I guess, had all this happened today and the choices a partner made in a relationship caused disasters such as homelessness, joblessness and unbelievable pain and suffering, the two could divorce citing "irreconcilable differences." As it was, Adam and Eve had to stick together or die out in the harsh realities of the big, bad world, because they literally had no one to lean on but each other.

Which could lead to a second scenario where Adam spent their remaining years together making comments (blatant or subtle) about "how things used to be ...," and "remember how nice it was ...," and "before you got us in trouble ...." As a result Eve would have become angry, bitter, and resentful of his behavior: "Adam, are you ever going to let this go and *just move on?*" In addition, as life has a tendency to do, the life of Adam and Eve had a significant amount of additional sorrow and disaster ahead. Things were pretty bad, but they weren't really going to get too much better. At least not like it had been when they were perfect and lived in paradise. This union, so wonderful and full of promise at the start, had the makings of one enormous train wreck.

> **Marriage is an interpersonal relationship with governmental, social, or religious recognition, often created as a contract, or through civil process. Civil marriage is the legal concept of marriage.**
> www.wikipedia.com

But even though Adam and Eve sinned, got thrown out of paradise and faced innumerable additional hardships over the course of their lives, they were and always remained a couple expressly designed for each other by God. God did not design Eve from the dust of the earth as He did Adam, but from Adam himself. God intended for them to be *as one.* The creative work of the creation of mankind were not complete until there was both a male and female counterpart. (Genesis 2:18) Marriage is synonymous with the term *oneness.*

Eve: A Heart of Perfection

Adam and Eve showed all of us that even with the quality of being perfect, the ability to exercise free will does not guarantee a happily-ever-after ending. After their first big mistake, Adam and Eve *had to* decide to make their life together work. They could sit down in the dust and cry, waiting for death to claim them. *And it would have.* The consequences of our actions rarely disappear even once we clue in and get on the right path: prison sentences still must be served, children conceived out of wedlock do not disappear, sexually transmitted diseases don't fade away, and reputations often live longer than we do. While God does forgive and completely forget, we must learn to live with the results of our actions.

And that is where new opportunities to shine arise. You see, at any point along the path we can change our hearts and renew our goals and begin to make God smile by our choices. *At any point.*

I particularly hold dear the part of the story in which Adam named Eve. You see, up until the point where the two exit The Garden they are *both* known to God simply as "Adam" – human. (Genesis 5:2) Adam, up until this point, had simply referred to Eve as "Woman." (Genesis 2:23) But standing outside paradise, chastised and alone, facing absolute and complete uncertainty, Adam felt compelled to rename his woman.

What would you have named the person who caused your career to end, your house to burn to the ground, and the most precious relationship you could ever hope to have to be permanently altered? "Disaster?" "She Who Listens to Snakes?" "I Told You So?" No, Adam looked at his partner, the woman God had made expressly for him and him alone, and recommitted to her amidst the smoking rubble they were standing in. He called her Eve, "The Mother of All Living." (Genesis 3:20) He recognized that they were in this together, this partnership was until death parted them, and that either one without the other was worthless. Adam loved Eve, he did not blame her, he was committed to her, and he acknowledged this with the name he gave her.

Q?

Why do we struggle so to be different from what we currently are within this moment of time?

31

Consequences ... Awww, do I have to?

Let's take a look at the consequences of Adam and Eve's disobedience in The Garden. God took each aspect of The Fall and dealt with it precisely and matter–of–factly.

Eve pointed a finger at the serpent when God inquired as to how she could have so blatantly disobeyed Him. "The serpent tricked me," she said, "that's why I ate it." (Genesis 3:13)

To the serpent, God said, "Because you've done this, you're cursed, cursed beyond all cattle and wild animals, cursed to slink on your belly and eat dirt all your life." (Genesis 3:14 MSG) What do you take from this? Since God is completely fair, I'm forced to conclude that the serpent, "shrewdest of all the creatures the Lord God had made" (Genesis 3:1) had some fault in all this. It was *not* an innocent creature, possessed by Satan, unable to withstand being used. However, it was in paradise that consequences for its involvement with Satan's deception resulted in its absolute reversal of fortunes. No longer shrewd, no longer above cattle and wild animals, no longer superior in appearance or style of living, the punishment for the serpent removed all traces of its ability for an advanced state. If God did that to an animal of limited intellectual knowledge, we can begin to understand how He feels with wicked and disobedient human beings gifted with His very own image.

To the woman, God said, "You will suffer terribly when you give birth. But you will still desire your husband, and he will rule over you." (Genesis 3:16 CEV) Pain and pleasure: that desire to be unified and one with your mate will result in pain and possible death giving birth to the children you conceive. Still charged with the responsibility to "be fruitful and multiply" and ingrained with all the physical and emotional qualities that go along with those desires, the final difficult result of childbirth will rest only with the woman. How could it have been in paradise before the fall if this is the revision after the fall? Man, wouldn't I just love to know!

Additionally, the equality initiated in paradise between man and woman will shift. No longer will male and female work easily in a unified, identical position, but forever there will be the concept of one being better, stronger, more superior and powerful. Women will always seem to get the short end of the stick and man will always seem to be control the rules.

Remember the next time someone implies a woman shouldn't teach a man or become a minister … this was *not* God's plan for us. (Christ, during His ministry here on earth was an outspoken supporter of women and their importance in His plan.)

For Adam, God said, "Because you listened to your wife and ate the fruit I told you not to eat, I have placed a curse on the ground. All your life you will struggle to scratch a living from it. It will grow thorns and thistles for you, though you will eat of its grains. All your life you will sweat to produce food, until your dying day. Then you will return to the ground from which you came. For you were made from dust, and to the dust you will return." (Genesis 3:17-19) No longer will work be a joyful, fulfilling experience. Now it will become a difficult job and absolutely necessary for survival. Besides life-sustaining fruits and vegetables, weeds and thorns will infiltrate your harvest causing complications and disasters. The pressures of providing, the fear of starvation, the specter of failure will haunt you right up until the moment of your death. Welcome to the school of hard knocks.

What cannot be overlooked, however, amid the smoking ruins of paradise lost, is the first glimpse of a way out. Yes, yes the path is much longer, dangerous, and tortuous now. Yes, had we been obedient and remained God-focused we would have achieved this glorious end with much more joy and efficiency. But, hey, Adam and Eve were given the ability to pick Door Number One or Door Number Two and they chose … the wrong door. To the serpent, God says, "I'm declaring war between you and the Woman, between your offspring and hers. He'll wound your head, you'll wound his heel." (Genesis 3:15 MSG)

Did you catch that? God issued a formal declaration of war on Satan in The Garden. Satan may have thrown down his gauntlet, he may have succeeded in successfully tempting God's precious creations, but God was not willing to concede anything. "You may cause pain and discomfort to Eve and her descendants, but Eve's offspring will deliver a death blow to you." (ST) Did Satan's fall begin when he moved to encourage Eve to disobey? Was Satan's fall sometime before all this, but was the instance in The Garden Satan's first blatant adversarial confrontation with God? Had the battle between Satan and God begun long before the creation of The Garden with Satan taking one third of the angels of heaven with him?

33

(Revelations 12:3-4) More questions we'll never know the answers to, probably.

Always remember this: no matter how bad things seem to be (and for Adam and Eve you've got to admit things were just about as horrible as they could get), God is in charge.

Relax, everyone. It's all under control.

The End ... Or is it the beginning?

And how did Eve react? I suppose she could have gotten righteously indignant once the dust settled and Adam and she stared at each other outside The Garden's gates. Hand on hip and finger pointed in accusation, Eve could have shouted, "Why didn't you stop me?" "Why didn't you remind me not to touch the fruit?" "Why did you tell God I gave you the fruit?" In addition, Eve could have whined, "Why couldn't He have given us a second chance?" "All the hard work, all the obedience, all we've faithfully done for Him and we mess up *once* and this is what we get?" "The punishment is too harsh! I was only trying to better myself!" "I hate God." "I'm done with God." Eve could have done the blame game and spent countless years refusing to face reality. She made a choice despite clear instructions to the contrary, and now she must deal with the consequences.

I don't think Eve did that. I believe that Adam and Eve, no longer perfect but still a team, trudged off into the sunset determined to recommit and determined to refocus. Let's face it, they knew exactly what they had lost. Faced with the inevitability of their situation they began to work towards survival and obedience, and with all their newly acquired knowledge, nothing would be as easy as it once had been before. Innocence lost means guilt acquired. The consequences were that they now bore the responsibility for their choices, their situation, and their future. All now rested on their shoulders. Welcome to ... hell.

Both Adam and Eve faded pretty quickly from the scene once they were banned from The Garden. But there was one last glimpse of them as a couple, and so I'm led to believe that this must have been the most important thing we, as readers of this journal entry, must take away from this story. The Bible recorded them making love and conceiving a child.

34

Actually, it's a little less romantically stated. "Now Adam had sexual relations with his wife, Eve, and she became pregnant." (Genesis 4:1) But then Moses wasn't competing for Top Romance Author of the Year award. What was it like for Adam and Eve to discover that they were going to have a child? I'm sure they had all the wonder and fear that comes with that discovery. Did both Adam and Eve remember the consequences of God's anger over their disobedience? Did Adam think, "How am I going to provide for a baby when I'm having enough trouble making ends meet for just Eve and me?" Did Eve think, "What is pain? Will I suffer long? Surely the child will be born healthy and strong? Can I do this?" Once again it was an experience that they went through together.

Together, Adam and Eve would weather the first murder between their sons Cain and Abel (Genesis 4:8) and would deal with God's punishment of Cain when he was banished to exist as a homeless fugitive for the remaining days of his life. (Genesis 4:11-12) They would follow God's directive and be fruitful and multipl, giving birth to countless male and female children.

At Cain's birth was the last biblically recorded thing that Eve said: "With the LORD's help, I have produced a man!" (Genesis 4:1b) Or, "God has given me another Adam!" (ST) Obviously, the circumstances of Eve's life had not taken God out of the equation. She attributed the wonderful occurrence of the birth of her child to God's help. Eve's life was radically different from when she first started out, but she had *chosen* to not exclude God when things had become less than perfect. She still knew *that God causes everything to work together for the good of those who love God and are called according to His purpose for them* (Romans 8:28) because she had seen both sides of that coin. And because of this, Eve kept God as a part of her life and of her relationship with the guy she loved.

For all you Eves out there …

So, what lessons can you apply to your life from the account of Eve and whom she hooked up with? First and foremost you must remember what Adam and Eve's perfection was based on. Nothing external. It was all internal. Their perfection was gone in the blink of an eye the moment they both chose not to allow God to rule their hearts and minds.

Eve started out hooked up with God, but then fell away from that perfect relationship. Blessed with her soul mate, Adam, she was able to get back on track and work towards getting back to the right relationship she needed to have with The One True God. We, as descendants of Adam and Eve, are creatures with an identical capacity for personal thought and childlike understanding. We also have the same God-given ability to choose to seek perfection … or not.

Q?

How can we determine the boundary between when God smiles and when He stops?

I like the way the apostle Paul talked about perfection. *"I don't mean to say that I have already achieved these things or that I have already reached perfection. But I press on to possess that perfection for which Christ Jesus first possessed me. No, dear brothers and sisters, I have not achieved it, but I focus on this one thing: Forgetting the past and looking forward to what lies ahead, I press on to reach the end of the race and receive the heavenly prize for which God, through Christ Jesus, is calling us."* (Philippians 3:12-14)

Forgetting the past …

Looking forward to what is ahead …

Pressing on to reach … the heavenly prize …

Sounds like a plan, doesn't it?

❖ **Good Choices and Bad:** Remember, Eve was wrong for her initial actions, but Adam was just as wrong for saying nothing to stop her. Doing *nothing* is doing *something*. Not speaking up and voicing The Truth or not correcting a wrong when it is being committed makes you culpable. Culpable as in "deserving of blame or censure, as being wrong, evil, improper, or injurious." (www.freeonlinedictionary.com)

❖ **Exemption:** Being superior in appearance, position, or ability does not excuse our guilt. Just as God created the serpent to be cleverer than any of the other creatures He had made, He also sentenced that same creature to eat dirt and die. Never, ever should any of us become complacent about our place within God's plan. We are necessary for what we can do for His greater glory and design, and nothing more. As soon as we pursue our own agenda we are spectacularly and frighteningly alone and undefended.

❖ **Focus:** Being perfect does not guarantee that you won't make mistakes. In fact, it might actually blind you into a false sense of complacency, so that when disaster sneaks up on you you don't even recognize it until after it's too late. Psalm 57:1-3 gives a good standard for how you should approach every step of your life:

Recognize You Can't Do It On Your Own:

Have mercy on me, O God, have mercy! I look to you for protection.

Know Where To Go In Times Of Trouble:

I will hide beneath the shadow of your wings until the danger passes by.

Know Whom To Ask For Advice:

I cry out to God Most High, to God who will fulfill His purpose for me.

Recognize Where True Power Lies:

He will send help from heaven to rescue me, disgracing those who hound me.

Understand The Reasons Behind It All:

My God will send forth his unfailing love and faithfulness.

❖ **Believe:** The person that you are is *exactly* the person God needs you to be. You must believe that for what God needs you to do right this very minute: You. Are. Just. Perfect. For. God. Right. Now. Your only flaws are the ones you perceive in yourself that keep you from following through with what God wants you to do. Rick Warren in his book *A Purpose Driven Life* says, "God never does anything accidentally, and He never makes mistakes." Stop focusing on what you're missing and concentrate on all you've got to offer.

❖ **Forgive:** Don't. Keep. Score. Dwelling on past mistakes prevents you from forging ahead positively into the future. You must learn to let go of your past failures as well as your mate's. God forgot your disasters as soon as you asked His forgiveness. Why can't you? King David, an abject failure as a husband and father but also known as "the man after God's own heart," sang about forgiveness in Psalm 32 (vs. 1-3 MSG):

Count yourself lucky, how happy you must be -
you get a fresh start, your slate's wiped clean.
Count yourself lucky - GOD holds nothing against you
when you're holding nothing back from Him.

❖ **Trust:** Just as Adam and Eve were provided with the perfect mate, you too have one out there somewhere in the

> Be the change
> you want to see
> in the world.
> Mahatma
> Gandhi

world. And *no*, before you ask, I don't believe you can find him or her on your own. That's where faith comes in: believing in something that you can't see or touch. Commit to pray for this person, commit to wait for this person, commit to believe that this person is doing the same for you, and commit to not settling for anyone less than the very best. Trust me, it will be worth the wait.

❖ **Commit:** Be determined to find the perfect heavenly-fashioned companion for yourself or work to create that sort of relationship with the person you are already with. He or she may not be as easily acquired as Adam found Eve, and yet you have every reason to believe that God's plan and desire for you is nothing less than "a perfect match." Remember what Adam and Eve had in common that promoted their success: a like-minded spiritual focus, a similar passion for the environment in which they chose to

> True freedom
> comes from
> obedience and
> knowing what
> *not* to do.
> NLT

live, a joint attitude of commitment, love and forgiveness, and a relationship rooted in innocence and purity.

❖ **Remain Vigilant:** Even the most perfect relationships must be nurtured and prized. Kind words never go out of fashion, loving expressions are always appreciated, and

thoughtful signs of appreciation are never wasted. Even if your mate is not yet suitable for the "perfect" category, what areas are pretty close? Have you shared that with him or her lately? Temptation to become complacent is a danger we cannot afford. Temptation in and of itself is not wrong. *Giving in to* temptation is the problem.

❖ **Stay Faithful:** Oswald Chambers says that, "Faith is the heroic effort of your life." It's pretty easy to be pleased with God when things are going well in your life and just as easy to blame God when things go down the tubes. You *cannot* be casual about your faith-walk in the day-to-day existence of your life only to become intensely spiritual when things start to get rocky. Your relationship with God is either a committed, loving relationship or it is a casual acquaintance. *You* and only you must set the standards.

❖ **Love:** Remember that the dominating emotion that was the force behind the creation of this world was *love.* Operating within that emotion towards *yourself* first and foremost, and then towards all others, redefines the world you live in.

How well do you know yourself? If you are unsure of what you want out of your life then you are on shaky ground trying to hook up with someone. Spend a few moments and work on the next few pages, which will make you think about yourself spiritually, emotionally, socially, and physically. Once you complete this list concerning yourself, you need to think about who will complement you best. What about your mate or the mate of your dreams? Do you know what you need? What you should be looking for? What qualities would ensure your success as a couple? Prayerfully and seriously consider these things. Don't just reach into the dating basket, randomly choose someone, and settle. Your choice of a mate should be *based on what God has given you and whom He would choose to be the best mate for you.*

Homework ... What makes you a uniquely perfect person?

Think about the person that you are, the person that God has specially designed. What makes you unique? Note that I did not ask what makes you perfect or superior or particularly wonderful in the *world's* eyes. I don't want comparisons. I'm simply asking what makes you *you*? What makes you *precious*? What makes you *one of a kind*?

You must begin to value and appreciate the person you are, the person God has created that is you. Embracing the

> Others were given in exchange for you.
> I traded their lives for yours because you are precious to me.
> You are honored, and I love you.
> Isaiah 43:4

uniqueness of yourself and delighting in the differences you have from everyone else is the first step towards being a vital person in any relationship, with mates, friends, colleagues, strangers, and most importantly, God.

Becoming perfect is like eating an elephant – seemingly impossible. But have you ever heard that joke? How *do* you eat an elephant? *One bite at a time.* The steps to becoming perfect in God's eyes begin by looking at yourself as God sees you and recognizing the things God has given you to enable you to do your job here on earth. Once you begin to value what you have and what you are capable of, then God begins to use you in marvelous and wonderful ways. Being really, truly perfect involves being focused solely on God and using all of your God-given strengths and weaknesses to His greater glory. *That's* a perfect life.

Oswald Chamber said, "God will never reveal more truth about Himself until you have obeyed what you know already." Eve's disobedience was based on her desire to be more than God had made her to be.

Take a few moments and do the next couple of pages on your own or with a trusted friend. Let me introduce you to a potentially perfect person ... *you.*

THE SOCIAL ME

What are the qualities that define you to the world? What strengths, passions, and abilities has God-given you to direct you to the place where He can use you best?

The social person you are determines **where** *God plans to use you in the world.*

Socially – WHERE You Belong

❖ What do the people you consider friends say about the person that you are?

❖ What words would others use to describe you?

❖ What do colleagues think of you? Friends?

Circle words below that describe the social person you are. There are no right or wrong answers. There are only words that describe. Feel free to add some additional words!!

Outgoing	Reserved	Flirty	Loyal
Good listener	Sound Advisor	Loner	Social butterfly
Silly	Wise	Advisor	Advice seeker
Extrovert	Introvert	Confidante	Gossip
Reliable	Unreliable	Life of the office	Obedient
Dependable	Flighty	Funny	Serious
Organized	Disorganized	Innovative	Staid
Honest	Exaggerator	Friendly	Confrontational
Dreamer	Planner	Listener	Talker
Problem solver	Problem maker	Available	Avoider
Optimistic	Worrier	Quiet	Loud
Opinionated	Unopinionated	Friendly	Colleague
Focused	Confused	Driven	Relaxed
Dependent	Independent	Maverick	Obedient

THE EMOTIONAL ME

What is your unique emotional make up? What do you have to offer that no one else has? What words describe the type of emotional individual you are? Remember that you have the God-given ability to reach certain people *that no one else can.*

The emotional person you are determines **whom** *you can best connect with as God uses you over the course of your life.*

Emotionally – WHOM You Can Reach

* ❖ How do you react emotionally toward yourself and others?
* ❖ What words describe your emotional state at the very **best** of times?
* ❖ What words describe your emotional state at the very **worst** of times?

Emotional	Cool	Compassionate	Hardened
Quick to laugh	Quick to cry	Carries a grudge	Forgiving
Angry	Calm	Withdrawn	Brave
Serious	Funny	Happy	Depressed
Good in stress	Bad in stress	Let it go	Talk it out
Listener	Talker	Sympathetic	Unfeeling
Impatient	Patient	Articulate	Inarticulate
Thoughtful	Delusional	Cool headed	Cool hearted

Use the words above, or some of your own, to describe what you are like in the …

Best of Times?	Worst of Times?

THE PHYSICAL ME

What God-given skills or talents do you have that distinguish you from others? How do you enjoy yourself? What do you define as fun? God wants to use these times of your greatest enjoyment for His purposes.

The person you are physically determines **how** *God plans to use you to His greatest glory.*

Physically – HOW You Perform

❖ What do your free time activities say about how "young you feel"?
❖ Do you have a goal or desire physically that you feel you could attain if you simply put more effort into it?

Circle the words that describe both the physical person that you currently are as well as the physical person you would like to be. Feel free to add some additional words!			
Athletic	Couch potato	Camping	Classy hotel
Hiking boots	High heels	Age defined	Attitude defined
Active	Passive	Outdoors	Indoors
New stuff	Same old	Willing	Hesitant
Able	Restricted	Ice Hockey	Crocheting
Craft Store	Sports Store	Mall	Museum
Fit	Unfit	Healthy	Unhealthy

THE SPIRITUAL ME

Where is your spiritual foundation? Do you even have one? God can only use you when your spiritual foundation is strong and solid. Are you rock-solid and sure or shifting and changing?

Your spirituality determines **when** *God can use you.*

Spiritually – WHEN You Will Go

❖ Is your life goal to please God and do what He desires for your life or do you have numerous agendas that you seem always to be juggling?
❖ In whom do you trust and believe in?

Who or what do you have to depend on? Circle from the list below or feel free to add your own.			
Family	Friends	Books	Television
Too many things	Too few things	Experienced	Something New
Minister	God	Holy Spirit	Therapist
Prayer	Mate	Just myself	No one

Where or to whom do you base your authority for right and wrong? Circle from the list below or feel free to add your own.			
God	Bible	Laws	Society
Public Opinion	Peers	Family	Friends
Just Myself	Nowhere	It depends	I don't know

So? Where does God plan to use you? Are you a quiet, one-on-one person, or are you a life-of-the-party person?

Who are you best prepared to connect with? Is it those loud, boisterous types who always seem to pull the cameras towards them, or will it be the shy, quiet types who often get lost or forgotten in the big picture?

How will you make an impact? Will it be sitting quietly in someone's living room over a cup of tea or will it be scaling the side of a challenging, rock climbing cliff?

When will you be ready to start doing what God needs you to do? Are you just barely equipped to begin to take yourself on a journey of discovery, or are you ready to lead a group into the exciting future of spiritual enlightenment?

Remember, if you don't fulfill the mission that God needs you to fulfill, those needs won't get met.

Questions To Discuss:

Q?

Have you ever felt specifically called
by God?
What constitutes a call?
Describe your ideal "call" by God for
you.

Sarah and The Guy She Was With For One Hundred Years

A Heart Of Patience

Sarah. The Hebrew matriarch. Or the woman who had a baby when she was ninety years old. But what has always stood out for me was that Sarah gave her husband to another woman for want of a child. Her inability to conceive was the key factor in defining everything she was about.

Through Sarah and Abraham's choices were born both the Israelite and the Islamic nations. Herbert Lockyer points quite an accusatory finger regarding Sarah and her apparent desire to have a child at all costs, "Sarah sacrificed herself on the cruelest altar on which any woman ever laid herself down; but the cords of the sacrifice were all the time the cords of a suicidal pride; still the sacrifice was both a great sin in the sight of God, a fatal injury to herself, to her husband, and to innocent generations yet unborn." (*Women of the Bible*) Whoa. I guess she and Eve share a lot of common ground, huh?

But there is so much more to Sarah's story than just a prideful, barren woman who wasn't patient enough to wait out God's perfect plan for her! She was an ancestress of Christ. She is one of only two women lauded for her faith in the "Great Examples of Faith" chapter in the book of Hebrews which says, "It was by faith that even Sarah was able to have a child, though she was barren and was too old. She believed that God would keep His promise." (Hebrews 11:11) Sarah's descendants were chosen to carry on the line of Christ's ancestry. She was a woman chosen by God to be the one to whom He would give His covenant to, so special that God distinguishes her by giving her a new name. Throughout the entire world it was Sarah and her husband, Abraham, who were chosen not by chance but because they had all the necessary qualities that God required.

Exquisitely beautiful, passionately loved, strong, intelligent, and independent, there is much about Sarah's story that we can learn from and apply to our lives today. Take some time with me and learn a little bit about pride and maturing in faith. Oh, and of course, patience. All of us can use a bit more of that … can't we?

First Things First

Scripture references you should check out:	Abram and Sarai's story begins in Genesis 12. Sarah's death is recorded in Genesis 23.
Question to ask yourself before you read any further:	What was the single most stressful/upsetting time of your life and was God pleased or displeased with your behavior during that time?
What her name means:	Sarai is one of just a few people who are specifically renamed by God. (Genesis 17:15) Names given by God are called "sacramental names" for they are a sign and seal of an established covenant (promise) between God and that person. "Sarai" means "princess" while "Sarah" (the name given to her by God) means "Chieftainness" or "Princess."

	With this name change came the covenant, "I will bless her and give you a son from her! Yes, I will bless her richly, and she will become the mother of many nations, Kings will be among her descendants!" (Genesis 15:16)
Connections:	Patience is something that all of us can improve on exponentially. Patience, in my way of thinking, is the difference between our personal time clock and God's. Our inability to understand, trust, and simply wait until God's perfectly planned moment is a human fault that pulls each of us down numerous times over the course of our lives. Maybe the phrase "needing more patience" should be better said as "needing more godly focused patience"?
What the Bible says about true patience:	**What it's better than:** Ecclesiastes 7:8 **How to increase it:** Romans 15:4-6 **Where it comes from:** Galatians 5:22 **How we prove ourselves:** 2 Corinthians 6:6 **How I illustrate Christ's patience:** I Timothy 1:15-17 **What profession teaches it:** James 5:7-8 **Why we should be so thankful for God's:** 2 Peter 3:15a

Questions We'll Never Know The Answers To:

❖ How did Abram relay all of his conversations with God to Sarai?
❖ At what point in her life did Sarai lose all hope of ever conceiving a child?

Did you know? Interesting Biblical Facts About Sarah

❖ **Ancestry:** Abram's (and Sarai's) lineage can be traced all the way from Adam through Enoch to Noah to Shem to Terah, Abram's father. (Genesis 5, Genesis 10, Genesis 11:10-26)
❖ **Hebrew:** While Abram was the first person in the Bible to be referred to as a "Hebrew" (Genesis 14:13) scholars do not agree on the origin of the term. Some attribute it to the Habiru, a race of people mentioned in clay tablets dating back to the 18th and 19th century B.C. Others believe that Eber, a descendant of Noah through his son Shem and

an ancestor of Abram, is the beginning of the term. As Eber means, literally, "on the other side of," it certainly is descriptively accurate of the nomadic life Abram, as well as many consecutive generations, lived.

❖ **God's Love and Patience:** First Adam and Eve disappointed Him (Genesis 3), then the entire world became so wicked that only Noah stood out (Genesis 6). It would seem that by the time Abram and Sarai come on the scene the world once again was on that slippery slope to wickedness. Was this the 'last chance' for the human race? Three strikes and were they *out?* Is it possible that only Abram, of the entire world's population, stood out for his faithfulness and goodness? It is inconceivable to me that God would choose someone to become "the father of a great nation" (Genesis 12:2) who hadn't already outclassed himself from all the rest.

❖ **Ur:** Ruins today of this city are located in what is now southern Iraq. The city of Ur during Abram and Sarai's time was a thriving metropolis at the height of its glory. Situated on the mighty Euphrates River, it was a prosperous center of religion and industry. Excavations have revealed a surprisingly advanced culture that had: writing, arts, crafts, beautiful jewelry, exquisite china and crystal, and advanced architecture. It is considered to be "the earliest known civilization in world history." (Wikipedia)

❖ **Barrenness:** Being barren was more than just a physical or even social problem. Because God had stated "You will be blessed above all the nations of the earth. None of your men or women will be childless, and all your livestock will bear young" (Deuteronomy 7:14) there was a religious stigma attached to the problem as well. In essence, if you were barren it was because God had punished you. Couples would then spend a great deal of time examining their spiritual well-being and offer sacrifices to cover all past sins. If they were still unsuccessful, there were 'love foods' you could try like the mandrake plant thought to produce fertility. (Rachel tried them unsuccessfully in Genesis 30:14-16.) But finally, if the woman was still barren after all these attempts, there were drastic final measures to try. One was to take another wife (Hannah's husband did this in I Samuel 1:5, even though the Bible clearly states "he loved Hannah.") The other was to use the wife's servant as a "surrogate." Yup, you read right. The husband

49

could have "relations" with the servant and any child born to a slave belonged to the mistress.

❖ **Family Connections:** Shocking though it might seem to us, marriages between half brothers and sisters as well as other near relatives was acceptable, and in some cases encouraged for religious reasons. Abraham sent his servant back to his homeland "to his relatives" to find a wife for his precious son Isaac (Genesis 24:3-4) and Jacob, one of Isaac's sons will return to the home of his grandfather to marry one of his uncle's daughters. (Genesis 28:2) Sarai and Abram shared the same father – Terah, but had different mothers, and *this* was the distinction that was critical. The role of the woman was critically important to tracing the hereditary line. The fact that Abram and Sarai *did not* share a mother was, apparently, the only critical distinction required to make their relationship acceptable. (Genesis 20:12)

The Core Story

Sticks and Stones … What is the worst thing to be called?

Any label would have been preferred: ugly, stupid, crude, unskilled, a lousy cook … Sarai would have taken any label upon herself but the one she was forced to bear. Sarai was barren. Mentioned for the very first time in the Bible in Genesis 11:29 as Abram's wife, in the very next verse it states, "But Sarai was unable to become pregnant and had no children." So extraordinarily beautiful that she will be taken in the future from Abram not once but twice by kings wishing to add her to the royal harem (Genesis 12:15 and Genesis 20:2), the defining feature of who she was, above and beyond anything else, was that *Sarai was barren.*

Q?

What area of your life is the greatest test for your patience? What does this say about you?

While in today's world we know that the problem of fertility could be with either the man or the woman, in biblical times the stigma of infertility almost always rested directly on the woman. Barren women were to be reproached for their sin and pitied for their absolute failure. I can imagine the whispers: "Sarai must be permanently cursed by the gods! I wonder what she did that was so bad? Do you know?" "I wonder if she's tried changing her diet? It worked for my sister." "Did you notice the new necklace Sarai is wearing? Do you think it is a amulet to ensure fertility?" "She must bring more offerings to the goddess Astarte. Only she is gracious enough to grant us the fertility we all want." "Do you think Abram will set her aside? I saw him speaking with Joash just the other day. Isn't Joash's daughter coming of age this spring?" "How many years have the two of them been married with no heir to show for it?" "What a wonderfully tolerant man that Abram is! I know of no husband who has been as patient for as long as he has. Does Sarai realize how fortunate she is?"

Sarai lived in Ur, *the* most cosmopolitan, progressive city of the day. Think London, Paris, or New York. She was part of a wealthy, prestigious family that could trace its lineage back to, literally, the dawn of time. Which should have guaranteed a dazzlingly happy future filled with joy and rainbows … except that whole unable to bear a child thing. Suddenly, being a part of this rich, world-renowned family was nothing but a huge depressing rock around Sarai's barren neck since she couldn't produce that all important heir to carry on the family name.

Yes, things would have been absolutely desolate if not for one very important thing. She really loved Abram.

And he really loved her. That was a good thing, right?

Love means … Yes? What does it mean?

There is no doubt in my mind that Abram and Sarai's was a love match. Culturally, there was not one reason for Abram to stay with Sarai outside of the equation of love. In fact, I would suspect that as time passed, Abram himself would have suffered for "not doing his duty" and finding someone more suitable than the beautiful, barren woman he had married. Even within the entire biblical account, few couples *chose* to die childless; instead they chose any one of a number of acceptable avenues to remedy the awful situation. Elizabeth and Zechariah in Luke 1 seem to be one of the only such couples biblically recorded willing to go to their graves monogamous and childless and were rewarded eventually with the birth of their son John in their twilight years. Indeed, *being* childless was a curse of the highest order and something to be avoided at all costs.

After many years together, Sarai and Abram would have probably gone through all the obligatory emotions that went with the issue of her barrenness: denial, fear, sorrow, despair, anger … am I missing any? With each of those emotions would have come the complementary emotional impact to the relationship: refusing to discuss things, attempting to shift the blame, tearful recriminations, depressed resignation …

I can hear Abram's words as he tried to comfort his wife, "It doesn't matter, Sarai. I don't care what anyone else says! I love *you*. You are my life."

"You don't understand, Abram! If they are not saying it to my face I see it in their eyes! I am a failure! You have married a worthless woman! Go find yourself someone else! Someone young and *fertile*. Someone that can carry on the precious family name. *It is your duty.*"

"I want no one but you, my love. No. One. If we are meant to have a child between us, we will. Otherwise, at least we will have the joy of each other …"

Abram and Sarai moved from Ur to the smaller city of Haran over the course of their marriage. Terah, Abram's father, just decided to move the family with no explanation recorded. Was Sarai glad to go? To have an opportunity for a fresh start away from all of the gossip and innuendos? We have no way of knowing.

Through the years, Abram and Sarai remained a monogamous couple despite social, familial, and personal pressures. Rather than let life pull them apart and destroy them, Abram and Sarai allowed it to bond them together, bind them so tightly that gradually they became insulated from the world and all it threw at them, and had only each other to rely on.

Solid foundations … Who do you rely on?

Here's an important part of the story about Abram and Sarai: when God chose to speak to Abram (God included Sarai in all His covenants but only once spoke with her directly) it wasn't because Abram was already a nice Jewish boy. He was a heathen, born of heathen parents.

I like this description of him, "He was a rough, simple, venerable Bedouin-like sheep master. He uttered no prophecy, wrote no book, sang no song, gave no laws. Yet ... he alone is spoken of as 'the father of the faithful' and as 'the friend of God.'" (Lockyer) The Bible didn't start mentioning anything about Abram, and God didn't call him until he was seventy-five years old. Did God just close His eyes, spin the earth and randomly pick someone? No, Abram, little heathen boy that he was, had somehow managed to distinguish himself before God. Think about it: without anything written down to study, without any specific instructions, *all on his own* Abram had managed to set himself apart from the depraved humanity that was populating the earth, the same

> **"Abraham, My friend ..."**
> Isaiah 41:8

humanity that God had already destroyed by a flood. And, the same humanity that God was once again shaking His head at over its wickedness.

The Bible doesn't specifically say what God saw in Abram and Sarai before He called them in Genesis 12. Wouldn't it be nice if it said, "And here are the qualities that caused God to choose Abram and Sarai and establish His covenant with them ..." Then we'd know, right? Well, *actually*, if you read through Abram's story the Bible *is* pretty clear on what God saw in Abram and his wife, Sarai. Things that we, too, can achieve.

Absolutely all we know about Abram before God calls him is this: "Terah was the father of Abram, Nahor, and Haran ... Abram married Sarai ... Sarai was not able to have any children ... Terah took his son Abram, his daughter-in-law Sarai, and his grandson Lot (his son Haran's child) ... and left Ur to go to the land of Canaan. But they stopped instead at the village of Haran and settled there ... Terah ... died ... Then the Lord told Abram, 'Leave your country, your relatives, and your father's house, and go to the land that I will show you' ... So Abram departed ... Abram was seventy-five years old ..." (Bits and pieces of Genesis 11:27-12:4)

On first blush it's not much, right? Of course, we have already established that Abram has a tremendous capacity to love. And he is uncommonly faithful and committed once he does love. And he does not let peer, familial, or societal pressures distract him from the course he has chosen.

Let's add a few more things to Abram's profile. He was a firstborn son. That put him a cut above the rest in all things: his father would have favored him, he would have been groomed for leadership from day one, he would have been taught differently, and the weight of his responsibility would have always been greater than the rest. (Uh-oh, let's add a bit more on Sarai's barrenness guilt while we're at it!)

Anything else? How about obedient? Nothing is recorded of either Abram (or Sarai) whining or complaining about being uprooted from all the comforts of a city like Ur to the much simpler life of the smaller town of Haran. Abram simply did as his father decided, his duty being with his father. (Which was also a perfect opportunity to "start fresh" with a new little woman and leave that barren Sarai behind in Ur ... but Abram didn't.)

> **Your most important decision you can make today is to settle this issue of what will be the ultimate authority for your life.**
> Rick Warren

So, are you keeping track? Suddenly, this sparse accounting of Abram's early life is brimming with striking personal qualities: loving, faithful, committed, knowledgeable, capable, obedient ... Sounds like some guy, huh?

Abram's only fault? Well, he was *heathen*. Both Ur and Haran were rich with idol worship. Ur was a center for religious worship recognizing many gods, but primarily the moon god, Sin. Still standing today in Ur (Southern Iraq) are the ruins of a ziggurat – a huge terraced platform on which temples were erected – to the moon deity, Nanna. Haran, which lay on one of the main trade routes, also worshipped Sin, the moon god. In all likelihood, Abram and Sarai recognized the authority of Sin (rather an ironic name, don't you think?) and worshipped at his pagan temple. Despite that one rather major flaw, it seems to be the *only thing* that God needed to change. Why buy a car when you have to replace the whole engine? Isn't it easier to buy one that runs fine, but does need a brand new paint job?

Yoo-hoo, Abram ... Are you listening?

The Bible simply says, "Then the Lord told Abram..." in Genesis 12:1. It doesn't talk about Abram's fear and trembling. Abram doesn't express skepticism, question his sanity, or try to ignore the godly conversation. There is no record of Abram expressing a list of logistical questions about the hows or whys or advanced details he needs to know before he begins this journey. It couldn't be that Abram misunderstood, because God was pretty darn specific: "Leave your country, your family, and your father's home for a land that I will show you." (Genesis 12:1 MSG) Nope, no doubt about what Abram was supposed to do.

In addition, God made an unbelievable promise, "I'll make you a great nation and bless you. I'll make you famous; you'll be a blessing. I'll bless those who bless you; those who curse you I'll curse. All the families of the Earth will be blessed through you." (Genesis 12:2-3 MSG) Well! How about *that* for a promise? Please note that Abram didn't cross his arms and say, "Just how do you define 'famous'? What specifically do you consider a blessing? How do I know

> **And Abram believed the Lord and the Lord declared him righteous because of his faith.**
> Genesis 15:6

you'll keep your promise, God? Can you provide me with some documented proof of all this? Can I see your references?"

We can add to Abram's already stellar list of qualities: belief, bravery, and trust.

Why do you think that Abram had to leave everything: his country, his family, and his father's house? Why couldn't God have accomplished all He needed to do right there where Abram was already safe, secure, and surrounded by (what seems to be) a positive and loving support system?

God does it with us all the time, you know, that asking us to step out into the dark unknown with only His protection and guidance. It's called *steps of faith*. Over and over the biblical theme is that God can do *everything* with *nothing*. He chose a barren woman (Sarai) to be the mother of his chosen race. He'll choose a shy stutterer (Moses) to be the spokesman for his people. He'll choose a scorned prostitute (Rahab) to champion His cause at the battle of Jericho. He'll choose a weak and reluctant man (Jonah) to challenge an entire city successfully to repent. He'll choose a poor nobody (Gideon) to judge His people. He'll choose a penniless, childless, widow ... well ... lots of times (Ruth, Anna, Naomi, the Widow of Zarepath) to champion His cause and bring forth The Truth. He'll choose a pile of issue laden men (Peter was impulsive, Matthew was a hated tax collector, Thomas doubted, Paul had poor health) to spearhead His earthly ministry. He'll choose women (who had no legal status in society) to be the chief witnesses and spokespeople of the Resurrection. I could go on and on ...

You see, if Abram had stayed with his family, even if he could have convinced them to embrace and love the One True God, all his newly acquired wealth and power and accomplishments would have always been attributed to the backing of his family and friends. Abram would never learn the truly awesome power of God's love, faithfulness, and authority. God told Abram to *step out on faith*, leave everything and everyone, and with absolutely nothing but Him set out to accomplish the impossible: becoming a great nation, becoming famous, and becoming a blessing to all the other families on the earth. Can you hear those people in Haran whispering to themselves as Abram and Sarai packed up and left the city? "It'll be a miracle if they survive out there in the wilderness!" "They'll be back." "They're crazy!"

Q?

How does your spiritual maturity help with your patience level?

How do you think Abram told Sarai they we're leaving? "Pack your bags, Woman. We're outta here. I'm not sure where we're going, but don't worry. This new God just spoke to me and made some great promises to me and I'm going to take Him up on His offer." Yeah, right, like that would work really well after over fifty years of marriage!

But what *did* he tell her? We only know what the Bible says, "So Abram departed as the Lord had instructed him, and Lot went with him. Abram was seventy-five years old when he left Haran. He took his wife, Sarai, his nephew Lot, and all his wealth – his livestock and all the people who had joined his household at Haran ..." (Genesis 12:4-5) Just in case you're wondering, Sarai was about ten years younger than Abram. (You can check the reference in Genesis 17:17.) Whatever Abram did tell Sarai, she went without any biblically recorded fuss or bother. Maybe, once again she was glad to have an opportunity to start fresh, away from the gossip and innuendos. Perhaps she trusted her husband's judgment about this new God.

Or maybe, just maybe, after all these years of being barren, finally through this promise from this new God, Sarai might really be able to achieve a child. The "become a great nation" part certainly had a promising ring to it, didn't it? Sarai had tried everything else. What did she have to lose?

God will reaffirm this promise to Abram and Sarai a number of times over a period of *twenty-five years*, becoming more and more specific with each instance. It was almost as if He told them only as much as they could comprehend at the moment. Or they deserved to know.

After they obediently packed up and left everything in Haran, as they entered Canaan, God promised, "I'm going to give this land to your offspring." (Genesis 12:7) or "Take a good look, guys, as we wander through. One day, this is going to be all yours!" (ST)

Years later, after their hasty departure from Egypt, God promised, "I am going to give you so many descendants that, like dust, they cannot be counted!" (Genesis 13:16) or "Be patient, there is a plan! You're going to have so many descendants it's going to make this all worth while!" (ST)

Decades later, after Abram finally settled in Canaan, God promised, "You will have a son of your own to inherit everything I am giving you." (Genesis 15:4) or "I haven't forgotten you're greatest desire to have a child. My promise will fulfill all of your hopes and dreams." (ST)

And, finally, almost twenty-five years after that very first promise, God changed Abram's name to Abraham, Sarai's name to Sarah and promised, "Sarah, your wife, will bear you a son. You will name him Isaac and I will confirm my everlasting covenant with him and his descendants." (Genesis 17:19) or "The woman that you love and have remained committed to through thick and thin, will have a son to call her own. You will call him Laughter because he will be the joy of your life and worth every moment of the wait." (ST)

Why *did* God wait so long? Why didn't He just spell it out to Abram and Sarai right from the start? Why didn't He say, "Now you two have to be patient because this child that will surely come isn't going to show up for another twenty-five years." (Actually, is it really patience if you know how long the wait is going to be?) Oswald Chambers said, "Faith must be tested, because it can be turned into a personal possession only through conflict." Just as love and trust, faith can grow. Or it can fade. God knew what was ahead not just for Abram and Sarai, but for their descendants as well: trials, tribulations, war, oppression, division, and unfaithfulness. God also knew what was present in the world at the time of Abram and Sarai as well as what was coming in the future: evilness, hatred, false gods, and famine. Maybe, as we gradually give more and more responsibility and knowledge to our precious children, God, too, was easing Abram and Sarai into the harsh realities of living as quickly as they could handle it all.

On the road again … Are we there yet?

When they initially started out on this godly adventure, Abram and Sarai would have had a substantial entourage as they traveled from Haran to where God had directed them. Plus they had their nephew, Lot, and all of his baggage and people. Let's just say it wasn't a quick and easy trip.

First stop was south and west a bit to the land of Canaan, a vast expanse that covered everything from dry, rocky mountainous areas unfit to sustain human life to fertile farmlands and lush river valleys and coastal plains. Named after Noah's grandson Canaan, the land was inhabited by all of those descendants who were called (here's a surprise) Canaanites. It was here that the Lord appeared to Abram and said, "I am going to give this land to your offspring." (Genesis 12:7) Did this statement puzzle Abram and Sarai considering the many decades of disappointment regarding having a child? Or, did God's promise fill both of them with hope and excitement and the inevitable question of, "When?! *When??*" Abram built an altar at the Oak at Moreh, near Shechem, in honor of God's visit.

> Goin' places that I've never been.
> Seein' things that I may never see again
> Willie Nelson

Next stop was southward again to the lush hill country between the cities of Bethel and Ai. Again, Abram built an altar and worshiped the Lord. Finally, traveling further south by stages, Abram brought his people towards the desert wilderness of the Negev.

When a famine gripped the land, Abram brought his entire family down into the land of Egypt to wait it out. Here they parked their camels and stayed for a while. I wonder about so many things concerning their trip ...

Do you think, each night as Sarai and Abram snuggled in their tent, they talked about the journey? "Did you see ...?" "Is it true what I heard ...?" "Do you think ...?" "Can we ...?" "Are we almost ...?" Did they laugh and giggle and roll their eyes at the day-to-day experiences? Were they young at heart enough to truly enjoy the adventure?

Do you suppose that their love life took on a renewed passion, with the promise from God, causing hopes and dreams to flourish once again? Did they recommit to each other, growing more deeply in love over the wonderful promise the two had been blessed with? Did they delight in the uniqueness that each had that made the day-to-day drudgery of the trip easier to bear?

Do you think with each unsuccessful monthly cycle that Sarai lost, little by little, that renewed spark of enthusiasm as her curse of barrenness appeared to be as strong as ever? Did Abram once again assume his role as comforter and encourager to Sarai? Did God's renewed promises at various stages along the trip - adding more and more detail each time - bolster the two of them up again and again as they trusted and believed?

> **Taste and see that the LORD is good. Oh, the joys of those who take refuge in Him! Fear the Lord, you His godly people, for those who fear Him will have all they need.**
> Psalm 34:8-9

Were there day-to-day events that awed and amazed this newly spiritual couple? Did God take the time along the way to reveal things about Himself so that both Sarai and Abram could see and feel and hear and taste the goodness of the Lord? Did they go from spiritual infancy, to toddlerhood, to teenagehood, to young adulthood? With each step that they took, did they understand more and more the might and power of the God that had called them?

Did Sarai or Abram ever once consider the magnitude of what they had gotten themselves into? Did they ever feel overwhelmed? Frightened? Regretful? They certainly had plenty of time to think things along the way.

This is my … He said she was *who*?!

For me it is rather surprising that for the very first time ever, as they prepared to enter Egypt, Abram expressed fear. It is in this part of the journal entry that we begin to hear not about Sarai's barrenness but about her beauty. Barely mentioned in earlier references (everyone was too busy reminding us how unfruitful she was), suddenly Abram seems to be desperate to literally throw a sack over her head. As they are approached the Egyptian border, he told his wife, "You are a very beautiful woman. When the Egyptians see you, they will say, 'This is his wife. Let's kill him; then we can have her!' But if you say you are my sister, then the Egyptians will treat me well because of their interest in you, and they will spare my life." (Genesis 12:11-13) She must have been some beauty. Remember, she was sixty-five years old!

Sigh. Oh, boy. This is one of those times where, if it was a made for television movie, you'd be looking at whomever you were sitting next to and rolling your eyes, big time. Abram's scheme had disaster written all over it. Can you imagine him looking at Sarai's incredulous expression, trying to look innocent and saying, "What? Why that look? It's not a lie, really …" Please note that not once did Abram mention praying and asking God for help, nor does Sarai encourage him to so. Despite the fact that this entire trip was God-directed, it seemed to not occur to either of them to ask God for help. While it was commendable that the two seemed to discuss this plan as a couple, the fact that God was completely left out of the equation was not only a big clue of impending disaster but a huge glimpse into how far they were from any kind of spiritual maturity. What was particularly disturbing about the plan is that Abram seemed more worried about his own skin than his wife's and that he appeared to be anticipate either financial or social gain as Sarai got shopped around. *Everything* about this stunk.

Q?

What role does trust play with regard to patience?

"And sure enough, when they arrived in Egypt, everyone spoke of her beauty." (Genesis 12:14) Sarai was so beautiful people were talking about her and singing praises about her to the pharaoh. Quicker than you can say, "Hey! That's my sister!" Sarai was taken into the royal harem. Somehow Sarai ending up as the next future Mrs. Pharaoh was not something I think either of them anticipated.

Abram had plenty of time to clarify things, but he obviously stuck with Plan A despite it going from bad to worse. In exchange for Abram's beautiful 'sister,' the Pharaoh gave Abram: sheep, cattle, donkeys, male and female servants, and camels. (Genesis 12:16) Wow, what a haul.

I am stunned at the absolute silence of Abram and Sarai. Don't you think they had to be absolutely terrified? Talk about a plan backfiring. But it does beg the question: What did Abram *think* was going to happen? Perhaps they did second guess the whole sister plan once Sarai was the newest flavor in the harem. Maybe they even second-guessed the whole "leave Haran and follow this new God thing." Whatever they were doing, God must have been observing all this with deeply frustrated sighs and disappointed shakes of His head. The Lord immediately sent such a terrible plague upon the Pharaoh's household once Sarai was present that this *heathen king* knew Sarai and Abram were the cause. "What have you done to me?" the Pharaoh shouted at Abram. (Genesis 12:18) Within a flash, Abram, Sarai, Lot, all their household and belongings were being escorted by armed guard out of the country! (Genesis 12:20)

Here's your wife, Abram, what's your hurry?

And, as a further example of how far Sarai and Abram had to go on the maturity and trusting God meter, more than *twenty years in the future* both will do the same thing *again*. Abram, by then called Abraham, will do *the exact same thing* with Sarah and King Abimelech, *with the identical disastrous results*, requiring God to *again intervene*. (Genesis 20) From this we can conclusively determine: 1) Sarah was some astronomically gorgeous woman, and 2) Abraham needed more than one try to learn anything of value from his mistakes. (Sigh … don't we all?)

Blessings, Covenants and Visions … But where's that baby?!

In case you think that God's promises over the course of their twenty-five year odyssey wasn't enough to confirm the validity of The One True God, and that Abram and Sarai were well within their right to doubt and blatantly disregard God's instructions and provisions, there were a number of other dramatic instances of God's authority.

Abram finally had the courage to address God regarding the promise of descendants "too numerous to count" and the inconsistency of Sarai's continued barrenness. "O Sovereign Lord, what good are all your blessings when I don't even have a son?" (Genesis 15:2) For me, this again shows a step towards spiritual maturity. God wants to hear our doubts and concerns. He wants a dialogue with us. True friends share deep hopes and fears, not just surface pleasantries. It is a mark of a deeper relationship when one begins to open up with another about things close to the heart.

> **"Blessed be Abram by God Most High, Creator of heaven and earth."**
> Melchizedek

That Abram honestly questioned God does not necessarily mean that he doubted God's plan, nor was he being disrespectful. He seemed to be simply clarifying the logistics of it all. For when God did indeed confirm that Abram would "have a son of [his] own" (Genesis 15:4), the Bible also records that "Abram believed the Lord, and the Lord declared him righteous because of his faith." (Genesis 15:6) The term 'righteous' means "morally upright, free from guilt or sin." (www.freedictionary.com) Obviously, God thought highly of Abram at this point and had no issue with his questions. And isn't that always the way it goes with a friend? You ask heartfelt questions, you share observations and explanations, and finally your level of trust and commitment increases as you become more personally intertwined. "Look up into the heavens and count the stars if you can. Your descendants will be like that – too many to count! … I have given this land to your descendants, all the way from the border of Egypt to the great Euphrates River." (Genesis 15:5, 18) Translations by today's map and country standards: all of Jordan, Lebanon, Israel, Syria, Iraq, Saudi Arabia, and Kuwait. That's one big parcel of land.

God caused Abram to have a "terrifying dream of darkness and horror" (Genesis 15:12) which seems to be a prophetic view into the upcoming years of struggling, oppression, punishment and enslavement for his descendants. Regarding these years of pain and suffering, God promised to "punish the nation that enslaves [your descendants], and in the end [your descendants] will come away with great wealth." (Genesis 15:14)

With this dream came the formal covenant with Abram, bound with an animal sacrifice and a vision representing the seriousness of God's righteousness and holiness. (Genesis 15:9, 17)

Please note by this point, how far Abram and God's relationship had progressed. From the basic minimum "leave … and go …" directions way back in Haran to dialogue, visions, and specific details. But the questions I have are about Sarai's faith. Did her faith grow in tangent with Abram's? Was her faith her own or more her husband's? Did Abram relay to Sarai in detail each and every contact he had with God? Did Abram and Sarai discuss the meaning and import of their call and the responsibility it entailed?

Relationships grow through the sharing of experiences, thoughts, worries, and joys. Did Abram and Sarai puzzle over the wonder and majesty of this whole experience so that they could share thoughts and perceptions from their different perspectives? Was Abram free to share his worries and confusion with Sarai? I have to believe that part of their strength as a couple chosen by God for this amazing journey had to be because they did such things. The sorrow and heartache of infertility had brought them closer as a couple and created a foundation of closeness that other couples cannot even comprehend. Did Sarai, as Abram had done for her during her lowest times, encourage and champion him? "Stop worrying, Abram, God chose you, didn't He?" "Come now, Abram, surely God would not have called you if He thought you would only disappoint Him." "Abram, God knows what a loyal, loving, faithful man you are for he has seen the way you have been with me."

The Final Straw … When is faith pulled so tightly that it snaps?

Through these years of traveling and adventure, Sarai appeared to be barren, beautiful and compliant (in that order). We never hear one word of complaint or one screech of impatience. We have no clue to her deepest thoughts regarding her infertility. Whether Abram shared his conversations with God with her in detail, or just the barest facts, I must conclude that

> Too often we want God's resources, but we don't want His timing.
> John Ortberg

she knew of The Promise and was cautiously optimistic regarding her part in it – for a time anyway. I suppose that with each monthly disappointment, she slowly slipped back into the pit of despair. As bright and promising as the first days on the road from Haran may have been, eleven years later when Sarai was over seventy-five it all must have been vividly clear that maybe *her husband* was going to be the father of many, but she wasn't going to be part of that equation.

Men having children into the late eighties and nineties was not as unusual as you may think. Abram's father Terah "was 70 years old" when he became the father of Abram. (Genesis 11:29) Going back through the family tree, Shem, Noah's son, had Arphaxad when he was 100. (Genesis 11:10) According to the list of Adam's descendants in Genesis 5, between the ages of 65 and 182 seem to be the times of each patriarch's greatest ... er, fertility! So, the fact that Abram at age eighty-five still had not had a son was not as disastrous as the fact that Sarai at seventy-five still had not conceived.

According to the biblical account, at the age of approximately seventy-five Sarai gave up completely all hope of personally conceiving a child. The journal account doesn't tell us why, but I would like to know why she waited until this ripe old age to finally toss in the towel. She is roundly condemned in various reference sources for her "lack of faith and patience" to which I want to scream, *she waited sixty years!!!* That in itself is a powerful testament to her faith and patience. It makes sense to me that, at this point in her life perhaps physically, Sarai's body simply signaled the end of its child bearing ability. Did she stop menstruating? Did the dreaded disappointment of the monthly flow suddenly seem far less worse than the awful realization of the cessation of her menstrual cycle? Was there one brief moment of brilliant hope, when Sarai did not have her period, that *perhaps, at last,* she thought a child had been conceived, only to be horribly disappointed by the cruel reality of her aging body?

Whatever it was, *something* significant happened at this time, because not only is Sarai recorded as taking action to remedy the lack of an heir but, at last, Abram seems willing to consider alternate methods as well. "So Sarai took her servant, an Egyptian woman named Hagar, and gave her to Abram so she could bear his children." (Genesis 16:2) After all these years of fidelity and hope (if they married when Sarai was a teenager as was the custom back then, they could have been together for over sixty years by then), Sarai said to Abram, "Go and sleep with my servant. Perhaps I can have children through her." (Genesis 16:2)

Now again, we have to read between the lines here. Sarai was *not* stepping down as wife and Hagar was *not* losing her status as Sarai's servant. Abram was *not* being told to have a child "with Hagar" but rather to *get* Sarai a child *through her maid.* Semantics are important here. All this was customary and proper in those days, and there were probably a pile of people in the camp who were breathing sighs of relief and thinking, *"Finally,"* at this entire arrangement. Hagar, in her capacity as Sarai's servant, had no real say in any of this, cruel as it may seem to us. However, within this world of status, rising from mere servant to second "servant wife" was a promotion of the highest order. Add in the fact that *should she* conceive a child and it be the precious son, then Hagar would be set for life. After all, for some women even today, status and prestige is what it's all about …

Q?

Think of examples of both success and failure with patience. How was your life impacted?

Take a minute and try to picture this. After *sixty years* of fidelity and hope, both Sarai and Abram gave up. What must it have been like for Sarai, laying alone in her tent the night Abram took Hagar to his bed? Was she relieved and hopeful? Did she cry in agony over her failure? Did she consider the ramifications of Hagar conceiving Abram's son? Did she try talking to God about her heartbreak?

Okay, so *it was* a lack of faith and patience on both Sarai's and Abram's part. We can't deny it. I just keep coming back to the sixty years of waiting, and am inclined to cut Sarai and Abram a bit of a break. (Please don't ever hold me up to such a standard, God!!) And, I suppose, while we're throwing stones, we should probably toss out "and they forgot to consult God about their plan" once again.

Trouble started almost immediately. Hagar conceived and "began to treat her mistress with contempt." Sarai went and complained to Abram saying, "It's all your fault! Now this servant of mine is pregnant, and she despises me, though I myself gave her the privilege of sleeping with you!" I find it particularly interesting that though God was apparently not consulted in the Abram/Hagar plan, Sarai didn't hesitate to bring Him into the mix when she felt entitled to retribution. "The Lord will make you [Abram] pay for doing this to me!" (Genesis 16:5)

We can almost say "Poor Abram," can't we? He gave the rather classic response of, "Hey, she's *your* servant. Do what you want with her." (Genesis 16:6 ST) Sarai then treated Hagar so harshly that the servant ran away into the desert, pregnant and alone. Things had gotten so out of hand that God chose to intervene. Hagar had the distinction of being visited by an angel, who gave her instructions to return, made promises that she was indeed carrying a son, his name will be Ishmael, and what he would be like as he grew to an adult. Hagar, to her credit, obediently returned and from thereafter referred to God as "the God who sees me." (Genesis 16:9-13)

Hagar obviously relayed the angel's visit to Abram, as the son she did indeed bear was named "Ishmael." I wonder how that went over? Did Abram and Sarai take it as a favorable sign that Hagar had this prophetic heavenly visitor? Did they interpret God's naming this child as His approval of their plan? Did Sarai as a result treat Hagar with more consideration? Did Hagar take on even more prestige within the camp as she not only gave birth to the precious heir but also had her son specifically named by God and was the one whom "God saw" and spoke to? (God had never spoken directly to Sarai, had He?) Was Sarai, after the apparent "success" of her plan to "get a son by her servant" unhappier than she ever could have imagined? Did Sarai ever regret her actions?

Or did Sarai finally become faithfully resigned to what God seemingly had planned all along? Did she finally *just let it all go*? As Sarai watched Ishmael grow and Abram delight in his son, was she able to finally release all of her guilt, sorrow, and anger? Was she able to smile with Abram as this little boy grew, and feel a measure of Abram's joy? Did Sarai somehow resign herself to maybe not being the biological mother of this child of promise, but the caring provider?

Whatever Sarai thought, the Bible does not tell us. But however she felt, she had plenty of years to get her head *and her heart* straight.

Ishmael, my son ... The Child of Promise, right?

Thirteen years went by. *Thirteen.* Ishmael grew up to be a strapping young adult, the precious heir to Abram's empire. *The* Child of Promise. The one that would carry on this godly plan. At least that's what everyone thought. I don't think that there was one single person in the camp who, after Ishmael was born, expected Sarai to conceive a child, do you? Whether Sarai continued to have ambivalent feelings toward Hagar and/or Ishmael, Abram would have treasured his son's presence within the camp. The boy would have had firstborn son status, coupled with "only son" value. He would have been spoiled, treasured, favored ... you name it.

I wonder if God was silent during these years? How often did He and Abram talk? Did Abram, simply by fact of Ishmael's birth and godly naming, assume that this was the son that God had always promised would come? Did Abram ever say, "Are you happy with the way things are going, Lord? Am I getting all this right?" Or did Abram just go whistling his happy tune as he and Ishmael went walking off into the sunset?

The biblical account is silent those thirteen years. It records Ishmael's birth and Abram's age of eighty-six (Genesis 16:15) and then in the very next verse Abram was ninety-nine and God was talking to him. (Genesis 17:1) It was a long conversation! God took the time to cover in detail: behavior rules of being faithful and blameless (Genesis 17:1), to clarify the whole mighty nation promise (Genesis 17:2-6), to officially change Abram's name to Abraham (Genesis 17:5), to reveal the duration of the promise through continuing generations (Genesis 17:7-8), to command the requisite sign of circumcision of all males, how, when, and who (Genesis 17:9-13), to spell out the consequences of disobedience (Genesis 17:14), and to change Sarai's name to Sarah (Genesis 17:15).

I wonder at what point Abraham began to get a wee bit confused. Maybe even start to sweat a little. All this talking from God and there's not one mention of Abram's precious son, Ishmael. You know, The Child of The Promise? Not one word. *Then* God changed Sarah's name. Uh, oh. How come she was being factored in? And then, God dropped the big bomb ...

"And I will bless Sarah and give you a son from her! Yes, I will bless her richly, and she will become the mother of many nations. Kings will be among her descendants!" (Genesis 17:16) While we have always been privy to the entire story and able to look back at things in retrospect, it is only now that God spelled it all out for Abraham.

Well, Abraham had kind of been hearing this all along, right? But, um, well, he and Sarah had solved this problem with the Hagar plan. The two of them had taken care of the whole 'child of promise' thing that had been made impossible with Sarah's infertility, hadn't they? Guess what Abraham did as God laid out the plans, including Sarah in the mix? *He laughed to himself in disbelief* as God talked about Sarah and her conceiving a son. He thought, "What? I'm going to be a father at age one hundred? And what? Sarah's going to be a mother *at ninety?*" (Genesis 17:17) Apparently, Abraham knew enough not to say this out loud, but didn't know enough, after all this time, to realize God already knew his thoughts. Hmmm, still growing spiritually, Abraham?

Politely, Abraham simply reminded God that, well, there already *was* a son. "Yes, may Ishmael enjoy your special blessing!" (Genesis 17:18) Or, "Yes, let's not forget that wonderful son, Ishmael, that you've *already sent me,* Lord!" (ST)

God, was probably rolling His eyes and shaking His head at Abraham. There Abraham was bowing down in the dirt before God thinking his thoughts were his and his alone. Ever patiently, God said to Abraham, "Sarah, your wife, will bear you a son. You will name him Isaac, and I will confirm my everlasting covenant with him and his descendants. As for Ishmael, I will bless him also, just as you have asked. I will cause him to multiply and become a great nation ... But my covenant is with Isaac, who will be born to you and Sarah about this time next year." (Genesis 17:19-21)

To his credit, Abraham once again believed. (Which, I'll remind you was why God chose him in the first place and called him righteous in Genesis 15:6.) Any doubts Abraham had fled with God's specific reassurance. He got himself up off the ground and first thing he did was have every male in the camp circumcised just as God had commanded.

Surely Abraham had to tell Sarah all about this conversation, didn't he? First, he ran around with a sharp knife circumcising every male in camp, then he insisted everyone call him Abraham, and finally he told Sarai that from now on God wants her to be called Sarah. I doubt he would have left out the baby boy that Sarah was going to have next year that they were required to name Isaac …

Poor Sarah. She'd been there and done that too many times! *She was ninety years old* and had been barren for *her whole life.* Can you imagine the look she must have given Abraham? Can you imagine what she must have said? I am inclined to think that it would be a major understatement to say that Sarah was not positively receptive to Abraham's newest message from God. Why do I think so? Because God went to the trouble of sending one more message. And this time, Sarah got to hear it for herself, without having to rely on Abraham's communication skills.

Laughter … Who says it's the best medicine?

While Abraham's entourage was camped at an oak grove, they suddenly had three visitors. Never let it be said that Abraham didn't know how to welcome a guest. He used the finest flour to bake some bread, he chose a fat calf and had it butchered and roasted, and he served cheese curds and milk and had a servant wash their feet as the guests rested under the trees. (Genesis 18:1-4) Sarah, for

> "They called him laughter, for he came after the Father had made an impossible promise come true."
> Michael Card

whatever reason, remained in the tent, out of sight but not out of hearing range.

As the meal progresseed, one of the men asked about Sarah's whereabouts and he was told that she was "in the tent." When this stranger made a prophetic comment about Sarah at this time the following year having a son, Sarah, listening to the conversation "laughed silently to herself." (Genesis 18:12) I can just imagine her thinking, another idiot man that thinks a woman of ninety years old can conceive and bear a child! The journal entry goes so far as to record her *thoughts*, "How could a worn-out woman like me have a baby? And when my husband is also so old?" Sitting in that tent all by herself, Sarah had a good chuckle over the whole thing. Gone was the hope. Gone was even the despair. Now the whole concept of Old Sarah ever having a child of her own was nothing but a huge joke.

Suddenly, according to the Bible account, the Lord spoke to Abraham and asked, "Why did Sarah laugh? Why did she say, 'Can an old woman like me have a baby?' Is anything too hard for the Lord? About a year from now, just as I told you, I will return, and Sarah will have a son." (Genesis 18:14)

Poor Abraham! Definitely clueless to his wife's antics, secluded as she was in the tent, he nevertheless got an earful from the Lord. Sarah, in the tent, must have been absolutely terrified. The Bible says she "was afraid" and whether she thought it or spoke it aloud Sarah denied that she laughed. Then the Lord spoke directly to her – the one and only time - simply saying, "That is not true. You did laugh." (Genesis 18:15) "Don't lie to me, girlfriend. I heard your laughter loudly and clearly." (ST)

> **It was by faith that Sarah together with Abraham was able to have a child, even though they were too old and Sarah was barren. Abraham believed that God would keep his promise.**
> Hebrews 11:11

Okay. So, Abraham and Sarah, renamed with covenantal names by God, Abraham bearing the distinctive bodily mark of circumcision in confirmation of this commitment, now had a hard and fast date for when their son, Isaac, was going to be born. It certainly could not be any more specific, can it? *Finally* Abraham and Sarah must have been on the straight and narrow, ready to forge ahead into the godly plan for the future. Their spiritual maturity had to have been at its ultimate level. Right?

Sigh. Wrong.

Despite all these godly conversations, signs, promises, and details, Abraham again introduced his still apparently astronomically beautiful ninety-year-old wife as his sister as they cross through the Negev desert, and she ended up in a heathen king's harem *again*. This time, God didn't bother with plagues like he did to the Egyptian Pharaoh. God was just blunt and to the point. "You are a dead man," the Lord told King Abimelech in a dream, "for that woman you took is married." (Genesis 20:3) Quick as you can say, "Here's your wife, what's your hurry," again Abraham was traveling on with his wife, sheep, oxen, male and female servants, and 1,000 pieces of silver to compensate them for any embarrassment. (Genesis 20:14-15) How could they do such a thing again, you might ask in stunned amazement? You know something? God must say that about us *all the time.*

And then, *finally*, after over seventy-five years of waiting, Sarah became pregnant exactly as the Lord had promised. She delivered a healthy baby boy whom they named Isaac, just as God had instructed them. Never let it be said that God doesn't have a sense a humor. The name "Isaac" means "he laughs." (Genesis 21) At Isaac's circumcision, Sarah declared, "God has brought me laughter! All who hear about this will laugh with me. For who would have dreamed that I would ever have a baby? Yet I have given Abraham a son in his old age!" (Genesis 21:6-7) Sarah, above everyone else in the world, appreciated the power of The One True God. And, obviously, Sarah also appreciated God's humor.

One Final Test ... Aren't I done *yet?*

If this were the movies, Sarah and Abraham's story would fade to black as the two elderly parents stood admiring their beautiful son on the top of a hill overlooking their vast wealth of sheep and cattle. The music would swell and then as the lights came on you'd feel good about the happy ending. But real life's not like that, is it? With each success and failure in life we add knowledge, strength, and skill to help us succeed when we face the next test. Oswald Chambers says that the idea of this life "is not that we do work for God, but that we are so loyal to Him that He can do His work through us."

God still had much to accomplish with Abraham and Sarah. It had taken this long to simply get them to a point where they were ready to have their son. Their loyalty, faith and obedience had to be absolute for what they and their descendants would face in the future. Why would God bother to test Abraham? Surely He already knew what the outcome would be? Personally, I think that when God tests us it is often for *our own benefit* rather than His, for that wonderful sense of accomplishment and strength we feel when we know we have made the right choice, as difficult as it might have been, and we have succeeded. Or for that moment of stark clarity as you stand among the ashes and think, "Uh-oh, I forgot to pray again." Stepping out on faith is a progression that builds on both its successes and its failures. We continue to be tested, and must continue to grow and learn right up until the moment of our death.

You would think with their precious Isaac in hand that Sarah and Abraham's commitment to God would have been absolute, right? But was that what it took? Would their faith be as sound had they not received the blessing of little Isaac? Shouldn't true faith hinge not as a reciprocal result of all the good things that we are given, but instead on the belief that there is no one but God worthy of our trust? And don't we sometimes only understand how strong or wise or patient or loyal or trusting or loving we *can be* when we are put to the test and are surprisingly victorious?

What would happen if God *had taken away* Abraham and Sarah's precious Isaac? Clearly this little boy was a miraculous gift from God and not something either of them had brought about on their own. Where would their faith have been then? Would their confidence in God have crumbled? Would they have turned away from God in anger and frustration? Each of us has suffered trying, terrible times when we wonder, "Why are you doing this to me God? Why me?" What would Abraham and Sarah have done in such a situation?

"Take your son, your only son – yes, Isaac, whom you love so much – and go to the land of Moriah. Sacrifice him there as a burnt offering on one of the mountains. Which I will point out to you." (Genesis 22:2) Well, God certainly didn't mince words, did He? Didn't try to blur any of the requirements or spare Abraham any angst. In fact, He gave Abraham ample opportunity to run in the opposite direction.

Over the course of this lifelong journey of learning and spiritual growth, Abraham had repeatedly taken the time to build an altar to the Lord. In addition, there had been a number of times in which an animal sacrifice had been necessary to "seal the deal." God had Abraham sacrifice a heifer, a goat, a ram, a turtledove, and a pigeon all at one time when He declared Abraham righteous for his belief in Genesis 15. But … *Isaac?* As a … *sacrifice?* As in … *killed?*

I'm not sure how old Isaac is when God called Abraham in Genesis 22 but he was old enough to travel and ask questions along the way. Called "one of the greatest acts of obedience in recorded history" (my New Living Translation Bible says in the notes), Abraham didn't hem, haw, stall, ask questions, whine, or offer alternative solutions. He "got up early" the next morning and set off with Isaac, his donkey and two servants. (Genesis 22:3)

What did Abraham tell Sarah? Maybe he told only a half truth. "I'm not sure why, Sarah, but I've got to travel to Moriah with Isaac. That's what the Lord has told me to do." I am inclined to ask, after all these years together, if he could have hidden such a thing from her. I can't imagine Abraham could have behaved calmly and rationally with such a huge secret. Sarah had already had Hagar and Ishmael sent permanently from the camp because Ishmael had been caught simply teasing young Isaac. She would have been a fierce, mother-bear in all aspects of her son's upbringing. Don't you think that Abraham would have had to answer nine million questions? "Where are you going?" "What do you mean you're going to 'some mountain' in Moriah?" "How long will you be gone?" "Why are you going?" "Can I come along?" "Why does Isaac have to go?" "Why are you bringing all that chopped wood?" "What's the hurry?" "Are you hiding something from me, Abraham?"

If Abraham told her the truth, then Sarah, too, was part of this great act of obedience. Perhaps Abraham went to her, anguish evident in every movement and every word he uttered, and told Sarah what the Lord had instructed him to do. Did they cry together through the night, holding and trying to comfort each other? Had they come so far that as they held each other they said, "It is not our place to question this. The Lord has given us Isaac and we must trust Him to do what is best"?

Throughout the entire journal account Abraham never hesitated. He placed the wood on Isaac's shoulders. He himself carried the knife and the fire. When Isaac pointed out that they have the wood and the fire but no lamb for the sacrifice Abraham simply said, "God will   provide ..." (Genesis 22:6-8). They walked *fifty miles* to the place that God directed. Abraham built an altar, placed wood on it, tied Isaac up, laid him on the altar over the wood, took the knife, and raised it up to kill Isaac ...

And a voice from heaven said, "Abraham! Abraham!"

"Yes, I'm listening," Abraham said.

"Lay down the knife ... do not hurt the boy ... now I know that you truly fear God. You have not withheld even your beloved son from me." Suddenly a ram appeared caught by its horns in the thicket and became the sacrifice to the Lord. Father and son together prepared and made the sacrifice to the Lord.

So Abraham proved his faithfulness, obedience, and loyalty to God. Abraham confirmed to himself that obedience to God was the only way to go. But what else did Abraham do? He provided a spectacular example to his young son, Isaac. An example of obedience in the most difficult of situations, of faithfulness in knowing that God would provide in all things, and of priorities in putting God first in life above and beyond all other things. *Wow.* Have you ever come close to such an example during the toughest times of your life? We all should aspire to such is a goal.

If Sarah didn't know the whole plan before they left, then she most assuredly would have heard the whole story once Isaac and Abraham returned. "Mom! Guess what happened on our trip ...!" "And then, after Dad put me on the altar and raised his knife there was this Voice ...!" "And Dad says that God provides always ..."

Belief, loyalty, obedience, trust, growth ... skills that Abram and Sarai had the *potential for* when God called them, and skills that Abraham and Sarah *developed* as their faith grew. Qualities that we too have the capacity for and should continually strive to improve.

For all of you Sarahs out there …

Abraham and Sarah's story is a lesson in patience, faith, loyalty, and obedience. I don't know about you but I am always *so thankful* that not one of these patriarchs and matriarchs was perfect. Where would that leave us? It's always reassuring to me as I read the biblical accounts to think, "Oh whoa, that's a mistake I don't think even I'd make." And yet these are the people that God chose. Not because of their perfection but because they had *potential.* These imperfect people had qualities that we ourselves can have as well. When you read their

> God does not give us hopes and desires that He does not intend to fulfill.
> My Mom

stories and take the time to really study them, you can glean lessons that you can apply to your own life.

God called Abraham righteous simply because he believed. Sarah is given a child because of her faith. Like our own precious children that cause us such heartache and worry, God loves us unconditionally, despite the fact that we repeatedly must drive Him nuts. Here's what you should take away from Sarah's story and who she hooked up with:

❖ **God's calendar and clock run differently than ours**. Ecclesiastes 3:1 says, *There's an opportune time to do things, a right time for everything on the earth.* (MSG) Because we do not know everything, we cannot assume to know what's best for ourselves or anyone else. Practicing godly patience requires trusting that God is in control and knows the best timeline for everything and everyone. I often hear people say, "I prayed about it and God did nothing!" We forget that God says, "Yes" as well as "No." We must remember that while we only know infinitesimally, God knows infinitely.

❖ **God is the perfect parent**. God has all the qualities of the perfect mother and father. He gives instructions - some gently whispered and some loudly shouted - and then lets us make mistakes as well as wise choices, realizing that this is the way we must learn and grow. *How often I have wanted to gather your children together as a hen protects her chicks beneath her wings, but you wouldn't let me.* (Matthew 23:37b) Through it all He waits patiently and loves unconditionally, grieving with us when we weep and rejoicing with us when we smile. His advice is always reliable, His promises are always kept, His reasons are always sound, and His presence is always guaranteed. Now, if we would just listen and obey …

> **Prayer does not fit us for the greater works; prayer *is* the greater work.**
> Oswald Chambers

❖ **When in doubt, pray.** Never plan without God in the equation. Your best laid plans are not always God's plans. You should do nothing – *nothing* – without first going to the Lord in prayer. The value and power of prayer is not appreciated nor utilized enough by any of us.

❖ **God does laugh.** Yes, He is the stern, immovable God that draws boundaries around what is right and what is wrong and expects us to behave according to His commands. That's what a loving individual does: teaches and reproves. But a loving individual also laughs and delights when a job is well done and when success has been achieved. Work to be friends with God, not just a distant acquaintance. "Friendship means identity in thought and heart and spirit." (Oswald Chambers) Practice making Him the first one you 'call' with good *and* bad news, the first one you seek for advice and counsel, and the only one you rely on in everything you say and do.

❖ **No Matter How Good You Are, Your Spirituality Is What**

> **Faith is not intelligent understanding. Faith is deliberate commitment to a Person where I see no way.**
> Oswald Chambers

Defines You. Abram and Sarai were probably the best the world had to offer, but even with that distinction their hearts were not centered on The One True God. Throughout their lives God worked with them patiently and lovingly to help them grow and improve so they were better prepared for what came next in their lives. Where are you on the spiritual maturity scale? Are you an infant, teen, young adult or mature warrior? Chronological age helps in the progress towards these states, but doesn't guarantee anything. Oh, and stepping out in faith never makes sense to our human way of thinking. That's why it's called *faith*.

❖ **Learn and grow from your mistakes as well as your success.** While it is critical that you continue to succeed, it is equally as critical that you don't need to make the same mistake more than once to learn your

76

lesson. We don't want God rolling His eyes and saying, "Not *again*. How many times do I have to explain this to you? How many times do you need to be corrected?" My father used to say, "I buy you books and buy you books but what do you do? Look at the pictures." Make a conscious choice that you are going to improve yourself in a manner pleasing and acceptable to God. Let the difficult times as well as the good times draw you ever closer to God.

Homework ... Where are you on the spiritual path?

Spiritual growth comes about in a variety of areas in your life through knowledge, experience, and service. In addition, it should always complement your God-given talents and interests (that's why He gave them to you). God doesn't need you to be perfect, but He *does* need you to always be growing. Paul in his second letter to the Corinthians said, "*We hope that your faith will grow so that the boundaries of our work among you will be extended.*" (2 Corinthians 10:15b) Growing is *life*, not growing is *death*. Be alive in Christ. Vibrant. Useful. Pleasing. All parents wish for their children to grow up successful, productive, and happy. God desires the same for us, and nothing less.

Q?

How can your strengths AND weaknesses help you improve your level of spiritual maturity?

So, the first step is to determine what level you are on. Then, the responsibility falls into your lap. Work, strive, pray, and dream yourself to the next level. Achieve success for yourself and make God smile in the process.

The Spiritual Infant Level

There is nothing wrong with being on the infant level of spiritual maturity, *unless you've been there all your life!* A baby isn't born able to fly an airplane or to make a gourmet meal. We start out slowly, with bits and pieces preprogrammed into us, our life takes us on a wild ride and we acquire even more bits and pieces. Along the way we hone skills and talents to make us functional and necessary to the life we end up in. Spiritual life is very similar, but unfortunately often horribly neglected.

> **There is one level *below* spiritual infancy. It's called "Dead."**
> McG

Perhaps you are on different levels regarding your knowledge, experience, and service. That's typical. Just as you have to understand yourself emotionally in order to improve and grow, you've got to do the same thing spiritually. Based on our God-given talents, some things are going to be much easier than others. It's important to remember that God wants us to fulfill the plans He has for us: He wants us to complete the job that only we can do. To do that we need to focus on what we're good at and capitalize on it, while at the same time strengthening the things we are weak at.

CHARACTERISTICS OF THE SPIRITUAL INFANT	
Area	**Infant Level**
Knowledge Level Devotions Bible Study Prayer Church Attendance	• Have a tentative belief. • Sometimes attend church and Bible study classes offered at church or small groups. • Begin to read your Bible. • Begin to do a devotional study on your own. • Begin to pray. Ask for spiritual wisdom, commitment, and the ability to follow God's directions. • Ask questions. Seek answers.
Experience Level Participation Sharing your Talents Sharing your Skills Sharing your Knowledge	• Sometimes attend Church and/or spiritually based activities such as dinners, musicals, plays, concerts … • Feel a desire or interest to participate or to share in "the fun." • View with a critical, capable eye things that could be improved or enhanced by you. • Ask questions. Seek answers.

Service Level	• Confirm your church's belief foundation of God and the Bible.
Church Maintenance Visitation Sharing your Professional skills Serving in Church 'Government'	• Make an effort to discover what type of church-supported opportunities are available that would interest you both within the church and within the community. • Ask questions. Seek answers.

The Spiritual Teen Level

The teen level of spiritual maturity is active, interested, and enthusiastic. It's asking provocative questions and then giving thoughtful consideration to the answers you receive. It's discovery time when you begin to determine likes and dislikes about your service preferences ("I'll never be able to sing a solo in front of the church but I'd love to design a new website for the church.") There's also a hesitant enthusiasm involved as well. ("You want me to help out with Vacation Bible School? Are you sure? I've never taught in my life ...") It's also a time when the church family begins to notice and approach you. ("Attend a Tuesday night Bible study at your home? Gee, what time? I don't get off work until 6ish ...")

Those at this level also tend to be rather emotional and unstable at times. ("I don't believe the assistant pastor is leaving! She's the one I liked the most here! Maybe I should attend church somewhere else.") Be careful with your impressions and opinions. ("Not one person has talked to me at coffee hour in three weeks! This church is so unfriendly.") And remember to exercise patience and restraint. ("That's it! I'm never

> **Being a spiritual teenager is just like being a chronological teenager. You think you know almost everything but you really know hardly anything.**
> McG

coming back here! I can't believe that old woman told me my son was distracting her in church!")

Before you react to a situation unfavorably, prayerfully consider if you are behaving like an adult or a teenager ...

79

CHARACTERISITICS OF THE SPIRITUAL TEEN	
Area	**Teen Level**
Knowledge Devotions Prayer Church Attendance Bible Study	• Assist an experienced instructor in a teaching capacity in church school or summer vacation Bible school. • Ask for prayer from your minister or Bible study leader regarding the direction God wishes you to go within the church and within your life. • Pray for your church and those you discover need your prayerful support. • Ask for suggestions as to what devotional you should try reading or biblical study you should try.
Experience Participation Sharing your Talents Sharing your Skills Sharing your Knowledge	• Offer to provide background help for an activity of your choice. • Begin to make acquaintances that could possibly become friends. • Cook for the bake sale, shop for the food bank, sign up for the walkathon, shop at the church based garage sale, have your car washed at the youth group event, donate your old clothes to the church sponsored mission … • Be watchful for opportunities in which your talents, skills, and professional knowledge may be useful to others in need.
Service Church Maintenance Visitation Sharing your Professional skills Serving in Church 'Government'	• Work to become aware of the different aspects within your church community that make your church 'tick'. • Become informed as to the outside areas that the church supports such as missionaries, community outreach services, and national and worldwide organizations. Become informed. • Learn how your church "works": its policies, its hierarchy, its spiritual and worldly authorities. Learn about them. Become informed. • When volunteers are asked for, *volunteer* for something that interests you. • Begin to give financially to the church.

The Spiritual Young Adult Level

I perceive the young adult level to be vibrant and alive. These are the people you see on committees, teaching church school classes, running youth groups, coordinating spaghetti suppers, and showing up on spring and fall clean-up Saturdays. They are the doers, the movers, and the shakers. They're the ones you think of when someone needs something done.

> **Think of the most welcoming person in your church besides your minister. Most likely that person is on the young adult level.**
> McG

This level has the most potential for burn out. Enthusiasm peaks and suddenly you become overwhelmed with all the things you've signed on to do. Resentment can set in because you start to feel as if you're being taken advantage of. ("Why don't they ask someone else for a change?") You might begin to feel as if you need to take a step back. ("I'm going to take the summer off from teaching church school.") You feel guilty for saying no. ("I am already a deacon, the junior youth group leader and on the entertainment and hospitality committee. There is no way I can teach church school this school year!")

During the young adult stage, the danger of disillusionment can be very real and every effort should be made to focus only on the things you enjoy doing the most. The saying really is true: quality, not quantity.

CHARACTIERISTICS OF THE SPIRITUAL YOUNG ADULT	
Area	**Young Adult Level**
Knowledge Devotions Prayer Church Attendance Bible Study	• Teach church school, volunteer in the nursery, help out with youth related activities, join a formal prayer group or email list, pass on devotional studies you have completed to others with recommendations and insights. • Complete devotional studies and Bible studies and begin new ones. • Approach people you have prayed for and ask them how they are doing? Refine your prayers. • Make suggestions for new studies or devotions based on your growing knowledge. • Find a prayer partner who will pray for and with you.

Experience Participation Sharing your Talents Sharing your Skills Sharing your Knowledge	• Formally serve on planning committees to help coordinate and execute an event. *Join* something. • Recruit and encourage new people to participate in church activities other than worship service. • Suggest a new activity or event based on your talents and skills. • Begin to share your opinions and ideas. Keep asking questions. Keep learning.
Service Church Maintenance Visitation Sharing your Professional skills Serving in Church 'Government'	• Formally serve on planning committees assuming some level of responsibility and commitment. • Visit, call, email, or write letters to elderly, missionaries, or the sick. • Recruit and encourage new people to attend and participate. • Offer assistance in those areas of your professional field or talents. Be dependable, accurate, and helpful. • Faithfully give financial support monthly.

The Spiritual Mature Level

Most spiritually mature Christians have a wealth of knowledge, experience and service under their belts. They've been there, done that, survived this, and coped with that. They've learned to say 'no', they've grown thick skins so that little things that may be said on purpose or unintentionally can be ignored, and they've become comfortable with their God-given talents and share them regularly.

> **Never become so mature that you are simply that "old dog" that cannot learn new tricks.**
> McG

The danger of this level is the compulsion to just coast along for the remainder. A feeling of complacency can creep in. ("I've done church school for thirteen years. I've served my time!") Entitlement can create a dangerous gap within the workings of the church. ("It's time someone else washed all the church table cloths. I've done that for what feels like a hundred years!") You can be perceived as being uppity and superior. ("I can't believe that young woman allowed her son to wear that football jersey on Easter Sunday!") You can forget what it was like to be a new Christian. ("Oh no, not *her.* She asks so many questions and makes so many prayer requests. We're never going to get out of here on time.")

Mature Christians must remember that their responsibility is not over until they're *dead.* And while roles change and opportunities shift, we are always called to be God's servants and make Him smile.

CHARACTERISTICS OF THE SPIRITUALLY MATURE	
Area	**Mature Level**
Knowledge Devotions Prayer Church Attendance Bible Study	• Lead your own Bible study class or group • Write your own Bible study course. • Initiate your own prayer group. • Be a knowledgeable, dependable presence in your study group.
Experience Participation Sharing your Talents Sharing your Skills Sharing your Knowledge	• Run the 'show.' • Write the 'show.' • Initiate the 'show.' • Head the committee. • Start the new group or activity.
Service Church Maintenance Visitation Sharing your Professional skills Serving in Church 'Government'	• Chair the committee. • Head the effort. • Provide the solution. • Be the point of expertise. • Become an elder, deacon, or Bible study leader. • Tithe (10%) your salary.

So, where are you? Are you an infant, teen, young adult, or mature Christian? You will probably discover that you are more mature in some areas than in others. Take a few moments to read through the next pages and rate yourself. *This is not meant to intimidate.* It is simply another tool to help you reveal the unique person that God loves and wants to work with. This isn't an exact science, merely a starting off point to help you discover more about yourself and your spiritual walk. Think: what would others say about you? Would they agree with your evaluation of yourself?

Remember, every level has benefits, opportunities, and pitfalls. Discover where you are in each category, what you need to watch out for, and what you need to do to continue to grow ...

Many people who have done this survey find that they are on all different levels: mature in some areas, young adult in others, and infant on some. Well, we can't all be top in every area, can we? That's what makes us *unique* and *special.* If we were all gourmet cooks or all opera singers or all charismatic leaders ... well, you get the picture, right? Think about your results this way: which score do you wish was higher? That should be your starting point.

One last thing: I noticed that when done privately, most people tended to be more critical of themselves and rate themselves lower that how other's viewed them. In my Bible study groups in which we've done this survey and shared our results, there was a consistent theme of, "You should have rated yourself higher!" "That score is ridiculous! Remember all the years you taught first grade Sunday school?!" Sometimes sharing your results with others opens up a whole new area of discovery for yourself: how God has allowed others view you. Try it sharing your results with a trusted friend. What you hear about yourself may be very enlightening.

Sarah: A Heart of Patience

MY SPIRITUAL LEVEL: KNOWLEDGE

0=Never   1=Rarely   2=Sometimes   3=Often   4=Almost Always

Spiritual Quality	0	1	2	3	4
1. I pray.	0	1	2	3	4
2. I read my Bible and do devotions.	0	1	2	3	4
3. I attend church.	0	1	2	3	4
4. I am working on now or have completed Bible studies.	0	1	2	3	4
5. When I don't understand something I ask questions.	0	1	2	3	4
6. When things are difficult in my life I ask for prayer.	0	1	2	3	4
7. I am teaching or have taught church school.	0	1	2	3	4
8. I am leading or have led Bible studies and/or prayer groups.	0	1	2	3	4
9. I am leading or have led youth groups.	0	1	2	3	4
10. I am attending or have attended Bible study classes.	0	1	2	3	4
TOTAL OF COLUMNS (Add totals of numbers circled)					

COMPLETE TOTAL (Add all columns):	
DIVIDE your complete total number by 10 to get your average spiritual knowledge level:	

0=DEAD, 1-1.9=Infant, 2-2.7=Teen, 2.8-3.4=Young Adult, 3.5-4=Mature

In regard to my spiritual level of knowledge, I am a(an):

Remember, the key word: G R O W T H!!

85

MY SPIRITUAL LEVEL: EXPERIENCE

0=Never 1=Rarely 2=Sometimes 3=Often 4=Almost Always

Spiritual Quality	0	1	2	3	4
1. In the past or currently, I have attended and assisted church sponsored activities such as dinners, plays, musicals, picnics, etc.	0	1	2	3	4
2. People at church know me by name as well as other pertinent information such as my profession, my family information, my talents, and other interests.	0	1	2	3	4
3. I know of and understand the workings of the hierarchy within my church and religion.	0	1	2	3	4
4. I have friends at church.	0	1	2	3	4
5. I have invited people to attend my church.	0	1	2	3	4
6. I am serving or have served on church committees.	0	1	2	3	4
7. I share or have shared my opinions and perceptions whether I am asked directly or not.	0	1	2	3	4
8. I am heading or have headed up major church related projects to their completion.	0	1	2	3	4
9. I am currently responsible or have in the past assumed significant responsibilities within the church.	0	1	2	3	4
10. I experience a joy for my active participation in church.	0	1	2	3	4
TOTAL OF COLUMNS (Add totals of numbers circled)	0				

COMPLETE TOTAL (Add all columns):	
DIVIDE your complete total number by 10 to get your average spiritual knowledge level:	

0=DEAD, 1-1.9=Infant, 2-2.7=Teen, 2.8-3.4=Young Adult, 3.5-4=Mature

In regard to my spiritual level of experience, I am a (an):

Remember, the key word: G R O W T H!!

MY SPIRITUAL LEVEL: SERVICE

0=Never   1=Rarely   2=Sometimes   3=Often   4=Almost Always

Spiritual Quality	0	1	2	3	4
1. I understand what makes my church different from other churches in regard to biblical and doctrinal topics.	0	1	2	3	4
2. I am participating or have participated in other church sponsored missions such as food, clothing, and other mission oriented activities with my time and/or my money.	0	1	2	3	4
3. I am supporting or have supported through prayer and financial donations our church sponsored missionaries.	0	1	2	3	4
4. I am fully aware of the outside organizations both nationally and internationally that our church affiliates itself with.	0	1	2	3	4
5. I am or have been dependable, accurate and faithful in all aspects of my service.	0	1	2	3	4
6. I support the church financially.	0	1	2	3	4
7. I have invited people to help at church with me.	0	1	2	3	4
8. I am serving or have served in a leadership capacity within the church.	0	1	2	3	4
9. People have asked me to assist in different projects and I have done so.	0	1	2	3	4
10. I feel that I assist or have assisted this church towards its active and vibrant ministry within this community and the world.	0	1	2	3	4
TOTAL OF COLUMNS (Add totals of numbers circled)	0				

COMPLETE TOTAL (Add all columns):	
DIVIDE your complete total number by 10 to get your average spiritual knowledge level:	

0=DEAD, 1-1.9=Infant, 2-2.7=Teen, 2.8-3.4=Young Adult, 3.5-4=Mature

In regard to my spiritual level of service, I am a (an):

So, how did you do? Do you feel your results were accurate? Were you surprised at your scores? Was it hard for you to evaluate yourself? Do you think, if you showed this to a close friend at church that they would agree with how you rated yourself?

The key in all of this is: *Don't be stagnant.* There is nothing wrong with any stage of a growing plant or a developing child, or even a building under construction. It's only when the progress *stops* that we throw the plant out, rush the child to the doctor, or start charging the contractor fees for being behind schedule.

Which, of course, is the most important part of a healthy heart ... *growth.*

GROW
REACH
OPEN
WORK
THRIVE
HOPE

Question To Discuss:

Q?

In what ways could you improve a situation that tries your patience that would be pleasing to God?

She may have been the first wife but she would never be the one her husband wanted.

Leah and Her Sister's Husband

A Heart Of Self-Confidence

Leah. A young woman who grew up with a cunning father, married a man who's name meant "deceiver," and lived with the consequences of her own deceit her entire life. Pretending to be her younger, more beautiful sister on the day of her wedding, Leah was forever relegated to being the unloved wife. The twisted dynamics of a family in which sisters became co-wives to a man that loved only one of them had all the makings of an unbelievable soap-opera plot.

While we will never know what prompted the sisters to agree to such a sham, the level of jealousy and lifelong animosity that grew between them could not be disguised in the biblical story. Leah and her sister Rachel's story is a classic example of a loving relationship between two women that fell apart because of a man.

But Leah, miraculously I think, managed to rise above all of this conflict and drama and make a real connection with The One True God. While her husband Jacob – the man whom God would rename Israel - seemed to spend a substantial part of his time coping with his crafty father-in-law, making babies with his four wives (yes, he added two more), dealing with his resulting recalcitrant twelve sons and one doomed daughter, and trying to get back to the family that he left for fear of his life, Leah slowly, quietly, and with great dignity became a woman after God's own heart.

It was Leah – not her sister - whom God chose to be an ancestress of Christ when her son was given the promise of "the ruler's staff." (Genesis 49:10) Of the twelve Israelite tribes, it was be from Leah's son Judah's tribe that Christ was born. Eve's promise, then Sarah's, is now Leah's, another woman worthy of such distinction.

Leah's story is not the kind of story produced by television and Hollywood with the picture perfect happy ending. Rather, it is a story of real life, told with genuine heartaches and beautiful joys. While we might feel momentary elation finishing a "happily ever after" story, the reality of life always eventually returns to us. But Leah's story is one we all can learn from. Read on, take notes, and enjoy this journal account. Because, you see, Leah over the course of her life gained the self-confidence to believe that she was absolutely priceless. And as a result, found something we all search for but sometimes never find: *true love.*

First Things First

Scripture references you should check out:	Genesis 25-34
Question to ask yourself before you read any further:	At times when you are at your lowest, where do you draw your strength?
What her name means:	"Leah" is Hebrew in origin and means "delicate," "weary," or "faint from sickness." As she is described in the Bible in reference to her eyes: "tender-eyed" (KJV), "eyes that didn't sparkle" (CEV), "weak eyes" (NIV) it seems as if there was some deficiency there.

Connections:	Leah grew up in the shadow of her exquisitely beautiful younger sister, Rachel. Even before Jacob came on the scene it seemed to have been the point of reference for everyone who knew Laban's two daughters. For Leah's entire life she was never able to measure up to the outward standard of beauty by which *everyone* seemed compelled to judge her. But to her credit, she discovered that it wasn't the outside that counted.
What the Bible says about confidence:	How you get it: Job 4:6 Where not to put it: Psalm 146:3 Where you should put it: Jeremiah 17:7-8, Hebrews 6:17-18 Be careful of what kind you have: Luke 18:9-14 What behavior should bring it about: 2 Corinthians 1:12 Warnings about it: James 4:13-17

Questions We'll Never Know The Answers To:

❖ Did Jacob ever grow to appreciate Leah and her love?

❖ Why did Leah and Rachel cooperate with their father Laban's deceitful plan?

Did you know? Interesting Biblical Facts About Leah

❖ **Polygamy:** God's intention for marriage was monogamy. Otherwise He would have created Adam, Eve, and Evette. "This explains why a man leaves his father and mother and is joined to his wife, and the *two* are united into *one*." (Genesis 2:24, my emphasis.) But just as we're not supposed to lie, cheat, steal, etc., this little rule about two becoming one was often put by the wayside by many of the Bible's esteemed patriarchs and kings (Abraham, Jacob, David, Solomon …). There is *not one instance* in which this scenario breeds love, happiness and unity. In his defense, Jacob didn't start out with a plan for polygamy. He shared the first biblically recorded kiss with Rachel in Genesis 29:11, and the journal entry clearly states "Jacob was in love with Rachel." (Genesis 29:18) *So* in love that the seven years he had to work to marry her to fulfill his bride price obligation seemed to him "but a few days." (Genesis 29:20) Unfortunately, things didn't go the way Jacob planned or wanted.

❖ **Concubines:** Concubines were females a man was lawfully allowed to have sexual intercourse with other than his wife. Sarai gave her maid, Hagar, to Abraham in her desperate attempt to gain a child, elevating Hagar to the level of "servant wife" or concubine. As children were greatly valued, a childless couple might resort to a concubine after years of infertility. Moses made laws protecting concubines (and multiple wives) not because God approved of it, but rather to protect innocent victims. (Exodus 21:10-11, Deuteronomy 21:15-17)

❖ **Names:** Jacob's name means "the supplanter" or, to put it in modern day terms the usurper, claim jumper, or wrong doer. He showed up at Laban's place (Leah and Rachel's father) because he was running from his twin brother, Esau. You see, Jacob had stolen his older brother's rightful birthright and familial blessing from his father Isaac, and was fearing for his life. At this point in Jacob's life, *despite the fact* that he is Abraham and Sarah's precious grandson and the one destined to continue The Promised Covenant with The One True God, he had a rather dubious track record.

❖ **Bride Price:** It was customary for a man to present a dowry or substantial gift to the family of his future wife. A compensation, if you will, for the loss of the labor of the young woman once she was married and gone. The bride price could be anything agreed to by the prospective bridegroom and the father of the bride: money, service, or, in the case of David trying to marry King Saul's daughter Michal, 100 Philistine foreskins. (I Samuel 18:25) David, just to show his mettle, brought King Saul 200 foreskins and got his girl. (I Samuel 18:26-27) Jacob agreed to work for Laban for seven years for the privilege of marrying Rachel – quite a steep price! Whatever Jacob would have earned as a shepherd – *for seven years* – was an astronomically high bride price compared to what would have normally been paid to a father. In agreeing to this arrangement without hesitation, Jacob showed what a high value he placed on his wife-to-be.

❖ **Weddings, Celebrations and Clothing:** On the day of the wedding everyone would have been dressed in their finest (just as we are today). A bridegroom wore a special "wedding suit" including a special headdress, and the bride would have been decked out in white robes, often richly embroidered. She would have worn all the family jewels, a bridal veil, and a garland on her head. (Isaiah 61:10) There would have been extensive celebrating with songs, music, and dancing, and the whole town would have probably come to the affair. A huge feast would have been served with extensive partying. And while the marriage would have been officially consummated that first night, the celebration would have continued for *seven days*.

❖ **Laban:** Laban kept turning up in the Genesis account kind of like a bad penny. Greedy and cunning, he seemed to always look out for number one, and his primary concern was the level of his wealth. (Genesis 24:30-31) He lived in Haran, the city from which Abram and Sarai had departed many years before by godly direction. Laban's father was Bethuel, the son of Abram's brother, Nahor. (Genesis 29:5) It was to Bethuel that Abram sent his most trusted servant to secure a wife for his precious son, Isaac. Isaac's wife, Rebekah was Laban's sister. When Jacob deceived his brother, Esau, Rebekah told him, "Go to your Uncle Laban in Haran." (Genesis 27:43)

❖ **Father's Blessing and Firstborn Blessing:** In Biblical times, the firstborn son got double the inheritance of all the others, and many other perks including his father's special blessing. Esau, as the firstborn of twins, was entitled to significant benefits. Esau has been criticized almost as much for not valuing his birthright (he sold it when he was hungry to Jacob for a bowl of stew) as Jacob has been criticized for his deceit (he disguised himself as Esau to trick their blind father into giving him Esau's blessing). A father's blessing, reinforced with the God-given spiritual covenant, had a prophetic quality. It "had the force of a will and was also thought to fix the future of the sons he blessed." (Lockyer) As a result, despite Jacob's deceit, he has been commended for having "enough faith to see the value of the spiritual. In this he contrasts with Esau, to whom the notion of a spiritual realm beyond what he could see and taste and feel seemed nonsense." (Richards)

The Core Story

Jacob ... This was God's chosen man?

Jacob knew enough about the family's birthright to risk everything to acquire it. A mama's boy right from the start, he was "the kind of person who liked to stay at home" and even liked to cook. (Genesis 25:27-29) There was no love lost between him and his twin brother, Esau, as the Bible reported that they fought with each other while still in their mother Rebekah's womb. (Genesis 25:22) When mother Rebekah complained about it to the Lord, she was told by God, "The sons in your womb will become two rival nations. One nation will be stronger than the other; the descendants of your older son will serve the descendants of your younger son." (Genesis 25:23)

Interesting, huh? Rebekah gave birth knowing that she would have twin boys and, in addition, knowing that the older would be dominated by the younger. I suppose this initial prophecy was what earned Jacob his name. (Esau, if you're curious, means 'hairy.') Was all this self-fulfilling prophecy, nature, or nurture? Probably a little bit of each. While Rebekah is not mentioned in Jacob's scheme to get the birthright from Esau (it is traded for some of Jacob's tasty stew), it was Rebekah who orchestrated the entire deception of the final blessing from old, blind daddy Isaac. "My son," Rebekah told Jacob, "do exactly as I tell you ..." (Genesis 27:8) She cooked the meal, came up with the disguise for Jacob to wear, and even promised to assume the curse that Isaac could rightfully impart on Jacob should he have been caught. (Genesis 27:9-13)

Jacob, good boy that he was, did exactly as his mother instructed and ended up with Esau's treasured birthright and paternal blessing, plus a brother who wanted him good and dead. Rebekah again intervened and slyly convinced Isaac to send Jacob back to her brother Laban's family and get him away from "the local Hittite women." (Genesis 27:46)

It is important to note that at this point in the story Esau already had a number of heathen wives (Genesis 26:34, 36:1-5) who "made life miserable for Isaac and Rebekah." (Genesis 26:35) In the end, Esau would have accumulated six wives, none of them on the right spiritual path. This is an important fact because as the firstborn, Esau was responsible for the spiritual temperature of the family. More than just a financial privilege, the birthright had a high spiritual value as well. It was the firstborn son who served as the family priest and was responsible for promoting the worship of The One True God. Between Esau's heathen wives and his equating the value of his birthright with a bowl of stew (no matter how good it was), Esau clearly did not have the potential for being the person that God needed to head the family blessed with The Promise.

On the road to his Uncle Laban, Jacob dreamed the famous dream about the ladder to heaven. He may have been far from perfect, he may not have appreciated exactly what he'd stolen from his brother, he may not even have believed all the hype and stories he'd heard all his life from his father, but on the road to Haran, at a place he named Bethel ("house of God"), Jacob got the full and complete message from God. If Jacob didn't understand what he'd stolen, by the time he woke up and made his way to Uncle Laban, he got it. "Surely the Lord is in this place, and I wasn't even aware of it … If God will be with me and protect me on this journey and give me food and clothing and if He will bring me back safely to my father, then I will make the Lord my God." (Genesis 28:20) While his wording might sound sort of conditional to us, Jacob was, in effect, confirming his belief in the promise that God had just made to him. "I get it God. I'm yours. It's a deal." (ST)

It would seem that the seed was planted in fertile soil.

Sisters … What bound them together?

Laban had two daughters: Leah and Rachel. As with most biblical accounts, the women's stories are often told as a secondary story to the primary account. The Bible's journal story focuses primarily on Jacob, the one with whom God will carry on The Promise. But just because someone isn't in the limelight doesn't mean he or she doesn't count. I don't know about you, but I haven't been on the cover of People magazine lately, nor have I been featured recently as the front page headliner. The majority of us are often "background players" to the huge big picture story. But I have news for you: those with renown couldn't make it without us. So while most of Leah and Rachel's stories are told through the sidebars of Jacob's life, how they did or didn't handle things is just as important a lesson as anyone else's.

Leah and Rachel were sisters. Leah the oldest, Rachel the more beautiful. Leah the one who saw to the home responsibilities, Rachel the one who traveled the countryside working as a shepherdess. Both were unmarried. The dominant wisdom over the years was that Leah had something nasty going on with her eyes. Were they dysfunctional? Deformed? Just plain ugly compared to her lovely sister? Translations vary

Q?

Why is self-confidence based on a godly assessment so much more powerful than self-confidence based on a worldly assessment?

from "pretty eyes" (NLT) to "dull eyes" (also NLT) to "delicate eyes" (NKJV), to "tender eyes" (ASV), to "weak eyes" (NIV). Hard to say for sure but something was definitely going on with her eyes! Within the same verse about Leah's eyes, the Bible says, "but, Rachel was beautiful in every way, with a lovely face and shapely figure." (Genesis 29:17) Sue Translation (ST): Rachel was *hot*, Leah was *not*. Jacob took one look at Rachel: capable, gorgeous, and outgoing, and

fell head over heals in love with her. Within a month Jacob was bargaining his time and skills for the privilege of marrying luscious Rachel. Daddy Laban probably couldn't believe his luck! He got *free labor* for seven years and married a daughter off! What a deal!

Absolutely nothing is told about those seven years that Jacob worked for Laban. Nothing except that for Jacob the time felt like "but a few days" because he was so in love with Rachel. (Genesis 29:20) Hmmm, the Bible doesn't usually wax this poetic about love, does it? Unless you're cruising through the Song of Solomon reading about "cheeks like rosy pomegranates" (Song of Solomon 6:7) and "breasts like twin fawns" (Song of Solomon 4:5), usually love descriptions consist of "Now Adam slept with his wife ..." (Genesis 4:1) or "David comforted Bathsheba, his wife, and slept with her ..." (2 Samuel 12:24) or "Isaac brought Rebekah into his mother's tent, and she became his wife ..." (Genesis 24:67) Obviously the author (Moses) wanted us to get the full scale impact of Jacob's love for Rachel. Jacob obviously *had it bad.*

But what did the sisters think of Jacob? Who knew? While the biblical account states on a number of occasions how much Jacob loved Rachel, and even makes a point to state "he loved [Rachel] more than Leah" (Genesis 29:30), it never added "and Rachel loved him back." Surely the two sisters talked about this man who had shown up and promised to work seven years for Rachel. Did they giggle and flirt with him? Tease and joke with him? Did one report to the other what Jacob was doing, where he was, and what he was wearing each day? Did they all share meals together, giving each other furtive glances? Was Jacob always trying to steal a few moments alone with Rachel?

When the seven years were up, Jacob said to Laban, "Now give me my wife so we can be married," and Laban invited the whole neighborhood to the wedding feast. (Genesis 29:21-22) I'm sure it was a huge bash with only the finest food and wine. The bride would have been exquisitely garbed in finely embroidered linen, jewels, and perfume.

Jacob had worked seven long years for the privileged delight of claiming Rachel as his wife. He was one happy boy on that wedding day, I'll tell you. He probably partied up a storm, too: wine, food, singing, and dancing. No one would have remembered seeing a bridegroom so happy or *so in love*. When Jacob finally got escorted to the marriage tent … well … Let's just say his senses would have been on overload between the wine and the love and *finally* getting his hands on beautiful, luscious Rachel.

It was not until he woke up the next morning that Jacob realized that not only was he married to *Leah*, but he'd also slept with her. He "rages" at Laban, "What do you mean by this trickery?" (Genesis 29:25)

Laban (you can picture him shrugging his shoulders in studied innocence) said, "It is not our custom to marry off a younger daughter ahead of the firstborn. Wait until the bridal week is over, and you can have Rachel, too – that is if you promise to work another seven years for me." (Genesis 29:26-27)

"So Jacob agreed to work seven more years. A week after Jacob had married Leah, Laban gave him Rachel, too … So Jacob slept with Rachel too, and he loved her more than Leah." (Genesis 29:28-30)

Sounds like a horrible arrangement doesn't it? Seems like a plan that has disaster written all over it. But one thing is crystal clear when you read between the lines of this journal entry: I can't see how this scheme of Laban's could have possibly been pulled off without both sisters agreeing to the deception. Leah and Rachel had to have agreed to their father's plan and cooperated implicitly to get it to work. And what does that tell us about those women?

I think the sisters honestly cared for one another. This plan wouldn't have worked if there was this huge pile of jealousy stewing on Leah's side and another huge pile of privileged entitlement on Rachel's. Did Rachel know that Leah's prospects were slim to none, and that if this opportunity with Jacob slipped by she could spend her life unwed and childless? Or, was there *another* husbandly prospect for Leah that for the sisters was *worse* than this scheme their father cooked up? Did Leah desire marriage and children so much that she was willing to risk her new husband's fury and settle for always being unloved? Had Rachel always looked out for Leah despite being the youngest, and did she see no reason to change things even with the prospect of her marriage looming? Did the sisters care for each other so much that the thought of being separated (as would surely have happened with Jacob going back to claim his inheritance from his father one day) make them desperate to ensure their lifelong togetherness? Did Laban have purely greed-based motives with this arrangement, or did he know that with Rachel, Leah's married life would have companionship and sisterly love and affection if nothing else?

Leah gambled the quality of her married future by agreeing to her father's arrangement. Rachel, on the other hand, gambled her future husband's passionate love and affection by being an accomplice to her father's deceit, and in the end they both got what they wanted.

But did they win or lose? Did beautiful Rachel ever imagine that she would one day be jealous of her "ugly" sister, Leah? Did Leah ever imagine the full extent of the heartache of being the unloved wife? Did Rachel ever conceive that life would not go exactly the way she planned? Did Leah ever envision a situation in which she would hold the upper hand in the way the cards of life would be dealt? Ahh, life. Always unpredictable … Always surprising …

Married Life … Is this the way it's supposed to be?

So, here's what Jacob had after a little over seven years of working for his Uncle Laban: first wife, Leah, along with her servant girl, Zilpah, second wife Rachel, along with her servant girl, Bilhah, and another seven years of obligation to work to pay off his debts. Over the years, Laban's family would have certainly heard some version of what brought Jacob to their door. Perhaps some of the deception and theft would have been filtered out or, given Laban's penchant for achieving wealth and power at all costs … maybe not. Certainly Jacob would have relayed the fascinating dream about the ladder from heaven and angels and the spectacular promise from The One True God! That would surely have impressed Rachel and her family, wouldn't it?

Did Rachel think, "Hmmm, now this guy is definitely husband material with all this spiritual blessing stuff guaranteed in his future!" Did Laban think, "Whoa, this guy's got potential. I'd better make sure he never leaves. Good things are going to happen to anyone who stays with this one!" Did Leah sit in awe and wonder and think, "Surely this man is chosen by The One True God! I can't wait to hear more of what he has to say."

Jacob apparently didn't learn any lessons from the mistakes his mother Rebekah and father Isaac made about the ugly affects of favoritism. After many years of infertility (yes, again), Rebekah and Isaac were finally blessed with not one but two sons. Isaac favored eldest son Esau as would have been fitting within the whole "firstborn son status" thing. But Rebekah favored Jacob, causing conflict and jealousy between the parents and the boys. Rebekah favored Jacob enough that she aided, abetted and encouraged the deception that Jacob perpetrated to secure the coveted firstborn blessing from his father and his brother.

We are products of our upbringing, are we not? Jacob, raised in favoritism and conflict, continued the pattern by blatantly favoring Rachel over Leah. Please note that the journal account does not imply in any way that Rachel ever encouraged this attention. At least not at first, anyway. Perhaps after an entire life of always

> No one can make you feel inferior without your consent.
> Eleanor Roosevelt

being the more beautiful one, Rachel simply expected the primary attention and consequently thought nothing of always receiving it. Conversely, Leah, having lived a whole life in her sister's shadow, would not have thought it odd to once again be in the position of being second best. But what both young women never factored in was the power of the heart when it comes to relationships and intimacy. That cannot be understood until it is experienced.

Based on the way the Lord responded to Leah, it would seem that while Leah may have been *accustomed* to being second best, she experienced true heartache once she became officially the unloved wife of Jacob. "Because Leah was unloved, the Lord let her have a child ..." (Genesis 29:31) Apparently, things were more difficult than Leah had comprehended they would be. She gave birth to a boy whom she named Rueben which means "look, a son!" (and also sounds very closely like the Hebrew for "He has seen my misery.") The Bible records her as saying, "The Lord has noticed my misery and now my husband will love me." (Genesis 29:32)

Whoa. Sounds like this girl was *sad*. But, based on the way things progress, Rueben's birth didn't make Jacob love Leah any more, although it certainly kept him returning to her bed. When Simeon, ("One who hears") was born, Leah said, "The Lord heard that I was unloved and has given me another son." (Genesis 29:33) When Levi ("feeling affection for") is born, Leah says, "Surely now my husband will feel affection for me, since I have given him three sons!" (Genesis 29:34) Leah's hope stayed alive through three pregnancies: close to four years probably.

> **Every small positive change we make in ourselves repays us in confidence in the future.**
> Alice Walker

But by the time baby number four rolled around, the dream for Jacob to love her seemed to have faded. The reality of what her worth was (good for bearing sons but not for love) seemed to have become crystal clear to Leah. After Leah's fourth son, Judah, ("Praise") was born, she said, "Now I will praise the Lord!" completely eliminating Jacob from the equation. (Genesis 29:35) It would seem that *finally* Leah had begun to focus on Someone worthy of her devotion.

100

I suspect that the reality of Leah's astronomical fertility caused Jacob more grief than joy. After the birth of her sister Leah's fourth child Judah, Rachel seemed to reach the end of her rope. "Give me children, or I'll die!" she shouted at Jacob. "Am I God?" Jacob shouted back at her. (Genesis 30:1-2) Uh-oh. Trouble in paradise. Probably for the first time in her life Rachel found herself jealous of her sister. I can only begin to imagine the emotions Rachel faced: the inadequacy of her infertility, while at the same time struggling with the green monster of jealousy for the sister to whom she had *always* been held superior.

It is at this point that the journal entry records that Leah stopped having children. Hmmm. Wonder why? Did Leah, recognizing her sister's distress, cease to seek out Jacob for familial relations? Did Rachel, jealous and hormonal, give Jacob an ultimatum, "Don't come to my tent if you're going to keep going to Leah's!" Did Jacob try to pacify his favorite wife by distancing himself from Leah? "I've already got four strapping sons. What's the harm in just concentrating on Rachel?"

Q?

What is your reaction to this statement? "Self-confidence is the best and brightest opportunity for Satan to be victorious."

Please note that not once was God consulted in any of this. There is no record of Laban, Leah, and Rachel "praying about a solution," nor do we hear Rachel praying about her barrenness. Jacob doesn't ask God for help solving this growing dilemma in his camp, but merely reminds Rachel (with a bit of angry sarcasm I wonder?) that God is "the only one able to give you children." (Genesis 30:2) Leah, in the naming of her last son, seems to be the only one of the group that seems to *finally* be cluing in to the correct direction of life: praising and honoring God. Good for her!

Life at the Jacobs', originally conceived (albeit incorrectly) in unity and compromise, had degenerated to misery, jealousy, and rage. Sigh. But we could have guessed that, couldn't we? And guess what? *It gets worse.*

I have a solution … Why not try this?

Rachel resorted to a solution that had been used in the family before. Sarah and Abraham had tried it. *Not successfully. Not within God's plan or pleasure.* But they did try it. Sarah gave her maid Hagar to Abraham in an attempt to "have a child through her servant." While a child *was* born (Ishmael), it was a disastrous move, causing complications and heartaches that we still feel today! Rachel took her maid Bilhah to Jacob and said, "Sleep with my servant, Bilhah, and she will bear children for me." (Genesis 30:4)

Are you saying to yourself, "Here we go again?" Bilhah conceived and bore a son whom Rachel named Dan ("to vindicate"). Rachel exclaimed at the birth, "God has vindicated me! He has heard my request and given me a son." (Genesis 30:6) Bilhah had a second son whom Rachel named Naphtali ("my struggle") because, as Rachel put it, "I have had an intense struggle with my sister, and I am winning." (Genesis 30:8)

Well. Sounds like *she* was on the right track, huh? (I hope you're picking up sarcasm in my tone.) Suddenly this whole childbirth thing is revealed to be a *competition* with her sister?! For the first and only time in her life, Leah had been more successful than her sister, and *Rachel couldn't stand it.* God's vindication that Rachel claimed at Dan's birth was not for the child Rachel so desperately wanted but, it seemed, it was because she was *at last* on the road to besting her sister. Which begs the question why did Rachel want a baby in the first place? Because she desired to be a mother or because she couldn't stand being in her sister's fruitful shadow?

Whether Leah was not conceiving because her body wasn't cooperating, or she was trying to mollify her jealous sister and not welcome Jacob to her bed, or Jacob was avoiding her because of Rachel's threats, Leah jumped on the "sleep with my servant and get me a child" bandwagon and good 'ole Jacob obliged. Zilpah, Leah's servant woman, conceived and bore a son whom Leah named Gad ("good fortune"). "See how fortunate I am!" Leah exclaimed at Gad's birth. (Genesis 30:11) Son number two for Zilpah Leah named Asher ("Happy") and Leah said, "What joy is mine! The other women will consider me happy indeed!" (Genesis 30:13) Hmm. I hope that Leah meant that sincerely and the real translation isn't, "Are you keeping count, Rachel? I'm up to *six sons!* Nah, nah, na, nah, nah!"

Are you tired? I am,

just reading and writing about all these kids. Jacob now had four wives and *eight sons.* (It was possible that the boys are all under the age of eight, too!) How confusing must it have been at night when everyone was going to their tents, scrambling to get all the children settled in their beds. "Jacob! It's my turn tonight!" "It is not! He was with you two days ago!" "You're a liar!" "Jacob, isn't it your night to be with me?" I can see Jacob standing there in the shadows of the sunset thinking, "What have I gotten myself into?"

But the primary wives were not finished yet. Rachel might have felt slightly vindicated and partially victorious, but the reality was she was still barren, and her sister was not. The fact that Leah was no longer conceiving didn't seem to make things any smoother. In fact, it only seemed to add to the drama.

One day Rueben, Leah's eldest son, found some mandrake roots during the wheat harvest. Mandrakes are a yellowish, sweet-tasting fruit that is a relative to the potato. It had a narcotic quality about it and may have been used for medicinal purposes. But what made it most valuable was that it was referred to as "the love apple," and was considered a type of love potion. Based on Rachel's reaction, mandrakes were not easily found. The Bible says she "begged" Leah to give some of them to her. (Genesis 30:14) Nothing else had worked to get her pregnant, maybe this would!

The claws came out though. Leah said in anger, "Wasn't it enough that you stole my husband? Now will you steal my son's mandrake roots, too?" (Genesis 30:15a) Ooo, don't hold back, Leah; tell us how you really feel. Finally, after all these years, Leah's calling her sister a ... thief! Whoa.

Rachel said in response, "I will let him sleep with you tonight in exchange for the mandrake roots." (Genesis 30:15b) No denial, no arguing back and forth. Rachel wanted those mandrake roots in a big way. And obviously, Leah's lack of child bearing was indeed directly related to Rachel controlling where Jacob was sleeping. Rachel had done more than steal her husband a week after Leah's wedding; Rachel had deprived Leah's husband from Leah's marital bed.

And Leah wanted Jacob and what he could give her. Not love. Not affection. Oh, no, she was long past waiting for those pipe dreams. But Jacob *could* give her another child - the source of her joy and fulfillment. As Jacob came in from the fields that evening, Leah walked out to meet him. Oh man, I bet his steps slowed as she came walking out towards him, full of purpose and determination. *"Now what?"* he was probably thinking. "Can't a guy get just a few moments of peace in his own home?"

Leah cut right to the chase. "You must sleep with me tonight! I have paid for you with some mandrake roots my son has found." (Genesis 30:16) "Paid for you" as in "hired" (NIV), "bartered" (MSG), or rented (ST).

Did Jacob realize what he'd lost? As the two stood there on the edge of the field, did Jacob look into Leah's 'different' eyes and see the *lack* of love she no longer had for him? Did Jacob begin to sweat, knowing that surely if Leah had gotten Rachel to okay this scheme, that there had to be something else brewing just around the corner? Could he feel the weight of dread press down on his shoulders? Did his nervous gaze flit over the entire camp, trying to determine when the other bomb would drop?

Leah got her wish, Jacob slept with her, and she gave birth to her fifth, son whom she named Issachar ("reward"). Without any means to "rent" Jacob again, Leah somehow managed to conceive again and give birth to son number six whom she named "Zebulun ("honor") saying, "God has given me good gifts for my husband. Now he will honor me, for I have given him six sons." (Genesis 30:20)

> **The more confident we are in God's loving gaze, the less driven we will be to win the loving gaze of others.**
> Cynthia Hicks

Note that Leah was not talking about love anymore in regard to Jacob, was she? Now she's aiming for honor. Honor as in: glory, respect, recognition, dignity, esteem, integrity, or distinction. Whoa. Seriously, who needs love when you can get *that* from someone, huh? Consistently, every time Leah named her children, she looked to the Lord for the blessing and honor it was. With each child she seemed to blossom with joy and happiness for what she had, rather than wither and die for what she had not. She was no longer basing her happiness and strength on something *outside her* – her loveless marriage. Leah was now drawing from a strength from within: delighting in what the Lord had equipped her with and given her to succeed. Step. Back. Jack!

Did Jacob's attitude change toward Leah? Did he notice this change in her? Was he with her long enough to begin to see the golden lining within? Did Jacob begin to grow tired of Rachel's complaints and begin to value and *honor* the worth of Leah? Had Jacob begun to realize that the outside of these two sisters was not what he should have noticed in the first place?

Leah with the sad eyes, first wife whom Jacob never appreciated or loved, had given *him* six fine sons. Over the years, rather than become bitter and hateful, she had become resigned to her place and confident of her worth. Surely, God was confirming His pleasure with her through giving her so many sons! Hadn't God kept His part of The Promise to give Jacob so many descendants that they would be as numerous as the dust of the earth? If God was truly with Jacob as He had promised, then wasn't it time for Jacob to recognize and appreciate what God had faithfully given? It would have been wonderful if Jacob had finally clued into Leah's worth, wouldn't it?

After all these boys, Leah's last child was a daughter whom she named Dinah ("Justice"). (Genesis 30:21) Interesting name, isn't it? Justice? For what? Did Leah finally become comfortable with herself and her life? Did she sit outside her tent watching her progeny and laugh to herself that poor, old, Leah with the weak eyes whom no one had wanted, had produced such a glorious, ruckus bunch of children? Was she able to delight in the glory of God's blessing and at the birth of her daughter, wishing for her nothing more than the joy she now knew? Did Jacob finally recognize Leah's intrinsic beauty rather than her outward deformity? Did the two finally reach an agreement of sorts to respect, honor, and treasure each other with or without the factor of "true love"?

Q?

What makes us dismiss what we have and instead wish for what we don't have?

God does everything for a reason. Nothing is random or haphazard. After all these years of infertility and drama, suddenly "God remembered Rachel's plight and answered her prayers by giving her a child." (Genesis 30:22) Did you catch it? God *answered her prayers.* Hello? That's the first time *anyone* in the Jacob family is recorded as praying. Isaac pleaded to God for Rebekah's infertility and "the Lord answered Isaac's prayer." (Genesis 25:21)   As many of us do, it seems after trying to solve her infertility with action, force of will, and magic potions, Rachel *finally* resorted to prayer.

Are you sitting there reading this thinking, "I pray all the time and don't get what I want"?   I was going to add that perhaps, at this time within the Jacobs, *many* circumstances were coming about to reinforce God's perfect timing.   Leah was *finally* confident and secure within herself.   Jacob was *finally* mature and in control of his life and his family.   And Rachel had, at last, perhaps come to the realization that life wasn't all about *her*.   When all the pieces were *finally* in the right place, the picture was perfect.

Rachel gave birth to a son and named him Joseph ("may He add") saying, "May the Lord give me yet another son."   (Genesis 29:24)   So every time she said her son's name would be a prayer asking for another child. Hmmm.   Nice.

Close to twenty years had passed since Jacob had run in fear for his life from his brother Esau. (Genesis 31:38)   Along the way, Jacob had acquired quite a bit: four wives, twelve children, numerous servants, thousands and thousands of sheep and goats, tents, equipment, camels, donkeys … Despite his father-in-law's greed and cunning, God had helped Jacob amass an amazing fortune.   Maybe it was time to cut those apron strings with Uncle Laban and wander on back to see if brother Esau was still mad enough to … kill?

I Want To Go Home … Is it time to go yet?

Jacob had matured a bit.   He had learned to keep a semblance of peace and control within the camp.   After sixty years he had learned a thing or two.   Rather than commanding his four wives to pack up, he did a very wise thing.   He sat down with Leah and Rachel and privately explained not only his rationale for wanting to leave ("Your father has turned against me and is not treating me like he used to"), but all of his private communications with God ("God of my father has been with me … God has not allowed [Laban] to do me any harm … God has made me wealthy …"), and what his goals for the future are ("God has said to me … leave this country and return to the land you came from…"). (Genesis 31:4-13)

106

Were we to tune into the story at this point, we would be suitably impressed with this level-headed, spiritual, and sensitive man, wouldn't we? The women responded maturely, saying "There's nothing for us here ... do whatever God has told you." (Genesis 31:14-16) In a flash, the tents were packed, the camels were loaded, the kids were herded up (all twelve of them!), and off Jacob set back to see Mommy and Daddy in the land of Canaan.

We've got to give Jacob quite a bit of credit here. He's listening to God, and returning to a place he had run from *in fear for his life.* Seemed as if Mr. Jacob had not only matured emotionally and intellectually, but had done some substantial spiritual growing these past twenty years as well. Good for him. Billy Graham once said, "Faith that saves has one distinguished quality; saving faith is a faith that produces obedience, it is a faith that brings about a way of life." It would appear that Jacob's faith had reached a point where obedience, even in the face of fear and adversity, was part of his character. And a faith like that (or, better said perhaps – a *change* such as that) would have been noticeable to others.

Could Leah and Rachel see the stark contrast between their father's greed and their husband's faith? In their conversation the women tell Jacob, "[Our father Laban] has reduced our rights to those of foreign women. He sold us ..." (Genesis 31:15) Ouch. Doesn't sound like the girls were willing to put up with any more of Laban's schemes, does it? It would seem that there was no contest between the "look-out-for-number-one-Laban" versus the mature and godly-directed Jacob.

As Laban was "some distance away shearing sheep" it took him three days to discover their departure, and then it took him seven days to catch up with them. (Genesis 31:19-23) Laban had worked twenty long years to keep this godly blessed Jacob tied to him one way or another. There was the fourteen years of obligation when he "sold" his daughters (their words, not mine!) plus the six additional years while Jacob earned his flock. Laban repeatedly tried to cheat Jacob out of acquiring an animal herd of his own by always trying to give him the lowest producing lambs, and had repeatedly breaking the wage agreement. Jacob had been required to pay for every lamb that was killed or stolen, whether it was his fault or not.

And over the course of Jacob's employment, Laban had *reduced* Jacob's salary *ten times*. (Genesis 31:38-42)

Well, well, it seems that Jacob had gotten some payback for his earlier life of crime and deception, huh? In addition, we can begin to appreciate a bit more not only Jacob's love for Rachel, but we can also stand in awe at his obvious patience as he waited out God's plan and God's timing.

Laban arrived at Jacob's camp shouting about sneaky behavior and prisoner daughters. He demanded an explanation for their secret departure and the reason for not giving him the opportunity to throw a big goodbye party – including tambourines and harps! (Genesis 31:26-28) I can see the sisters looking at each other and rolling their eyes. Then Laban laid in the threat about being capable of destroying Jacob, except for the fact that Jacob's God had sent a really scary dream to warn Laban against such behavior. Lastly, Laban accused someone of stealing his household gods. (Genesis 31:29-30)

Huh? Household gods?! Also called teraphim, household gods held a lot of significance in a home. They were small figures made of wood or metal, they would have had a rude representation of the human form, and could even have been the likenesses of distant ancestors. They were thought to have prophetic qualities, and have been able to offer advice in times of need. In addition, they were believed to protect the home that sheltered them. Passed down though generations, family heirs were given the household gods, and with them could rightfully claim the greatest piece of inheritance. To steal them would have been a serious charge. To be in possession of them would have in effect secure that person's future claim against all that Laban had worked and schemed for.

Jacob clearly knew nothing about the gods. He acknowledged that he had snuck away because he was afraid that Laban would "take his daughters by force," but in reference to the gods he said with righteous indignation, "Let the person who has taken them die! If you find anything that belongs to you, I swear before all these relatives of ours, I will give it back without question." (Genesis 31:31-32)

Laban was no dummy. He hadn't gotten where he was by being trusting! Besides the apple doesn't fall far from the tree, right? Leah and

Rachel *were* his daughters. He meticulously searched each and every tent: Jacob's, Leah's, and the two concubines without success. When he showed up at Rachel's tent, she was sitting on her camel saddle and said, "Don't mind me, Dad, but I can't get up because I'm having my period." (Genesis 31:35 ST) As men of those times considered women "unclean" during their period, as well as anything they touched, wore, or sat on (Leviticus 15:19-24) there was *no way* Laban was going near Rachel in his search. Hmmm, do you smell a rat?

The household gods never showed up, despite Laban's thorough search. When Laban began to shed false tears over the loss of his only daughters and grandchildren, Jacob called it just like he saw it, and spent a goodly amount of time venting. "God has seen your cruelty and my hard work." (Genesis 31:38-43) The two men did eventually make a peace treaty, and both agreed not to cross into each other's territories to cause harm. Once everything was settled, Laban kissed everyone goodbye and went home. (Genesis 31:55)

Guess where those idols were? Yup, Rachel was sitting on them. She'd stolen them when they'd departed. (Genesis 31:19b) Why? What was her agenda? No matter what reason I come up with, *none of it showed good will or good faith.* Perhaps she took the household gods because she believed that with them Laban would have been able to discover the path that they were taking in escape. (Lack of faith in God.) Maybe she wanted to secure her chance of gaining an inheritance at Laban's death. (Greed.) Maybe she wanted to insure continued the success Jacob had achieved in the presence of her father and his household gods. (More lack of faith in God.) Did she wish to pass the idols on to her son Joseph, and secure headship of the family? (More greed.) Did she want to level one final kick, right where it would hurt, her father for his lifetime of self-indulgence and avarice? (Vengeance.) This one brief incident reveals a glaring flaw in the heart of what was important to Rachel. Beautiful on the outside, inside she lacked faith and was selfish, greedy and opportunistic. Uh-oh, sounds a lot like her father, doesn't she?

Q?

What makes one heart receptive to The Truth and another heart hostile?

Thinking harshly of Rachel is justified. She knew her actions were wrong because she hid her deed from everyone who was important to her. We teach our children about these kind of things; we call them "bad secrets." Rachel put herself and her family at great risk physically, as Laban was willing to fight for the gods' return. She damaged her own and her family's character forever, casting a shadow of suspicion and doubt on them. Rachel was forced to lie and deceive her father – the very same trait for which she found fault in him less than two weeks earlier. (Genesis 31:16) And she put her husband Jacob in a position of unwitting accomplice, "You have chased me as though I were a criminal. You have searched through everything I own. Now show me what you have found that belongs to you! Set it out here in front of us, before our relatives, for all to see." (Genesis 31:37) Those gods stayed with Rachel. There is no record of her ever returning them ... or rejecting them.

The remainder of the trip to Canaan was eventful, to say the least. A group of angels met them on the way, Jacob spent one whole night wrestling with a "man," and Jacob eventually had a successful reunion with his brother Esau, who turned out to be a pretty decent, forgiving guy after all. (Genesis 32-33) Wow, can you imagine what the videotapes of that trip would have been like?

It's the wrestling match that needs to be looked at the closest. (The angel visit no one seems to be able to figure out. I like to think it was God's way of showing delight in Jacob's obedience before his entire caravan.) But the fight Jacob had with this "man" was odd.

It was the night before Jacob was to be reunited with his brother Esau. How tense do you think that night would have been? Would you have slept a wink? Jacob sent his wives, kids, and all his possessions across the Jabbok River, and stayed alone on the other side. Too uptight to sleep or deal with wives, kids, or servants, he just *wants to be alone*. The journal entry doesn't say Jacob prayed. It says, "All alone in the camp, a man came and wrestled with him until dawn." (Genesis 32:24)

It was a long, dark night. Jacob wrestled with a man ... was it in some ways himself? Did the deceiver Jacob had always been fight with the man of truth he wished to be? Did the mamma's boy's memories try to drag down the man who faced Laban and his army and *won?* Was the fearful man who had run from his brother's wrath opposing the obedient man who was now returning to face whatever was in store? Was the man of cunning Jacob used to be trying to turn aside the man of faith Jacob had worked so hard to become? In the light of dawn, exhausted and wounded, the battle was declared a draw.

"Let me go!" the man says, "It's dawn!" ("Enough already. This isn't going to be solved." ST)

Jacob refused and gasped out, "I will not let go unless you bless me." (Genesis 32:25-26) ("Oh no. I'm ending this on a positive note. Give me something affirmative: your approval, your appreciation, your support, wish me well for the future … *something.*" ST)

The only blessing Jacob had ever gotten was from his father through deception. Jacob hadn't earned it and didn't really deserve it. *This* blessing, Jacob wanted - badly enough to hang on to even though he was exhausted and wounded. Unlike the angels, earlier on the trip, that Jacob recognized instantly as messengers from God, this "man" was obviously different. Jacob's *heart* had recognized something unique in "him" and caused Jacob to latch on to and not let go. Jacob maybe didn't understand it all completely, but in his heart of hearts he knew *this was important to not mess up.* Jacob realized the only blessing that counted was this one from God.

The man asked Jacob his name and Jacob told him. You remember what Jacob's name means: the usurper, the claim jumper, or the wrong doer. Like a big scarlet letter A on his chest, Jacob's name for these past sixty years had declared his deepest darkest secrets.

Q?
Think about those you call friend. Why have you chosen them? More importantly, why have *they* chosen you?

"Your name will no longer be Jacob," the man told Jacob, "It is now Israel, because you have struggled with both God and men and have won." (Genesis 32:27-28)

Was this what Jacob expected? At that moment, as he was still gasping for breath, did Jacob look at this "man" and suddenly see "him" for what "he" really was? *The one who struggles with God and men and wins.* Wow, some name change, huh? I kind of equate it with a professional wrestler's moniker: The Ultimate Victor of All.

"What is your name?" Jacob asked the "man." I'm guessing Jacob had got a pretty big clue by now but just wanted to hear the "man" say it out loud.

"Why do you ask?" the man replied, and then blessed Jacob there. (Genesis 32:29) ("Why do you need to ask? *You know already in your heart. Here is the blessing you have hungered for all your life even before you knew what it really was about. Now it is truly yours and yours alone.*" ST)

> **Even in the womb, Jacob struggled with his brother; when he became a man, he even fought with God.**
> Hosea 12:3

Jacob named the place Peniel, which means "face of God." The journal entry recorded him as saying, "I have seen God face to face, yet my life has been spared." (Genesis 32:30)

Jacob, now called Israel, certainly had a lot to tell the wives when he got to the other side of the Jabbok River. Did he look different? The Bible said he limped because of his injury. What a precious gift God gave Jacob just at a time in his life when he needed the greatest boost: to face his greatest fears, to confirm the changed man he was determined to become, and to encourage him on to the next far more difficult journeys of life that lay ahead.

"Hello, my name is Israel. I am God's chosen man. Let me introduce you to my wives and children ..."

The end ... How much further?

Jacob arrived back in Canaan and, well, life continued on! There were battles (to avenge Dinah's rape – Genesis 34:2), deaths (Rachel in childbirth – Genesis 35:16 and Isaac of old age – 180 years! – Genesis 35:28), more babies than can be counted (Genesis 36, 46), and significant accounts of the good, bad, and ugly behaviors of all twelve of those boys ... (Genesis 35:21 – Genesis 48:22).

On his deathbed, Jacob blessed his twelve sons and "each received a blessing that was appropriate to him." (Genesis 49:28) Jacob's life is a perfect study in a person that grew closer to God with each experience. And while he never achieved perfection, at the end of his life he could rightfully claim obedience to God.

It was through Jacob that the twelve tribes of Israel were created, and the structure of the formal Jewish religion was set in motion by Moses.

Rachel's servant, Zilpah's sons Gad and Asher formed two of the twelve tribes.

Rachel died in childbirth when her second son, Benjamin was born. Jacob, much more spiritually and emotionally mature but still a flawed human being, favored both of his beloved Rachel's sons so much that jealousy caused Leah's sons to sell Joseph as a slave and stage his death just to get rid of him. As it was God's perfect plan all along, Joseph flourished in Egypt, marrying and having two sons, Manasseh and Ephraim. So, from Rachel came three more tribes: Benjamin, Manasseh, and Ephraim. From Joseph's line came an impressive list of famous Bible personalities: Joshua the warrior, Gideon the judge, and Samuel the prophet, while Benjamin's line included King Saul, Queen Esther, and the apostle Paul.

Leah's servant Bilhah's two sons, Dan and Naphtali, made up two more of the Israelite nation's tribes. The judge Samson (yes, Delilah's guy), Barak (the faithful general that helped the only female judge, Deborah, achieve victory), and Elijah (the prophet) descended from these tribes.

Israel's priestly line came through Leah's son, Levi and were known as the Levites. They were unique in that they were a tribe without a land claim, as their duty was priestly service throughout the other tribes. Look at a map of the twelve tribes; you will not find "Levi" anywhere. Levite descendants included the first high priest Aaron, Moses, and John the Baptist.

Leah's sons Rueben, Simeon, Issachar, and Zebulun made up four more tribes. (Are you keeping track? We're up to eleven now.)

But it's Leah's son, Judah, that took the big prize in the end, as the ancestry of Christ came through this line. As God does not choose favorites, nor is He a God of chaos, His selection of Leah and her son Judah cannot be considered coincidental. I would like to think that Judah's choice to have this blessing: "The scepter shall not leave Judah; he'll keep a firm grip on the command staff until the ultimate ruler comes and the nations obey him," (Genesis 49:10 MSG) had a lot to do with Leah. You see, Judah wasn't that much of a prize in his early life. (There's a chapter coming on him in this book, too, and you won't believe how messed up the Judahs were.) In comparison, Rachel's son Joseph was pretty darn perfect throughout his life. From a human perspective, the choice between Joseph or Judah for wins the "You Made God Smile Prize" goes hands down to Joseph. But only God knows our hearts and who is best fit to serve.

It's important to note that there's no clear distinction here between the women and their children. All of one wife's children don't excel while all of another wife's children are miserable failures. It's *real life* as opposed to movie life. Despite good examples or bad examples, some children succeed and some fail. It all boils down to individual choices, just as it does today, I might add.

Take Laban for example. He watched as his sister Rebekah was chosen to be Isaac's wife, and their son Jacob flourished through blatant divine intervention. Yet he never signed on to The One True God's cause, did he? Laban kept to his own selfish agenda, quite content to keep scheming and acquiring.

Aren't we all like that? I know people who are astronomically blessed in their lives and yet attribute it all to "luck" or "hard work." I've seen miracles in people's lives, only to hear them reduce such happenings to "amazing good fortune" or "being in the right place at the right time." Our whole life is about watching, listening, learning, believing and applying. But it's all up to us.

Leah was part of the whole Laban 'scheme and grab' culture when she first came on the scene. She participated in the wedding day deception and spent the rest of her life dealing with its consequences. Throughout her early married life she practically turned herself inside out trying to get her husband to love her, without success. She distanced herself from those around her – her sister, her servant, and her husband – and instead began to draw on this God that, to her, seemed real, true, and just. When other women would have become bitter and full of hatred and jealousy she – *miraculously* – transformed herself into a spiritual woman after God's own heart. And while she watched some of her sons take paths that caused her sorrow, while she watched her daughter's life be destroyed through rape,

114

while her husband continued to favor her sister Rachel, and then, consequently her sister Rachel's children, she rose above all of this and became a strong, confident woman who apparently pleased God mightily.

It's to Judah, *Leah's son*, that Jacob gives The Blessing and The Promise. The promise of the Savior that will come. The same Savior that God promised Eve (Genesis 3:15), the same Savior that God promised Abraham, Sarah, and Isaac (Genesis 17:19-21), and the same Savior that God promised Jacob (Genesis 28:14). Leah with the sad eyes, unloved by her husband, second best to her beautiful younger sister, was the one with the heart whom God recognized, honored *and chose.*

While Jacob outlived both his wives, it was Leah he requested to be buried with, along with his father, Isaac, his mother, Rebekah, his grandfather Abraham, and his grandmother Sarah. (Genesis 49:29-32) In death, Leah is first wife, side by side with her husband, leaving a legacy that will *save the entire world.*

For All You Leahs out there …

Would you say that Leah's life had a happy ending? Do you think that she was more often joyful than sorrowful? Do you think that she was more content in her life than her sister Rachel? Do you think she liked the person she was?

> The greatest use of life is to spend it for something that will outlast it.
> William James

I am inclined to answer "yes" to all of these questions. On first blush her story seems sad and full of lost love, but when you really study it, her story is more a story of victory. Just as Jacob became known as "the man who struggled with God and men and won," Leah, too, could be called the woman who "struggled with God and women and men and won." Her life ends on a victorious note that resounds through the centuries well after her death. We can all be Leahs, each one of us. We doubt our self and our worth, we constantly judge ourselves to be second when compared to others, we desire things that we do not have and dismiss things we do have. Rather than becoming bitter, we need to work toward becoming victorious. Forget what's on the outside and make sure that our insides are glorious. And have confidence in God and what He has planned for us. *No eye has seen, no ear has heard, and no mind has imagined what God has prepared for those who love Him.* (I Corinthians 2:9) Appreciate that verse. God wants good things for us that *we cannot comprehend.*

❖ **Prayer Motivation:** Make sure your prayers are for the right things. Are your desires toward improving yourself in God's eyes or are they towards measuring up by the world's standards? And remember, your motives, no matter how deeply hidden, are crystal clear to God. You might as well just own up to them all and determine their worthiness … or not.

❖ **Godly Plans:** Keep God in focus as you plan your life. Let all you work toward be for His praise and honor. In keeping that perspective, you cease comparing yourself to others and finding yourself exemplary … or lacking. He's already got plans for you. You've just got to choose to follow them. *"For I know the plans I have for you,"* says the LORD. *"They are plans for good and not for disaster, to give you a future and a hope."* (Jeremiah 29:11)

> But everyone knows that you are obedient to the Lord. This makes me very happy. I want you to be wise in doing right and to stay innocent of any wrong.
> Romans 16:19

❖ **Obedience & Faith:** They go hand in hand. Are you obedient to God's instructions and advice? Do you heed His still small voice, or does He regularly have to use a baseball bat to get your attention? Are your prayers full of thoughtful introspection and insight, or just a jumble of disasters you're hoping to fix and/or avoid? What does your life reveal about your faith and your obedience to The One True God? Do those who surround you know who you obey?

❖ **Children:** The person we are in this life directly influences our children, and they are more observant than we often give them credit for. Worse yet, it's the difficult times that will stand out in a child's memory more than anything else. Make a conscious choice to be a wise example, have a dialogue with your child when things go well *and* when things go badly. Remember, what they see is how they learn to behave. It's up to you to give them the right tools to be able to discern the truth. What legacy do you wish to leave your children? How do you wish them to remember you? *I could have no greater joy than to hear that my children are following the truth.* (3 John 4)

❖ **Secrets:** Secrets you keep from those closest to you are never secrets from God. "Integrity is built by defeating the temptation to be dishonest; humility grows when we refuse to be prideful; and endurance develops every time you reject the temptation to give up." (Rick Warren) What secrets are in your heart? While

> **Would not God find this out? For He knows the secrets of the heart.**
> Psalm 44:21

you may think that they are safe and hidden, they are the things that God focuses on! How scary is *that?*

❖ **Good Things Are Worth The Wait:** Jacob labored for twenty years for his lousy father-in-law Laban. It doesn't seem as if work conditions were ever great, and rarely were they more than bearable. But Jacob was able to appreciate what God gave him as a reward for his faithfulness and honest hard work: loving wives, numerous children, and wealth above and beyond what the average person would have expected in similar circumstances. Learn to recognize, even when things are bad, the good things God is sending your way. *We can make our plans but the Lord determines our steps.* (Proverbs 16:9)

Homework … How is your self-confidence level?

The qualities that you have are those things the Lord specifically wishes for you to use to His glory. But if you can't recognize them, let alone appreciate them, then you've got a lot of work to do!

Below is an activity designed to help you recognize those unique qualities that have been especially assigned to you. Take a few moments to see what it reveals about you.

> **But blessed are those who trust in the Lord and have made the Lord their hope and confidence.**
> Jeremiah 17:7

WHO ARE YOU?

Take a few minutes to read through the following list of personal characteristics.

Decide which of these characteristics you exhibit. Do the test quickly. Don't over think it.

Is this hard? Too hard? Call a friend to help you. Get some advice.

This is who you are. Who God has designed. Your strengths are by His design, as are all the other areas as well.

Be proud of *all* your characteristics.

Be confident that you have *everything* you need.

Like Leah, you need to realize that everything the Lord values, you've already got.

I see myself as someone who:	Almost Always	Often	Some-times	Almost Never
1. is talkative				
2. tends to find the positive in others				
3. does a thorough job				
4. is almost always positive				
5. is original, comes up with new ideas, an innovator				
6. is reserved				
7. is helpful and unselfish with others				
8. is usually very careful				
9. is relaxed, handles stress well				
10. is curious about many different things				
11. is full of energy				
12. rarely starts a quarrel with others				
13. is a reliable worker				
14. is relaxed				
15. is ingenious, a deep thinker				
16. generates a lot of enthusiasm				
17. has a forgiving nature				
18. tends to be organized				
19. worries				
20. has an active imagination, is a big thinker				
21. tends to be quiet				

I see myself as someone who:	Almost Always	Often	Some-times	Almost Never
22. is generally trusting				
23. tends to be productive				
24. is emotionally stable, not easily upset				
25. is inventive, a mastermind				
26. has an assertive personality				
27. is warm and welcoming				
28. perseveres until a task is finished				
29. rarely is moody				
30. values artistic, aesthetic experiences				
31. is sometimes shy, inhibited				
32. is considerate and kind to almost everyone, a nurturer				
33. does things efficiently				
34. remains calm in tense situations				
35. prefers work that is routine				
36. is outgoing, sociable				
37. is never rude to others				
38. makes plans and follows through with them, a leader				
39. does not get nervous easily				
40. likes to reflect and plan first				
41. has artistic interests				
42. is cooperative				
43. is rarely distracted				
44. is sophisticated in art, music, or literature				
45. has high self-esteem				
46. is very religious				
47. is usually on positive terms with others				
48. is skilled at counseling				
49. is considered a go-getter				
50. works well and encourages others to improve, a mentor				
51. is a peacemaker				
52. likes to make others smile, a performer				
53. has a talent that is unique and special				
54. has a skill that is unique and special				
55. can do a job that is unique and special				
56. has the ability to plan out solutions to problems, a strategist				

I see myself as someone who:	Almost Always	Often	Some-times	Almost Never
57. can always get the job done, a provider				
58. can fix just about anything				
59. is analytical, logical and objective				
60. is decisive, driven and energetic				
61. caring, helpful, and supportive				
62. is complex, thoughtful, and sensitive				
63. is cautious, thoughtful, and loyal				
64. is inquisitive, independent, and contained				
65. is lively, enthusiastic, and energetic				
66. is expressive, talkative, and friendly				
67. is realistic				
68. is efficient				
69. is imaginative				
70. is visionary				
71. focus more toward the "head" than the "heart"				
72. focus more toward the "heart" than the "head"				
73. is more spontaneous than planned				
74. is more planned than spontaneous				
75. is more an extrovert than an introvert				
76. is more an introvert than an extrovert				
77. is more impressed with facts than ideas				
78. is more impressed with ideas than facts				
79. has a hobby that gives me great joy				
80. can do something that gives me great personal satisfaction				

This is a good snapshot of who you are. The "almost always" columns that you checked are your strengths and the qualities that God can make the most use of. Don't be quick to dismiss the other columns. Just as a skeleton is the frame of strength of your body, you are not a whole person without all the other traits – big and small, they make up the physical body that you have. So too are the 'other columns' (I don't like to call them

> **You are a custom-designed, one of a kind, original masterpiece.**
> Rick Warren

weaknesses) important in making up the whole snapshot of who you are by God's design.

Do not minimize these things. They are the precious qualities that you have been given that make you special and precious to God. God can use these abilities, and if you are seeking to have Him in your heart, then these are the tools to do it with.

Question To Discuss:

Q?

What is something unique about yourself that
others seem not to possess?
Do you value this? Utilize this? Share this?
Is God pleased with your use of this?
How is your self-confidence reflected in this?

Tamar and The Guy She Picked Up on The Side of The Road

A Heart Of Strength

Tamar's story is one you may not be familiar with. I'll also make a guess that at some point as you read about it now you'll crack open your Bible (hopefully not for the first time, but probably ...) because you just won't be able to believe that her story *is really in there*. To put it bluntly, Tamar had a sucky life. She suffered abuse, betrayal, abandonment, false accusations, and was forced to absolute rock bottom until the men in her life finally clued in and stepped up to the plate of accountability and responsibility. At the mercy of the cultural dictates of the day, she was absolutely and completely defenseless. Called "the woman with a pathetic history" (Lockyer), Tamar truly had more to complain about than most.

Which make the lessons in her story all the more startling. Unprotected, heathen, and literally unwanted *by everyone in her life* she rose to the exemplary status of being "more righteous" than the man chosen to carry on the covenantal promise of God. You see, all on her own with no one to teach her, help her or coach her, Tamar seemed to have *gotten it*.

122

Over the course of her horrible life, Tamar learned of The One True God. Did she believe in Him, embrace Him, and choose to dedicate her life to Him? Or was her determination to survive so all-consuming that she accidentally accomplished what God's man Judah failed to do?

In doing the right thing, God honored Tamar and elevated her above all others. For you see, she joined the elite "Ancestress of Christ" club. Even though she was a heathen. Even though no one saw any value in her. Even though at one point her father-in-law thought her worthy of being *burned to death*. God saw her goodness and value. He recognized her strength. Tamar's story drives home the point that even if no one wants you or thinks you are worthy, it's only what God thinks that counts.

And as you read Tamar's unbelievable story, I'll caution you about one important thing. I pray you don't need to go through all she did in order to gain the same critical understanding she came to. God speaks to us with a still small voice, but sometimes, if we don't listen carefully, He might be forced to use a baseball bat. Come, learn about a woman whose life helped her grow a heart of strength.

First Things First

Scripture references you should check out:	Genesis 38
Question to ask yourself before you read any further:	At your most desperate of times, who or what do you turn to?
What her name means:	"Tamar" means "a palm tree." The palm tree was one of the most important trees and evokes feelings of beauty and wealth when used as a female name.
Connections:	Tamar led a frighteningly solitary life, facing tragedies, terrors and humiliations completely on her own. Along the way she heard of The One True God. Purged by fire, she survived to be worthy of admiration. Strong and committed, she did not allow her trials to break her, but instead let them perfect her.

What the Bible says about true strength:	Where it comes from: Exodus 15:1-3 When we should use it first and foremost: Deuteronomy 6:5 Why Strength Alone Will Get You Nothing: I Samuel 2:9 Who Is Eligible To Have It: Psalm 29:11 What Saps Your Strength: Proverbs 17:22b On Human Strength: Jeremiah 17:5

Questions We'll Never Know The Answers To:

❖ Where, when and how did Tamar hear about the One True God?

❖ Was Tamar motivated merely by survival or did she eventually embrace the tenants of the Jewish faith?

Did you know? Interesting Biblical Facts About Tamar

❖ **Levirate Law:** The Israelites of biblical time honored the custom of the Levirate Law (from the Latin word *levir* meaning husband's brother) or the principle of the Kinsman Redeemer. (Deuteronomy 25:5-10) Simply stated, this custom required that if a man died before his wife conceived a son, the widow must become the wife of one of the dead man's brothers. (Yes, in some cases this resulted in multiple wives.) The first son of such a union was considered the child of the dead brother, to carry on the dead man's line and inherit his property.

❖ **Israelite Nation:** Although it was Abraham who is considered the father of the Jewish nation, it was Jacob, Abraham's grandson, who fathered the twelve sons that made up the twelve tribes of Israel. God renamed Jacob 'Israel' in Genesis 32:38 because he "fought with God and man and won." ("Israel" means "God fights.")

❖ **Jacob's Family:** The family of Jacob/Israel consisted of twelve sons (and one daughter) who were the product of Jacob's marriages to four women (two of them sisters). The sons, in order of their birth, were: Reuben, Simeon, Levi, Judah, Dan, Napthali, Gad, Asher, Issachar, Zebulon, Joseph, and Benjamin. Now this might surprise you (yes, you are detecting sarcasm), but the family of Jacob was somewhat dysfunctional. Despite the fact that the first son traditionally received the greatest blessing, Reuben lost the honor when he became romantically involved with one of his stepmothers. The next two in line, Simeon and Levi, were condemned by their father for the massacre of an entire town. Consequently, on Jacob's deathbed it was Judah who received the greatest blessing, and it was through his family line that the ancestry of Christ can be traced.

❖ **The Land of Canaan:** To clear up any confusion, the following terms *all* apply to the *same plot of land*: "The Land of Canaan" was the term used for the land when it was inhabited by the Canaanite people. "The Land of Israel" or "The Promised Land" was the title of the land when it was inhabited by the twelve tribes of Israel. "The Land of Judah and The Land of Israel" was the name given when the Jewish nation divided after King Solomon's death. The tribes of Judah and Benjamin went south (with Simeon's tribe joining later) and all the rest of the tribes making up Israel were in the north. "Judea" was the Greek/Roman name for the land of Judah ("Judea" comes from the adjective "Jewish"). "Palestine" was the title of the land given by the Romans after the Jewish revolt of A.D. 135. "The Holy Land" is the modern title given to this area today.

The Core Story

Judah, MVP in Town ... What skeletons were in his closet?

Judah moved away from the family farm before his father Jacob died and bestowed any of the treasured blessing referred to above. Perhaps he was trying to distance himself from the drama that a home with four wives, thirteen children, numerous servants and thousands of sheep and goats must have created. Or maybe he couldn't stand hanging around looking his father in the eye as the old man mourned the supposed death of his favorite son Joseph. (Genesis 37:31-34) Or even better, Judah may have hoped to escape the guilt of having convinced his brothers to sell their annoyingly favored younger brother Joseph to Ishmaelite slavers. (Genesis 37:26-27) Who knew? Maybe it was a combination of all of those things or something else.

Anyway, Judah up and moved further into the Land of Canaan. Note that the land was called by this name because it was filled with Canaanites. The Israelites at this time were just one very large, very wealthy, dysfunctional, nomadic family eeking out an existence by shepherding sheep and herding goats.

Judah married and settled down with a nice Canaanite girl, a big no-no. Though there wasn't anything resembling a biblical guide at the time (not even The Ten Commandments were around yet), Judah most certainly knew that the family would be displeased with this match had they been consulted. He had to have heard the story of how his great-grandfather Abraham had made his trusted servant pledge an oath to secure a wife for his beloved only son, Isaac. Abraham had made the servant promise, "Swear by the LORD, the God of heaven and earth, that you will not allow my son to marry one of these local Canaanite women. Go instead to my homeland, to my relatives, and find a wife there for my son Isaac." (Genesis 24:3)

But even if Judah had never heard that story, by the time he married his Canaanite wife, Shua, his brothers Simeon and Levi had already massacred an entire town of Canaanite men because the prince of that city had the audacity to want to marry their sister, Dinah. (Genesis 34) I think we can safely assume that Canaanite and Israelite unions were definitely discouraged and Judah knew it. Was Judah sowing his wild oats? Taking a stand to be different and separate from his wild and crazy family? Rejecting his family's God and all that it stood for? The Bible doesn't tell us. In fact, at first glance there seems to be very little information given about the Judahs in those early years. But by reading between the lines we can surmise that things were pretty good. In fact, they appeared to be excellent.

We are told that Shua conceived and had one son whom they named Er (which means "awake" or "on the watch"), then another son whom they named Onan ("strong" or "pain"), and finally a third son whom they named Shelah ("peace" or "prayer"). Three healthy sons were considered an enormous blessing as children were the measure of a man's wealth and a woman's worth, with male children being the epitome of success. (Female children were almost always considered a liability.) Judah knew *first hand* about a woman's fierce desire for male children, having watched his mother, Leah, and her sister, Rachel, compete fiercely for his father's attention in that area. Things got so far out of hand that both Leah and Rachel had eventually offered their servant women to Jacob (who then became his third and fourth wives – Bilhah and Zilpah) just to keep the baby count climbing. Children delivered by a female servant could be counted as the headwoman's child. (Genesis 30:1-8)

Besides three healthy, strapping sons, the Judahs would have been a wealthy family, having surely taken a large portion of father Jacob's extensive holdings. (Jacob prays in gratitude for a household large enough to fill two camps in Genesis 33:10.) Even though Judah had not received the final blessing from his father, eldest brother Rueben had already done the big no-no with his stepmother Bilhah (Genesis 35:21), and elder brothers Simeon and Levi had already been severely chastised by their father for their violence. (Genesis 34:30) Hence, Judah was definitely at the top with "favored son" status floating all around him, and would have been suitably rewarded when he set out on his own to make a go of things.

When the Judahs settled in the town of Kezib the family's penchant for violence was surely known, as his brothers Simeon and Levi had the blood of the entire male population of the town of Shechem on their hands. Arriving with flocks of sheep and herds of goats, servants and supplies, you can imagine the town buzzing about who had shown up and what was known about Judah and his extended family. Wealth and notoriety would have ensured for Judah a level of welcome and a guarantee of popularity that the average traveler would never had anticipated.

Finally, as Jacob and his family were the chosen race (yes, you're allowed to ponder just how bad all the rest were if they were the crème of the crop), God had caused a "great terror" to come over "all the towns of that area." (Genesis 35:5) This permitted Jacob and his sons to live in an awe-inspired cocoon of safety.

Wow. The Judahs had wealth, notoriety, popularity, and a spiritually induced force field! They must have appeared to be some fantastic family to get involved with, huh? Wouldn't you like your daughter to marry into that kind of power and prestige? I can imagine that every available female in town had eyes on Judah's three boys.

Not until Judah sought out a wife for his eldest son, Er, does the Bible start the family again, and then we get a glimpse of just how bad things *really* were with the Judahs …

The Bad Seed ... How far reaching can bad choices be?

Wealth, power, and prestige ... Couple that with what was surely an astronomical ego at being "God's chosen race on earth" and it sounds to me that Er, as Judah's eldest son, was probably 'big man on campus' in his small corner of the world. The Bible gives no specific genealogical information about the woman Judah chose for his firstborn son, but it would be a safe bet to assume that Tamar, the young Canaanite woman who won the dating game, would have been of similar social status.

> **And all the girls dreamed that they'd be your partner**
> **They'd be your partner...**
> **You're so vain!**
> Carly Simon

I can just imagine the wedding. Probably the whole town turned out for the festivities. Judah's brothers and their wives and children as well as the patriarch, Jacob, and his wives and servants would have come for the party. The celebrations probably went on for days.

The Bible is silent, however, about any of the details of the marriage except for one very telling thing: "But Er was a wicked man in the Lord's sight." (Genesis 38:7a) I always want specific details when the Bible gives none. Do you do that? But the Bible is relatively consistent about the level of detail given whenever something or someone is referred to as wicked: *it lets the word speak for itself.* Man was described as "wicked," causing God to initiate the worldwide flood in Genesis 6:5. The men of Sodom and Gomorrah were "exceedingly wicked," causing God to completely destroy both cities in Genesis 19. You've got to be pretty high up on the badness scale to qualify as "wicked," and trust me on this one: you *do not* want God to view you as such. Somehow Er reached the wicked level of badness and just like that, the Bible simply says that the Lord took his life. (Genesis 38:7b)

As I read the biblical account - just that one very brief verse - I feel a real gut clenching fear for Tamar. Questions that cannot be answered roll through my head: Why was Er described as wicked *after* his marriage? Why was Er's life taken only *after* marriage? I think of rape, abuse, and terror for that young woman and I thank God for His mercy.

Unfortunately, just when Tamar might have thought she was safe, Judah would have recounted the customs of his people and the "kinsman redeemer" clause that was in the marital contract. You know, those people whom Judah had moved away from and married outside of. Seems as if you can take the boy out of the family but you can't take the family out of the boy ... Poor Tamar. Once she married *one* Judah, she seemed in reality to had married *all* the Judahs.

Did Tamar's people practice the kinsman redeemer custom of marriage? Other tribal-based people did have similar practices. Whether such a tradition was familiar or not, very shortly Tamar found herself married to her brother-in-law, Onan. Like it or not Tamar was in this marriage for the long haul. Forever, in fact. Who knew that some marriages didn't end with "until death do us part"?

Help ... ! Where do you go when there's no place to turn?

It was Onan's duty to have sexual relations with Tamar so that she would be able to conceive a male heir to carry Er's ancestral line. "Why bother if Er was so wicked?" you might ask. But perhaps, as only *we* have been given the privilege of reading this biblical journal entry, only *we* know that Er was taken because of his wickedness. Well, us and Tamar anyway.

While Tamar was breathing a sigh of relief, maybe the rest of the Judahs were in full blown mourning for the loss of the precious firstborn son. Shua, the grieving mother, would be constantly teary over Er's possessions that still littered the tent. Judah would suddenly be scrambling to look towards Onan now as the heir apparent, desperate to ensure he was prepared for his inevitable duty. Onan would have been suddenly thrust into the limelight. And little brother, Shelah, maybe was frightened that someone else in the family was going to die again soon.

Q?
What was the motivation behind the hardest thing that you ever had to do *and* failed? How did that influence future opportunities for strength?

And Tamar ... well what would Tamar be doing? I doubt she would be doing the happy dance and telling tales about just how awful Er was and just how wonderful it was that he was gone. I can see her gathering her courage, preparing herself for her ... upcoming responsibility to wed Onan. Was she emotionally, mentally, physically and spiritually damaged? Did anyone even care or ask? Was she scrambling to find something, *anything* that would get her through the next few days ... or weeks ... or *years?*

If you were Tamar, what would you have done? What are your resources when you are absolutely painted into a horrible, terrifying corner? How do you react when you are really terrified? Do you have family to turn to? Friends? Do you research on the Internet so you can make an informed decision? Do you speak with your therapist? Do you just go to bed? Here something novel you might try: Do you pray?

Did Tamar begin to pray somewhere along the course of her life? Did she begin to attempt a dialogue with The One True God? Had she begun to hear about Judah's family's God? Despite the obvious dysfunction within Judah's family, was Tamar intrigued with the power and might of their God? Perhaps, during the overwhelming grief of Er's death, someone within the family compound dragged themselves back onto the proper spiritual road and started talking the right talk and walking the right walk. Or, perhaps not.

However Tamar heard of The One True God, whenever it happened, if it did, it would have been at some point while she was with the Judahs. Maybe it wasn't at this moment, but it certainly would have been the perfect time for her. Why? Because low points in our lives often bring us crawling to God, don't they? The Judahs' would have been seriously grieving over the sudden death of the firstborn son. And Tamar, well Tamar had *absolutely no one.* She was a stranger in a strange place with a family that worshipped a different God and embraced different customs. And, unfortunately, it was be time for her to do her duty (again) and have intercourse with the brother of a man who had been so wicked that God decided the world was better off with him dead.

Take Two ... Could it be any worse?

So, do you think Onan was any better than his brother? No vocal objections were recorded when he and Tamar were wed. In fact, once again as far as the family probably was concerned, Onan was a dutiful son and a willing new husband. Only Tamar would have witnessed the depths of her new husband's duplicity. For while Onan was quite willing to perform the sexual act with Tamar, he was unwilling to follow through on its true purpose. The Bible states that he simply did not want to have a child that would not be his own heir, and is particularly graphic with how he accomplished this: "whenever he had intercourse with Tamar, he spilled the semen on the ground to keep her from having a baby who would belong to his brother." (Genesis 38:9)

Please note that God gave Onan at least a few chances to have a change of heart regarding this behavior. The biblical account doesn't talk about the *one and only* time that Onan chose to take advantage of what Tamar dutifully had to offer. No, the Bible clearly states, *"whenever* he had intercourse..." This guy saw an opportunity, as well as a convenient solution, and took it. Over and over again.

Calling Onan selfish would have drastically oversimplified his actions. Yes, he was unwilling to shoulder the responsibility of a child that he would never be able to claim as an heir. What we, in this day and age don't appreciate, is what "firstborn" status meant back then, and why Onan was so intent on holding on to it once he received it.

To be a firstborn son guaranteed a multitude of perks: your parents loved you in a special way, you had unique rights and privileges your entire life, you automatically were expected to assume a position of leadership within the family, and upon your father's death you received a *double portion* of what everyone else got. This birthright was assured to you at the moment of your birth. By the time Moses rolled around and wrote down all the rules and regulations that were to distinguish the Israelite people from all others, the privileges of being a firstborn son were specifically outlined

> **Figuratively speaking, the term firstborn stands for that which is most excellent.**
> Lockyer

and protected. (Deuteronomy 21:15-17) So precious was the status of being the firstborn that God called the nation of Israel His firstborn. God instructed Moses to tell the Egyptian pharaoh, *This is what the LORD says: 'Israel is my firstborn son. I commanded you, Let my son go, so he can worship me.'* (Exodus 4:22)

Throughout biblical history the firstborn was always uniquely special. Abel brought his firstborn lambs as an acceptable sacrifice to God, (Genesis 4:4) which prompted Cain's jealousy over his unacceptable offering. God's greatest punishment to Egypt was the death of all firstborn sons (Exodus 11:5) – which I must point out even included all firstborn males of Egypt's *livestock*. God literally *claimed* all firstborn males – human and animal – for Himself. (Exodus 13:2) Perhaps most fascinating, when Moses set up the structure that would become the Jewish religion, God instituted the tribe of Levi to *replace* His claim to all firstborn sons. God had Moses literally count how many firstborn sons there were (22,273 one month or older), then count how many Levites there were (22,000) and then set up financial worth for the 273 firstborns that He was owed (5 pieces of silver each), which was then to be paid to Aaron (the High Priest) as a redemption fee. (Numbers 3)

Q?

Think about the worst advice you've ever received. Now think about if you followed it or not. What does this say about the strength of your heart?

You might wonder whether firstborn status was such a big deal, if men fought over it or used it as a bargaining tool. They did! Onan's own grandfather Jacob was *not* the first son of his father Isaac and it galled him. Big time. Jacob's name meant "deceiver" and he did a good job at living up to it, too. He goaded his older (twin) brother, Esau, into trading his birthright for a pot of stew. (Genesis 25:34) And before you say anything, you should know that Esau was roundly condemned in the Bible for not valuing his birthright and selling it so lightly (yes, you *could* sell it). Jacob disguised himself as his much hairier twin and got his very old and very blind father Isaac to bestow the final important blessing on him. Then Jacob ran like heck because he was afraid of his brother's fury. (Which landed him in the place where he fell in love with one sister and ended up married to both…) Firstborn status could also be taken away as punishment for bad deeds, which was how Judah's brothers Rueben, Simeon and Levi lost their rights to it and how he eventually ended up with it.

But, even after all this, you might wonder *still* why firstborn status was so important. It held an almost mythical quality. It was as if you didn't quite know why it was so terrific or what was so important about having it, but you did know that if you had it, it was *really* special. Especially in this family. For remember, as wicked and dysfunctional as they were, they were *God's Chosen Race*. The One True God had spoken to Great-grandfather Abraham, Grandfather Isaac, and the current patriarch Jacob and promised, "I am El-Shaddai - 'God Almighty.' Be fruitful and multiply. You will become a great nation, even many nations. Kings will be among your descendants! And I will give you the land I once gave to Abraham and Isaac. Yes, I will give it to you and your descendants after you." (Genesis 35:11-12) Oh yeah, being firstborn in *this family* promised unimaginable wonders. Onan's father, Judah, was currently the favored son in the line of succession. With Er's death, Onan had everything to gain. Had this been a monarchy, Onan would have suddenly found himself with the unbelievable luck of being the crown prince. No way was he going to let this opportunity slip through his fingers. It was the understatement of the year to say that ensuring that Er's firstborn line continued was definitely not in Onan's best interests.

Here We Go Again… Is there any goodness to be found?

So, here Tamar finds herself, again, stuck with a horrible man. Maybe this one wasn't outwardly abusive or cruel to her. Perhaps he was even kind to her in his own self-absorbed way. I guess it was possible that she might have felt a bit of relief over the way things had turned out.

Except she was never going to have a child, was she? Maybe this was when Tamar began to hear about The One True God. Did the other women of the settlement whisper to her with excitement, eagerly anticipating the child she would most certainly be conceiving soon? Tamar would have surely heard the family stories about Great Grandmother Sarah's miraculous pregnancy at age ninety (Genesis 21:6), about Grandmother Rebekah's tender love story (Genesis 24:67), and the titillating account of matriarchs Leah and Rachel (Genesis 29:16-30). Did she listen intently? Did she ask questions? Was she curious? Intrigued? Skeptical? Maybe this One True God inspired her with awe over His faithfulness, patience, and love. Was she initially so disbelieving that she laughed to herself over the gullibility of some people? When Tamar heard about the promises of greatness and the command to be fruitful and multiply, did the realization of what her husband was doing cause her to worry? Did her role within this wild and crazy family, as first wife of the firstborn son of Judah, son of the patriarch Jacob, now renamed by God as Israel, and the responsibility of carrying on the family line cause her to feel as if she had the weight of the world on her shoulders? Was the fear of infertility now magnified by the possibility of spiritual retribution from this family's God? Did she finally begin to pray *then?*

The Bible doesn't tell us how long Tamar's marriage to Onan lasted. It takes just two verses to tell of Onan's deed, God declaring it wicked and taking Onan's life just like his brother Er's.

So once again the Judahs are in mourning. Once again Shua grieves over the death of her son. Once again little brother Shelah worries about death. And once again Tamar is a widow.

Only *this time* Judah, in typical denial mode, takes a good long look at this woman who has been married to both of his dead sons and thinks, "Maybe this girl is the reason my sons have died." (Genesis 38:11) There's *no way* that Judah is going to risk his last surviving son with this woman! Judah once again ignores the rules, ignores what needs to be done, and ignores what is the correct thing to do. Hey, this has been his Life's Theme, why should he change now? Judah tells Tamar that the wedding to the third brother – will have to be put off – he's just too young right now - and Tamar gets sent back home to her parents.

The Widow... Have we finally hit rock bottom?

That was lucky, wasn't it? Finally poor Tamar escaped those horrible Judahs and was able to go back home to her family. So what if Judah never intended to call her back to marry Shelah, right? Who cared? Maybe that was a blessing in disguise! The youngest boy was probably just as bad, if not worse, than the other brothers. Now she could just recover and go on with her life, right?

Wrong. Believe it or not, Tamar was now in an even worse situation than before – with either husband. You see, she was a *childless widow*. Back in ancient times a woman enjoyed her status either as a daughter, a wife, or a mother. Sorry, that was the way of things. (Hence the importance of child bearing being the measure of a woman's worth.) What male a woman was associated with dictated what rights or privileges she was eligible for. The ideas of independence, women's liberation, or even freedom of choice were not concepts anyone considered. Because

> **Widows without children ... have no hope for the future since they have no one to support them.**
> Victor Matthews

of a widow's perpetually sorry state, instructions on how to care for them are given by Moses (Exodus 22:22) and to 'make your wife a widow' was a curse of the highest order. (Exodus 22:24)

In returning to her parent's home, "to remain a widow" (Genesis 38:11) Judah condemned Tamar to a life of abject poverty, eventual homelessness, and a social status lower than a prostitute. *And he knew it.* (Hey, prostitutes at least have a way to support themselves, don't they?) Tamar returned to the unwelcoming atmosphere of her family (remember, women were liabilities, so they would not have been happy to see her) under a grim cloud of suspicion and a dark shadow of despair.

Most assuredly, by this time, Tamar had at least heard of The One True God. Perhaps she had not chosen to believe in Him yet. Was she bitter or angry at this family and their God? As she struggled with the reality (and I suppose desperate hope) that things could not get any worse, she had plenty of time to think about everything she had heard, seen and experienced. Lots of time.

Time passed. A significant amount of time. Again, the Bible doesn't give us a specific number of years but it recounts events such as Shelah growing up (Genesis 38:14) and Judah's wife dying and the period of mourning passing (Genesis 38:12). Tamar, during all these years would have been at the mercy of her family's hospitality (whatever it did or did not entail) wearing the uniform of a widow.

And she did wear a uniform. Clothing, just as it is today, was a status symbol. You could tell, by a glance who were the haves and who were the have-nots. "Changing clothes did not simply reflect a practice of good hygiene but a change of labels or status. Those who changed clothes were preparing to play new roles." (Matthews) To a great extent we still do that today. If you are going to an important job interview you will dress carefully, make sure your hair and make-up are just right and be attentive to details such as body odor and food stuck between your teeth. You do that to make a good impression on those you are meeting, which is another way of saying you strive to present yourself at the highest possible status at which you can be viewed.

Tamar's status was that of a childless widow residing in her parents' home due to shameful circumstances. Her dress would have communicated that to anyone who viewed her. She had no money to buy fine things, no opportunity to secure new robes, and no reason to wish for such. Just one glance at her would have confirmed her social status loudly and clearly: she had none.

The telling sentence, "Tamar was aware that Shelah had grown up, but they had not called her to come and marry him" (Genesis 38:14) suggests to me that she was well aware of the miserable reality of her life. Had she known immediately upon being sent back to her family of Judah's true intentions or was there a moment later on of horrible, dawning realization that *this was it*? Just how innocent was she? Virginal and full of hope and excitement when she arrived at the Judahs, by the time that family was well and truly done with her she had all the wisdom of the world.

Q?

What was the motivation behind the hardest thing that you ever had to do *and succeeded?* How did that influence future opportunities for strength?

Quiet and passive throughout this entire journal account, it seems that suddenly Tamar snaps when she hears that Judah and his friend Hirah have gone to the town of Timnah to supervise the shearing of Judah's sheep. Perhaps she was at the well, a favorite spot for town gossip, doing the endless, back-breaking job of hauling water for the family. The town well was the place where the woman met to socialize and gossip, usually in the cool of the morning and the evening. I can picture Tamar, in her poor widow rags, a stark contrast to the various other women congregating to laugh and talk. Despite the fact that she could only have been in her early twenties, everyone in town knew that she had nothing to look forward to. "Hey Tamar! I hear your father-in-law has gone to Timnah to shear his sheep." (Genesis 38:13 MSG) Was there laughter? Giggles? Were there sly innuendoes or subtly dropped hints about how difficult a job it was for Judah with only one son and his wife's death? Had the subtle or not so subtle digs been going on *for years?*

What the Bible records in the next verse is equivalent to Clark Kent rushing into a phone booth and coming out as Superman. Tamar walked back to her home, changed out of her widow's clothing, covered her face with a veil to disguise herself, and walked down the road. Parking herself at the entrance to the village of Enaim, which was on the route that her father-in-law had to take to get to Timnah, Tamar waited for Judah to pass by and … assume she was a prostitute and proposition her. (Genesis 38:14)

What?! She dressed herself up like a whore with the intent of seducing her *father-in-law?* Yep, that's what she did. (Ha, I bet there are some of you reading this who are trooping over to your Bible to check my references! *Good for you!)* This woman was fed up. This woman was desperate. This woman recognized the one and only opportunity to right the series of wrongs she had been dealt. How she planned to do it … well, she must have been pretty darn desperate.

Tamar had two choices: continue living as she was (with no expectation for change) or take drastic (and completely unacceptable) action to make the situation different. Was her entire incentive because her life and her future were so unbearably bleak? Survive at all costs. Were the Judahs merely the lesser of two evils? (Just how bad was her family if that was the case?!) Did the fact that Tamar knew that *she* was the only one to legitimately carry on the esteemed line of Judah, nee Jacob nee Isaac, nee Abraham give her any motivation? She *was* the necessary vessel to secure the only legitimate family seed.

Whatever her impetus, at some point Tamar decided that if Judah wasn't going to let her have Shelah, she'd take matters into her own hands.

Hey, Big Boy... Are we done yet?

Are you wondering how she could have possibly managed to do such a thing? Even if her status as a childless widow was already as nameless and shameless as being a prostitute ... well, it couldn't have been an easy charade. For us, we have trouble comprehending the distinction, but for Tamar, it was a brutal truth. I would like to think that she hadn't let the Judahs get her down and that she was simply that desperate to find a way out. But the reality is, in posing as a prostitute to seduce her father-in-law, Tamar behaved exactly as the Judahs had communicated to the world she was worth.

> In reality, her status – as low as a prostitute - was exactly what the Judahs had made of her.
> McG

I wonder if Tamar was worried that Judah wouldn't take her up on her offer as she sat outside the city gate? Did she have a Plan B? She needn't have been concerned. Sure enough, the Bible states, "Judah saw her and assumed she was a prostitute since she had veiled her face. He left the road and went over to her. He said, 'Let me sleep with you.'" (Genesis 38:16 MSG). Please note: Tamar did *not* call him over with a come hither crook of her finger and a breathy, "Hey, big fella." *He* was the one who propositioned *her.*

Tamar was all business. She negotiated a price (one young goat), secured promise of payment (Judah gave her his identification seal, cord and walking stick – the equivalent of his photo ID), and allowed Judah to sleep with her. When things were all said and done, Tamar went home, took off her veil, and put her widow's clothes back on.

I find it interesting that the Bible records the fact of her pregnancy before it elaborates how she went home and returned to the status of widow: "she then let him sleep with her, and she became pregnant." (Genesis 38:16-18) Did she know enough about her womanly cycle to be aware that she was fertile? Or did she just cross her fingers and hope? Because surely the pregnancy was the intended goal, not the young goat!

Never let anyone accuse Judah of not paying his debts. As soon as he met up with his friend, Hirah, Judah instructed him to take a young goat and pay "the prostitute who was sitting beside the road at the entrance to the village." (Genesis 38:21) Seems as if interacting with a prostitute was nothing unusual and certainly nothing to be ashamed of. As long as you were on the up and up and paid, of course.

Poor Hirah did his best to locate the prostitute. When he couldn't find the prostitute where Judah had said she would be, he went so far as to question the men of the village. (Can you see him dragging the young goat around by a rope saying, "Hey, where's the prostitute who usually is at the gate? I owe her this goat...") Completely unsuccessful, Hirah returned to his friend Judah explaining, "The men of the village claim they've never had a prostitute there."

My Bible (New Living Translation), has Judah *exclaim*, "Then let her keep the pledges! We tried our best to send her the goat. We'd be the laughingstock of the village if we went back again." (Genesis 38:23) I picture him throwing his hands up in the air as he shouts, while Hirah stands there still holding that goat. Isn't it interesting that Judah wasn't embarrassed about visiting a prostitute, just worried about being a laughingstock when he wasn't able to find her and settle his debt with her? And something tells me the reason he was shouting was because it was going to be a lot of trouble to replace his important seal, cord, and walking stick. A few moments of pleasure had turned out to be a major inconvenience. Poor Judah.

By this time in her life, Tamar was a master at waiting. As there were specific rules and regulations about how women were to behave when they menstruated, within no time her family would have been shocked by the fact that Tamar *did not*. And, of course, being a widow, *if* she was pregnant *then* it would immediately be assumed that it was because she had been behaving immorally. Did her family even question her to hear her side of the story? Was there concern that she had been attacked or did they immediately assume the worst? But here's the saddest question: Would Tamar have bothered to respond had she been asked?

Based on how Judah was told about Tamar's pregnancy, I don't really think Tamar received any sort of care or concern. "Your daughter-in-law has been playing the whore—and now she's a pregnant whore." (Genesis 38:24a MSG) And based on Judah's response to the news, I think he probably saw a quick end to an annoyingly persistent problem. "Get her out here. Burn her up!" he yelled. (Genesis 38:24b MSG)

Hey Tamar, the bad news is your father-in-law's not happy about your pregnancy. The good news is things finally can't get any worse.

Double Standards ... Is life ever fair?

For those of us reading this biblical journal entry, this is the defining moment for both Tamar and Judah. Nothing before and nothing after will be more important than what these two decided to do at this point in time. Again, I ask you, what would you have done?

How galling was it that what Tamar did sentenced her to be put to death, and what Judah did caused mild embarrassment and inconvenience? But please, if you are going to be furious at Judah about his blatant double standard, make sure you're angry about him for the right offense.

You see, it goes back to the whole status within the community thing. A person was only as much as the status he or she had. Judah had status. Judah, in his eyes and probably most of the rest of the culture of his days, did nothing wrong by visiting a prostitute. (Yes, yes, God saw it as wrong, but remember that there were scant rules and regulations at this point.) You see, *prostitutes had no status.* They didn't matter. There was no family line to sully because they had no family connection. *They were nobodies.* Children from this type of union were worthless because they were *nobody's heirs.* Judah's availing himself to the pleasures of the flesh now and then was not wrong as long as he kept it all on the up and up and did it with *nobody who would be hurt.*

> **Q?**
> **Why did something acceptable for Judah become a death sentence for Tamar?**

Anyone associated with Judah through blood or marriage shared his status. Tamar in marrying into that family gained the same status that the Judahs had. Her most precious function was the bearing of children and maintaining the pure family line. That's why she was stuck marrying Onan and was currently "on the shelf" waiting for Shelah. It was all signed and sealed. She had arrived at the Judahs a virgin (it would have been confirmed) and she was expected to remain pure to the line of Judah *for her entire life.* Yeah, I know. But Judah sent her back! Judah didn't want her! Judah condemned her to childless widowhood. And *that's* the double standard you should be annoyed about. Now do you get it?

I don't know about you but if I had been Tamar I would have been screaming my head off as they dragged me out into the center of the town square to set me alight: "It wasn't my fault! It's not fair! What did you expect me to do? It's the Judahs! They started it all! I don't deserve any of this! I've done everything that was expected of me right from the start!"

> No person ...
> shall be
> compelled ... to
> be a witness
> against himself.
> The 5th
> Amendment

Here is Tamar's defining moment: Tamar said none of those things. As they came to take her away to *burn her*, she sent a message to Judah, which simply said, "The man who owns this identification seal and walking stick is the father of my child. Do you recognize them?" (Genesis 38:25) Experience has made Tamar wise beyond her years. The brutal experiences over the course of her young life had made her remarkably astute, and perhaps resigned to her inevitable fate. For while Judah had the right to demand her death, Tamar *acknowledged his right* to do so. Here now, as they tied her up, was the final end for Tamar. Nothing she could have said would have changed her situation. There was no human being on the face of the earth who could influence the course of the next few moments of her life ... but Judah.

A messenger, breathless from running (he would have needed to hurry to get back to see the burning!) rushed into Judah's presence with Tamar's final words. "Here! Sir! The whore who is your daughter-in-law says these things belong to the man who is her child's father! She suspects you recognize them. What should we do?"

Judah didn't have a lot of time. The torches were lit. The woman was tied up and ready. The only thing holding people back was probably the opportunity to burn two for the price of one. I'm sure in those brief few moments, Judah's life flashed before his eyes in brutal clarity. Maybe he remembered the words of regret of his father Jacob as he spoke of his early life of deceit and the horrible weight of its consequences. Perhaps Judah had a flash of his brother Joseph's tearful face as the Ishmaelite slave traders tied him up and dragged him away. Could Judah still remember the sounds of his father as he grieved for his firstborn son's staged death? Did he have a flash of clarity regarding just how terribly wicked both his dead sons had been? Or maybe Judah recalled the resigned look on Tamar's face when he told her that she needed to go back to her family ... to wait until Shelah was older ... and remembered how even then knew he was lying.

> My father taught me,
> "Take my words to heart.
> Follow my commands, and
> you will live.
> Get wisdom; develop good
> judgment.
> Don't forget my words or
> turn away from them.
> Don't turn your back on
> wisdom, for she will protect
> you. Love her, and she will
> guard you.
> Proverbs 4:4-6

The messenger was still standing there before Judah. Still breathing hard. Was he frowning in confusion over Judah's thoughtful hesitation? Were his ears straining to hear if the crowd was shouting because the burning had begun ... ?

Here indeed was an opportunity to make a wise decision: Judah's defining life moment. A decision that would be unbearably painful with its acknowledgement of truths, lies, and betrayals. Talk about a secret worth keeping to preserve your reputation! We all know what he *could* have said, "Nope, don't recognize that seal." Or "She's a whore! Why should we listen to anything she says?" But instead, amazingly, Judah said simply, "The seals are mine." The messenger must have been speechless with shock! Who knew the action at Judahs would be better than at the burning? "She is more in the righteous than I am because I didn't keep my promise to let her marry my son Shelah." (Genesis 38:26) Or, "This Canaanite girl put more importance on the continuation of my godly line than I myself did." (ST)

Please note that Judah publicly commended her! *Acknowledged her righteousness.* Judah redeemed Tamar's reputation by validating her actions: for appreciating the magnitude of her responsibility above all else, for pursuing by the only means left available to her to continue Judah's godly line; and for forcing him to finally face all the esteemed responsibilities that being favored son stipulated.

Whoa.

Epilogue... So, what happened in the end?

The Bible doesn't specifically say, but I would assume that Tamar went back to reside with the Judahs. Certainly her family didn't want her, and as she was carrying the heir to the Judah dynasty it would be appropriate. What the Bible does state is that "Judah never slept with Tamar again." (Genesis 38:26) I wonder how the Judahs explained Tamar and her child to visitors?

The last we hear of Tamar she was delivering not one but *two* sons with a midwife in attendance. That whole "firstborn" thing must be pretty darn complicated with identical twins, huh? The Bible account of Tamar's delivery showed things could be even more complicated than usual. The first child's hand appeared and the midwife quickly tied a red thread around his wrist for distinction at being firstborn, but then the child drew back his hand. Oddly, when a boy was finally born, he *did not* have the red thread around his wrist! It was the second child that appeared with that red marker. The first child was called "Perez" which meant "breaking out" while the second child was called "Zerah" meaning "scarlet." (Genesis 38:27-30)

> Faith is the confidence that what we hope for will actually happen; it gives us assurance about things we cannot see.
> Hebrews 11:1

Would you say that Tamar's story had a happy ending? Perhaps in our romance filled world you might think the answer is 'no.' I would assume that she lived out the remainder of her life without sexual relations with *any* Judah. But, given her experience, that was probably a good thing! She would have reverted back to her esteemed status as the mother of the heir to the line of Judah. Was she Judah's official wife? Or Shelah's? Who knew? The Bible doesn't say, and things have gotten way too complicated for me to speculate.

Was Tamar's life finally filled to overflowing with contentment? Did she enjoy the kind of satisfaction that came from making it through the fire and surviving? Was there any kind of godly fulfillment from finding the key to not only surviving in this hard world, but also thriving? Was she ever privy to the realization that comes when you have made some incredibly hard choices that turned out to be right? Did she ever understand the extent to which her choices, in the end, would bring about all kinds of wonderful things?

There were some positive changes within the Judah family after Tamar's and Judah's defining moments. For Tamar, she had her two beautiful, healthy sons, Perez and Zerah. Her future was secure having done her duty and producing not one but two legitimate heirs. Firstborn Perez will be mentioned only once after the interesting account of his birth, in Matthew 1:3 (as is Tamar, I might add) as part of the genealogy of Christ! And why *is* Tamar mentioned anyway? Tamar joins Rahab, Ruth,

Q?

Did Tamar's life have a happy ending? Is it fair for us to expect one?

Bathsheba, and Mary as the only other women named. In the genealogical list of Matthew 1, Tamar is in the company of women who exhibited, over the course of their lives, an exemplary kind of faith and complete trust in The One True God. Could she merely be the odd woman out? Could she be the only one who didn't understand The Truth? Was her story just so darn interesting that she couldn't be left out of

the list? Personally, I don't know where or when or how Tamar got it, but somewhere over the course of her very difficult life, I believe that Tamar acquired the most important quality of all: faith. How you acquire your faith doesn't really matter, does it? Whether it's done in retrospect, or in the heat of absolute chaos, or over a long lifetime process, in the end, understanding The Truth is all that matters.

The other visible, powerful change that came about was in Judah. After this journal entry, the Bible account picks up with the wild and crazy ride that Judah's brother Joseph has as a slave in Egypt. Joseph's a good kid and God sees him through a whole pile of near fatal disasters (it's reminiscent of a good Indiana Jones movie!). Years pass and although there are no specific examples of Judah's "change in heart," when you look closely you can see a rather stunning before and after distinction.

For example, there was the subtle comparison between Judah and his elder brother Rueben in Genesis 42-43. Rueben pleaded with his father, Jacob, to allow the youngest son Benjamin to travel to Egypt with the brothers when they went to beg for food from the Pharaoh during a time of severe famine. Jacob, having "lost" favorite son Joseph (through a jealous scheme perpetrated by the brothers) was adamant about not letting Joseph's youngest, full-blood brother (and only surviving son of Jacob's favored wife, Rachel) Benjamin out of his sight. Rueben literally offered the lives of his two sons should he fail to bring Benjamin back from Egypt unharmed, but Jacob refused. (Genesis 42:37-38)

But when Judah approached his father with the same purpose, he simply said, "I personally guarantee his safety. You may hold me responsible if I don't bring him back to you," and Jacob finally relented. (Genesis 43:9) Seems as if Judah's word became his bond, while anything Reuben says just wasn't quite good enough.

But my favorite picture of Judah, overshadowing all the other horrible things that are recorded about him, happens once all the brothers travel to Egypt. Much to their horror, Benjamin is accused of stealing and the Pharaoh's second in command demands that the young man remain in Egypt as a slave for punishment. Guess who among all those brothers had the courage to step forward and plead his case? (Genesis 44:18) Guess who among the brothers offered his life in place of his young brother's? (Genesis 44:33) Guess who among the brothers spoke so sincerely and so eloquently that the Pharaoh's representative was moved to tears? (Genesis 45:2) It was Judah, of course. His speech has been called "one of the noblest pieces of natural eloquence in any literature, sacred or profane." (Lockyer)

Judah redeemed himself in his defining moment with Tamar, and set his life on a course that remained admirable and respectable. On his deathbed, Judah's father Jacob said, "You, Judah, your brothers will praise you … honor you… The scepter shall not leave Judah; he'll keep a firm grip on the command staff until the ultimate ruler comes and the nations obey him …" (Genesis 49:8-12 MSG) To Judah, Jacob gives the definitive prize: *the line of Christ will come through his descendants*. It seems after everything is said and done it's not what you *did* that was important, but what you *chose* to do.

For all you Tamars out there...

Defining moments, crossroads of life, life-altering decisions … however you choose to label them, are in retrospect, the stand out times of our existence: good *and* bad. If we are fortunate, the good ones outweigh the bad. How's your tally so far? Are you groaning with embarrassment, glad no one knows the reality of your world? Do you have any room for improvement?

> **Don't let the best you have done so far be the standard for the rest of your life.**
> Gustavus F. Swift

Just as Eve taught us about achieving perfection, Tamar taught us about achieving strength: strength of character, strength of faith, and strength of commitment. Physically isolated at the beginning of her Biblical tale, she was, technically still physically isolated in the end. Tamar would always be that Canaanite girl the Judahs brought into their midst, who married two or three times (who knew for sure? – roll your eyes), who gave birth to her father-in-law's heirs by playing the whore, and who managed to reclaim a solid, if highly tarnished, status in well-bred society.

But, the person who Tamar was at the start was exponentially different from the person Tamar was at the end. I believe she achieved a closer level of perfection by accepting and honoring The One True God. She exhibited a commendable level of courage under pressure that would put most of us to shame. And she learned the precious skill of being able to discern what was worth fighting for and what was not. I think Tamar learned what all of us can learn: that the things of most value are eternal.

❖ **Who Do You Rely On:** When that gut wrenching panic grips your stomach, when worry invades your days *and* your nights, when your heart pounds with fear and trembling, when you are so filled with dread that you would rather not leave your bed, let alone your home, what do you do?

> **All that is not eternal is eternally useless.**
> C. S. Lewis

Who do you rely on? Perhaps you have a precious friend, or a loving mother, or a caring workmate who will listen to your tale of woe and offer some sincere insight and advice. But do you always do what they suggest? Do you become filled with doubt as to which words of advice are sounder?

Sometimes do you think that others have no idea what you're going through? Well Someone does understand *exactly* what you're going through because *He knows your heart and your mind. God would surely have known it, for He knows the secrets of every heart.* (Psalm 44:21) Rely on the advice of Someone who knows you inside and out, where you've been, where you're going, and how you're going to get there. Make a conscious choice to learn more about Him, abide by His rules, and listen to His still small voice. Come on; give it a try at least.

❖ **Courage/Strength:** We cannot do it alone. The courage and strength that is required to survive this life is not something that any one person is capable of. Circumstances and people batter us from all sides until sometimes we crumble. "How come this always happens to me?" "I can't deal with anymore stress and trouble!" "I've never been so afraid in all my life!" "What am I going to do?!" "I'm lost." "I'm frightened." "I'm alone." Not only does the Bible promise courage and strength from God, but along with it we receive a peace that cannot be truly comprehended. *Don't worry about anything; instead, pray about everything. Tell God what you need, and thank Him for all He has done. Then you will experience God's peace, which exceeds anything we can understand. His peace will guard your hearts and minds as you live in Christ Jesus.* (Philippians 4:6-7)

❖ **Hard Times:** Every person in this world faces hard times. No one is immune. Wealth, power, intelligence, and skill do not protect or prevent trials and tribulations. And you know what else doesn't guarantee a life that's a bed of roses? *Being a Christian.* Take a look at any person in the Bible, talk to any missionary, or consult any minister or faithful Christian that you know. Being a godly person doesn't keep the hard times at bay. What being a Christian *does do* is give you an extra, super-charged power source that the average Jane does not have. *Do not* diminish God's capacity to guide, protect, and save. *God is not a God of disorder, but of peace.* (I Corinthians 14:33)

I arise today
Through God's strength to pilot me,
God's might to uphold me,
God's wisdom to guide me,
God's eye to look before me,

147

God's ear to hear me,
God's word to speak for me,
God's hand to guard me,
God's way to lie before me,
God's shield to protect me,
God's host to save me…
From everyone who shall wish me ill,
Afar and anear,
Alone and in multitude.
From, *The Deer's Path, St. Patrick,*

❖ **The Best Kind of Satisfaction:** We spend a major portion of our lives trying to gain approval – from our parents, our mates, our superiors, our friends, our colleagues… But the reality is, the only place we should really strive for approval is from God. Does He approve of you? Of your life? Of your choices? Of your goals? Do you make Him smile? We were created out of His great love to bring Him pleasure through obedience and companionship. If that is not your focus, you are not on the right track.

> The smile of God is the goal of your life.
> Rick Warren

❖ **Faith:** At some point over the course of the horrors that Tamar was experiencing, I believe she found faith in The One True God. Rather than see what she was experiencing in the here and now, Tamar chose to look forward to what she *knew* she was heading towards. True faith believes in things that have not been seen or experienced. At some point Tamar *chose* to believe that God would see her through the fire of her life and bring her to something safe and good on the other side. While there may be many defining moments in our lives, the single most imperative one is to believe in The One True God. *So be truly glad. There is wonderful joy ahead, even though you have to endure many trials for a little while. These trials will show that your faith is genuine. It is being tested as fire tests and purifies gold—though your faith is far more precious than mere gold. So when your faith remains strong through many trials, it will bring you much praise and glory and honor on the day when Jesus Christ is revealed to the whole world.* (I Peter 1:6-7)

Homework... Who Do You Have?

God should be your first and foremost source of advice and comfort in times of stress, trouble, and sorrow. You know to say that (at least after reading this chapter) even if you don't readily do it. In addition, God also surrounds you within your life with people that He embraces and speaks to as well. Did *someone* take the time to speak with Tamar, answer her questions, and patiently guide her to the point where she could believe? How about you? Besides

> **You are truly blessed if your lists have:**
> - **Your mother and/or father**
> - **Your mate**
> - **The same person listed more than once**
>   McG

seeking out God through prayer, Bible study, and church attendance, you should consciously work to surround yourself with people who give you *sound* advice, guidance that would cause God to smile and nod His head in agreement, choices that would make you so strong that you become almost invincible against anything the world has to throw at you.

Who has God provided in your life? In your work? Now, don't panic. It's quality that's best, not quantity. One sound person is better than ten damaged ones. Plus, you are much better off recognizing a void in one or more areas of your life and making wise choices to fill it than grinning like a Cheshire cat oblivious to the sinking ship you're happily rowing.

Would God agree with those people you surround yourself with? Pretend it was up to God to choose your top three advocates in each area of your life: personal, worldly, professionally, and spiritual. Who would He pick? Write those names on the next pages. Take time to pray and be thankful for what you've got, to pray and ask for guidance to fill in gaps and, most importantly, to pray and ask God to give both yourself and these lifelines wisdom in all that is said, thought, and done.

So, in regard to HUMAN BEINGS you are acquainted with, think about them in terms of these four categories:

Personal	Worldly	Professional	Spiritual

MY PERSONAL LIFELINES

Personal Life
• With whom do you share your most private thoughts and worries?
• Who understands your sense of humor?
• Who knows about your personal demons?
• Who loves you enough to take you aside and speak firmly to you when they see you making serious mistakes?
• Who is the #1 person you trust when seeking advice about your personal life?
• With whom do you have your longest personal relationship?

Personal/Private Of all the people I know, God would choose:	1. 2. 3.

MY WORDLY LIFELINES

Worldly Life
• Who do you trust to give information about dealing with the world you live in: financial, automotive, medical, educational ...
• Who is concerned enough for you to take you aside and speak firmly to you when he or she sees you making serious mistakes?
• Who is the #1 person you trust when needing advice about your worldly life?
• Who has taught you the most about dealing with the world you live in?
• With whom do you have your longest worldly relationship?

Worldly Of all the people I know, God would choose:	1. 2. 3.

MY PROFESSIONAL LIFELINES

Professional Life
• Who in your professional workplace provides you with sound advice? • Who is interested enough in you take you aside and speak firmly to you when he or she see you making serious mistakes? • Who is the #1 person you trust when seeking advice you about your professional life? • Who has taught you the most about your professional career? • To whom do you owe the most gratitude? • With whom do you have your longest professional relationship?

Professional Of all the people I know, God would choose:	1. 2. 3.

MY SPIRITUAL LIFELINES

Spiritual Life
• Who can answer your questions about God? • Who would take the time to listen to your doubts and fears about God? • Who would you trust to really mean it when they say, "I'll pray for you." • Who loves you enough to take you aside and speak firmly to you when they see you making eternal mistakes? • Who is the #1 person you trust when seeking advice about your spiritual life? • With whom do you have your longest spiritual relationship?

Spiritual Of all the people I know, God would choose:	1. 2. 3.

What do you think of your lists? More importantly, what do you think *God* thinks of your lists? Is it possible that the area of your life that is in the greatest trouble is the area that has the weakest lifelines?

How can you fix this?

Always start with prayer. Ask God to put wise people in your life. Ask also that the Lord will give you a discerning spirit: that is the ability to tell good advice from bad.

What if you have *no one?* Spend a number of days simply praying and watching those around you in your life. Who do others go to for advice? ("I love Kathleen, she's the greatest person to unload on. She's always positive and willing to listen.") Who do others *stay away from?* ("Don't believe a word that Pauline says. I don't think she's ever said a truthful thing in her life!")

Take baby steps. This is a foundation you are building and it will be as weak or as strong as you determine to make it. Ask one person a question and weigh the response. Does he or she take time with you? ("Why don't we have lunch and talk? I've got some ideas, but not enough time to talk about them right now.") Does he or she seem to really give your question thoughtful consideration? ("Well, let me think for a moment. Answer some questions for me first so I'm sure I understand the whole picture ...") Does that person acknowledge his or her strengths and weaknesses while still providing an opinion? ("I'm not the greatest when it comes to financial advice, but I found a really great financial advisor at a seminar I attended. Here, let me find his phone number ...")

And don't dismiss anyone! You know that God has a sense of humor. Don't put yourself on such a high horse that you can't see whom you're riding by.

Question To Discuss:

Q?

What role must faith play in your level of personal strength?

The movie "Pretty Woman" would have been her favorite flick.

Rahab and The Guy Who Got It For Free

A Heart Of Belief

Rahab was a whore. She was a heathen. She betrayed her own country to the enemy. She saved her own skin and that of her family while her entire city – every man, woman, child, and animal – was utterly destroyed by the attacking army. If you were an Amorite, you would probably spit every time you said her name. And if it's possible to make matters worse, she wasn't shy, quiet, or at all submissive.

Independent and astute, Rahab appeared to thumb her nose at polite society, cultural mores, and the whole 'woman submit, respect, and obey the man' mantra. And although unlike anyone we've seen before along the historical route of God's prefect plan, Rahab is exactly what God wanted in His ancestral line of Christ.

I get a kick out of how Herbert Lockyer describes her: "Rahab ... was a woman who yielded herself indiscriminately to every man approaching her. Rahab indulged in venal wantonness as traveling merchants came her way and were housed in her ill famed abode." (*Women*

154

of the Bible) She probably did additional disgraceful things like leaving her hair uncovered, allowing her bare arms and bare ankles to be seen, and permitting men to speak with her while she was out running errands during the day. She was a real baddie, a woman you would have protected your children from and crossed the street to avoid.

Rahab's colorful life was riddled with pertinent lessons that we can apply today, such as: no excuse is too big, no mistake is too disastrous, no secret is too horrible, and no history is too bleak for God. In fact, if Rahab is any indication, the lower you are to start creates just that much more glorious a contrast when you win the top prize at the end.

The lesson of Rahab's life cancels out all excuses we may have for not embracing and following Christ. Sorry. If Rahab was acceptable as an *ancestress of Christ* - pass her the torch, Tamar - then every single one of us has got to be okay to join the club of God's followers. Do you get it *yet?* God doesn't care about the outside; He only cares about what's on the inside.

Enjoy Rahab's story about a woman who didn't care a whit about what the world thought of her, just what The One True God thought.

First Things First

Scripture references you should check out:	Joshua 2:1-21; 6:17-25; Matthew 1:5; Hebrews 11:31; James 2:25
Question to ask yourself before you read any further:	Do you have things in your past that you feel cannot be forgiven and/or forgotten?
What her name means:	Her name means "storm," "arrogance," "broad," or "spacious." The first part of Rahab - "Ra", was the name of an Egyptian god. As an Amorite, Rahab belonged to an idolatrous people.

Connections:	Every one of us makes the mistake of comparing ourselves to others. Worse yet, we must continually deal with the comments, opinions, and critiques of family, friends, and strangers. Maintaining our own level of self-worth is a daunting task that sometimes can leave us exhausted … and defeated. Rahab dealt with the worst that could be thrown at her but still managed to hang onto her self-respect. Better yet, she learned to bend when things got tough, but never break. Intelligent and intuitive, she let her heart guide her away from all she knew, to believe in The One True God.
What the Bible says about belief:	**In God:** Isaiah 43:10 **What You Can Accomplish Through It:** Mark 9:23, Luke 1:45, John 1:12, John 3:16 **Vs. Unbelief:** Mark 9:24, Mark 6:11 **What It Accomplishes:** Mark 16:16, John 6:47 **Levels of Belief:** John 3:11-13 **And Judgment:** John 3:18, 36 **In Christ:** John 6:35, John 14:10 **The Ultimate Question:** John 16:31 **And The Bible:** John 20:31 **How It Changes Us:** Romans 3:22 **And Winning:** I John 5:5

Questions We'll Never Know The Answers To:

❖ What events brought Rahab to a life of prostitution?

❖ How did Rahab end up belonging to the Israelite tribe of Judah?

Did you know? Interesting Biblical Facts About Rahab

❖ **Prostitution:** There were different classes of prostitutes back in biblical times. Temple prostitutes, male and female, performed sexual acts in heathen temples (Hosea 4:12-14) symbolically acting out the fertility rites of the cycle of nature. A second kind of prostitute may have owned a bar or inn and had sexual relations with the patrons who desired her services. Whether or not Rahab actually owned an inn, she was this second kind of prostitute.

❖ **Amorites:** Amorites (often also referred to as Canaanites to keep us all confused) were one of the major tribes living in the land of Canaan when the Israelites, led by Joshua, showed up. The Amorites claimed extensive land west of the Euphrates River including all of what is now Palestine, Lebanon, and Syria. Major biblical cities such as: Jerusalem, Hebron, Jarmuth, Lachish, Eglon and Jericho were all, at one time or another, Amorite strongholds. Amorites by the time of the Israelite kings became the servants of the Hebrews. (I Kings 9:20-21)

❖ **The Israelites:** No longer just a large, dysfunctional family, the Israelites by the time Moses led them out of Egypt were a *nation* of over a million people. "That night the people of Israel left Rameses and started for Succoth. There were about 600,000 men, plus women and children." (Exodus 12:37) Judah was the largest tribe with 76,500 men (Numbers 26:22) while the tribe of Simeon was the smallest with 22,200 men. (Numbers 26:14) With an army of 40,000 strong (Joshua 4:13) they were now not only a force to be reckoned with, but a force to be *feared*.

❖ **Joshua:** Joshua, AKA Hoshea, was a man on a mission. Taking over after the death of Moses, he was charged with conquering The Promised Land, supervising the division of the territory among the twelve tribes, and leading the Israelites into a renewed covenant with God (Joshua 1-22). Leader of the Israelite tribe of Ephraim, he was a stellar example of godly empowered leadership. (Numbers 13:8) He, along with his equally commendable partner Caleb, leader of the Israelite tribe of Judah, distinguished themselves early by being the only spy team who believed with complete certainty that with God's might and assistance, The Promised Land could easily be conquered. *Of the entire nation of Israel* that departed with Moses from Egypt (over a *million people*), only Joshua and Caleb would earned the privilege to set foot in The Promised Land. (And that even included Moses!) Hey, one last Joshua tidbit: guess what the Greek equivalent of his name is? *Jesus*.

❖ **The Promised Land:** One man named Abraham was given a promise 600 years before (give or take a couple of decades). He and his barren wife were promised the land, and that their descendants would become too numerous to count. From Abraham and Sarah's perspective, the story had a rather desperate, how could it possibly ever be? quality to it.

157

From Joshua's perspective, as he led his million plus group into The Promised Land to conquer and take possession of it, it was simply a logistical, tactical exercise. They had the might, the reputation, the leadership, the experience, the wherewithal, the spiritual drive and the direction ... Suddenly the timing seemed to make perfect and complete sense. Hmm, does God ever say, "I told you so"?

❖ **The Ark of the Covenant of the Lord:** The Israelites had a fully established religion by this time with The Ten Commandments and a multitude of rules and regulations to obey. The Ark of the Covenant was Israel's most sacred treasure and a symbol of God's presence and power. Covered entirely in gold, it was a rectangular box with two angels (cherubim) on the lid. The box contained the original Ten Commandments, a jar of manna (the bread that miraculously appeared in the wilderness that fed the Israelites while they wandered), and Aaron's (Moses' brother and the first high priest) staff that actually *bloomed*. Only the Levite priests could carry the Ark. (Exodus 37:1-9) Today, its whereabouts is unknown, having disappeared when Nebuchadnezzar's armies destroyed Jerusalem in 586 B.C.

The Core Story

My name is Rahab ... Won't you come in?

Harlot, whore, prostitute ... There were a few other unfavorable names that applied to her as well, but Rahab probably had pretty tough skin by the time she showed up on the scene in the biblical journal. She was a woman who made her living selling her body for sexual purposes to strangers. I don't think anyone in the prostitution profession (then or now) could ever be labeled as delicate or sensitive.

We have little information about what had brought her to this profession. Some commentators believe she actually ran an inn and that, as a sideline, for the right price you could spend some quality time with the proprietress as well. The Bible isn't specific, though. Her place would have been in the seedier part of town, where no one "of quality" wanted to be. She'd apparently managed to find a place literally in the wall of the city.

Think about it: who'd want to live *in the wall*, as in the first place to be attacked and/or destroyed and farthest from the town center? For Rahab, it would have been better than living on the streets. That she managed to eek out a livelihood is, well, pretty darned amazing.

She also kept flax (a plant that grew over a meter tall and was used for making cloth) on her roof (it was where people put it to dry before weaving it) and had possession of "scarlet cord" which indicated the ability to dye fabric as well. Did she have an additional way to make money when business was slow, or was she attempting to find a new career that was significantly more reputable? No one knows.

Rahab was not a prostitute because she had been orphaned. Part of the happy ending to this story was that she rescued her family – mother, father, sisters, and brothers - as well as herself when the Israelites invaded her home city of Jericho. (Joshua 2:13) It's also definitely not because she was mentally challenged, because throughout the entire Bible account she's sharp, calm, collected, and intuitive. And while I suppose that she could have made the choice to become a prostitute because she always wanted to be one when she grew up, I find such a scenario hard to believe. The movie "Pretty Woman" is a fairy tale today, and was definitely a fairy tale then … Or was it?

More than likely, some circumstance beyond Rahab's control caused this drastic change in status. Abuse or rape would have made her "unsuitable" for a proper marriage (no, they wouldn't have cared about the reason why or the circumstances). Rejection by a suitor or husband because of something real or imagined (such as infidelity or ineptness) would have rendered her "unsuitable" as well. It's possible she simply refused to bend to her father's will in a planned marriage and was consequently disowned. (If that was the case, the prospective groom must have been awfully bad to have Rahab choose prostitution over marriage.) Remember, a woman's status in biblical times hinged completely on the man she was attached to: first father, next husband, and then son. Take these away those, and society pretty much shrugged its shoulders, wiped its hands, and turned its backs on you. *Hey, you weren't their problem* …

Rahab was some woman. Tough as nails; she was a survivor who had apparently made the best of a bad situation. In sinking to the bottom of society she rose above its ability to control or hurt her. She was a business woman using the skills she had to the best of her advantage. Everything she did: in business, socially, and personally, was completely and permanently tainted with the status that she bore: *she was a whore.* In fact, throughout the biblical account, "whore" pretty much becomes her last name. (Joshua 2:1, Hebrews 11:31, James 2:25) Her exact address was: Rahab The Whore, Home In The Wall Of The City, Amorite Stronghold, City of Jericho, The Jordan Valley, Canaan.

What would her life have been like, apart from her professional "duties"? She would have been shunned by "reputable" people, so her peers would have been other castoffs of society: fellow prostitutes, criminals, the sick and handicapped, beggars, and widows without anyone to provide or care for them. Life would have taught her not to judge a book by its cover; that everyone had things deep inside that they kept hidden. Would she have been tolerant of others, or accepting of no one? Would she have become a good judge of character, or simply mistrusting of everyone? Would she have had friends who accepted her for *who* she was as opposed to *what* she was, or was she a loner, enjoying no one's company but her own?

Q?

What do you think of this statement? "It is more dangerous to be lukewarm in opinion than to be hot or cold."

With no welfare, food stamps or rental assistance she would have been forced to be frugal, wily, industrious and astute. Life would have taught her that you never knew what was around the corner, so you'd better always be prepared. Everything she had claim to would have been earned through – literally – her very own blood, sweat, and tears. She would have been able to spot a con man from a mile away, a thief simply by the glint in his eyes, and a hypocrite by their smell.

Her associations with the questionable side of society would have made her worldlier and more informed than the average, sheltered young woman of her time. Rahab would have seen and heard more about what was beyond the walls of Jericho than even some of the city men. She would have met many interesting people as a result of her profession: businessmen, travelers, vagabonds, warriors, criminals, politicians, and probably even a few temple priests. Nothing would have surprised her anymore.

Beyond everything else, Rahab would have been the epitome of self-reliance in a society that subscribed to the belief that if you were not good enough, you were just as well dead. Self-sufficient, cunning, and worldly, there was nothing left in this life that could impress Rahab the whore. Or so she thought …

Those Israelites … Uh, oh! Are they here yet?!

For a while, the biggest bit of gossip around Rahab's and the market was about a group of escaped Egyptian slaves that were cutting a huge path through Canaan. At first, there had been fanciful stories relayed with complete cynicism. "Hey, Rehab! I would have gotten here sooner but I couldn't manage to find an Israelite to part the Jordan River, so I had to cross the usual way!" "Hey Rahab, there's no Israelite to make water come from rocks so could you bring me another cold one?"

Gradually though, accounts of the Israelites' battle successes cut into the jokes. *Some* customers began to discuss the seemingly "miraculous" battles: a magical staff of God causing victory in battle (Exodus 17:9), stories of slaughter and Israelite occupation of cities previously thought invincible (Numbers 21:24), and phrases like "not a single survivor" spoken in hushed tones when talking about kings that poets had actually written *poems* about. (Numbers 21:35) While more than one customer still mocked about "the Israelites will get you if you don't watch out" only to collapse in hysterical, supercilious laughter, more than a few patrons no longer saw the humor in it all. And *lately*, there had been nervous, furtive glances and whispered comments about who had the latest confirmed news, and speculation about where "those accursed Israelites" were headed next. Real fear would have set in when it was learned that the Israelites were headed *toward Jericho*.

Rahab heard all the words, but more importantly had observed the change in attitude. *Never* had Rahab heard of such a thing before: the complete transformation of a person's status (forget about an entire nation) from slave to free to warrior. Who had ever heard of someone going from being the butt of jokes and laughter to the object of genuine fear and worry? Rahab was living proof that you were dealt a course of life and *you were stuck with it* no matter how hard you tried to change things. And yet here, vividly, seemed to be proof of the fallacy of that statement. How could such a thing be?

Rahab would have heard fearful whispers of a powerful god. One that was not visible, had no image, and yet was attributed with this entire nation's miraculous alteration. Could such a god exist? If it were true, then Rahab would have been ready to sign on without looking back. She knew about the supposed power of gods because she'd been to the heathen temples. She had seen the sacrifices, listened to all the superstitious mucky-muck, and probably even had a bunch of the "sacred relics" displayed around her place. Hey, if it worked, why not? Heck, she even knew a few of the priests *really well*. But this Israelite god ... it seemed as amazing as its followers. With a passionate curiosity, Rahab would have made every effort to learn all she possibly could about this amazing ... phenomenon.

Jericho was one of the oldest inhabited cities in the world, situated 800 feet below sea level in the valley of the Jordan River near the Dead Sea. During Rahab's lifetime, it sat high up on an imposing pear-shaped mound. Its climate was tropical, meaning temperatures could get quite high, and very little rain fell. A beautiful oasis, Jericho was known for its date palms, banana trees, balsams, sycamores and henna. In fact, on a number of occasions the Bible refers to Jericho as "the city of palm trees." (Deut. 34:3, Judges 3:13)

After Moses' death, the Lord had told Joshua, "You must lead my people across the Jordan River into the land I am giving them. I promise you what I promised Moses: 'Everywhere you go, you will be on land I have given you' ... No one will be able to stand their ground against you as long as you live ... I will not fail you or abandon you ... Do not be afraid or discouraged. For the Lord your God is with you wherever you go." (Joshua 1:2-9, select parts)

Joshua had already proven himself to be a man after God's own heart. He was strong, decisive, obedient, and willing. Already he was a seasoned warrior, having led Israel to victory against the Amalekites (descendants of Jacob's brother Esau!). (Exodus 17:9) Most surely he would have been a participant in the successful battles against the Canaanite

162

king Arad (Numbers 21:1-3), the Amorite king Sihon (Numbers 21:21-30), and Og, the king of Bashan. (Numbers 21:33-35) The nation of Israel had transformed itself from a collection of escaped slaves to an army of experienced warriors.

Joshua's plan was to leave the women, children, servants, and supplies on the east side of the Jordan River, and take 40,000 able-bodied and fully armored warriors, across the Jordan River to conquer it. "We will fight until the Lord gives us possession of *all* the land He has promised us." (Joshua 1:14-15 ST) The Israelite nation, on the right spiritual track, told Joshua, "We will do whatever you command us and we will go wherever you send us. We will obey you ... And may the Lord your God be with you ..." (Joshua 1:16-17) Sounds like a recipe for success, doesn't it?

Two men were chosen to spy out the land, in particular the area around Jericho. Israel had used this tactic years ago (Joshua was one of the spies) to scope out The Promised Land. The earlier spies had brought back reports of a land flowing with "milk and honey" as well as being inhabited by giants who made the spies feel "like grasshoppers." (Numbers 13:27, 33) All of the earlier spies, except Joshua and his partner Caleb were struck dead for their negative reports. In addition, the entire nation of Israel was punished to wander forty years in the wilderness (one year for every day the spies had spied) for their failure to believe in God's promises, and their faithlessness in doubting God's abilities. Consequently, I would suspect that these two spies sent out by Joshua were carefully selected and particularly aware of the magnitude of their job.

Salmon was one of the chosen spies. We don't know a lot about him and he isn't specifically named in the initial plan outlined in Joshua 2:1, but because he was named in future lineages we can put two and two together. His partner, though, remains forever nameless. I imagine both of these guys to be young, fearless, confident, and extremely physically fit. Sort of like the special ops guys we see in the movies or read about in our romantic suspense novels. They set off and make their way into the busy, teeming, corrupt streets of Jericho to gather some Intel. Hmmm, let's think. Where would be a good place to go in which they could gather information but be confident no immediate suspicions would be raised and no specific questions would be asked? Hmmm, how about a whore's house?

Seems as if Rahab was going to add *Israelite Spies* to her list of Interesting Men I've Met Over The Course Of My Profession.

Rahab's Place ... Was there any vacancy?

Salmon and his partner showed up at Rahab's. Traveling through the city they would have, most assuredly, made every effort to "blend in" as much as possible to ensure their success. Their ability to do such would have been one of the qualities that led to their choice for the mission. Yet

> I am the LORD
> your God, who
> has separated
> you from the
> peoples.
> Leviticus 20:24b

the sheer, unadulterated sinfulness of it all must have just about bowled the two men over. At this point, all Israelites had spent at least *forty years* wandering the land separate and apart from all heathen cultures except during battle and other brief, unplanned encounters. They wore different clothes, ate specific foods, avoided certain behaviors and practices, and even went so far as to worship an unseen God who refused to have even a graven image of Himself erected. Literally every aspect of their lives had been altered to make them a "separate and distinct people."

I picture the two spies as doing the whole furtive behavior thing: staying in the dark corners, keeping their hats pulled down low and their eyes downcast. Most people wouldn't have given them a second glance. But Rahab would have immediately picked up all kinds of clues about who they were from their appearance, behavior, and "never been in these parts before" personas. She was a student of the world and had gotten an A+ in "Reading People: Body language And Other Telling Clues."

Whether Rahab knew immediately or clued in later, the biblical account records that the two spies made arrangements to spend the night at her place. Was it their unique accents that made her take note of them? Was the cut of their clothes so strange? Did they fumble with the strange coins or offer odd ones that peaked her curiosity? Maybe their obvious lack of experience at making arrangements to stay for the night in a whore's house sent up a red flag? Perhaps she offered to serve them a food they weren't allowed to eat and glimpsed the panic in their eyes? Did she make flirtatious overtures to them and watch in stunned fascination as they both blushed?

By this time, Rahab knew an extensive amount of information about the advancing Israelite army. She would have heard the gossip and worked diligently to separate fact from fiction. Intrigued with each new discovery, her interest would have grown. Privy to multiple pieces of the full puzzle of what the Israelites were all about, it was possible that Rahab knew immediately who was standing making arrangements to stay with her, and couldn't believe her luck. Boy, did she have a pile of questions she needed to ask these guys!

Unfortunately, there were others watching for suspicious characters. Before the city gates closed for the night, the biblical journal records someone telling the king of Jericho, "Some Israelites have come here tonight to spy out the land." (Joshua 2:2) Immediately, the king sent a representative to Rahab. She must have definitely been the "go to" place, huh? The king's representative said, "Bring out the men who have come into your house. They are spies sent here to discover the best way to attack us." (Joshua 2:3)

But this was Rahab they were dealing with. Rahab knew her clientele and her neighborhood. Observant as ever, Rahab had already anticipated the king's representative and taken care of the spies. Batting her lashes and maybe winking at a few of the soldiers accompanying the king's representative, she said, "The men were here earlier, but I didn't know where they were from. They left the city at dusk, as the city gates were about to close, and I don't know where they went. If you hurry, you can probably catch up with them." (Joshua 2:4)

Off the king's men went to look along the road leading to the spot that has the shallowest crossing for the Jordan River. As it was spring time and the Jordan River was at flood stage, there was only one place where the river could be easily forded. As soon as the king's men departed, the city gates were shut for the night.

Okay, so she lied. Big time. Rahab knew *who* the men were. She knew *where* they were, too. They were up on the roof hidden under her piles of drying flax. While the king learned about the presence of the two spies within his city walls, Rahab was having her defining moment. And while I suppose it could have been a spontaneous, spur of the moment decision to betray her people, her country, her king, and her family, not to mention risk her life with the charge of treason, I think Rahab had already made her personal choice long before the two spies showed up at her place.

Rahab had listened, questioned, done her research, and thought long and hard about these Israelites. And I believe that sometime before Salmon and his partner walked into her home, Rahab had already clued into The Truth: the Israelites had The One True God. Without advice from anything but her common sense, without the availability of books, Internet, or Bible tracts, and without thought to her deeply tarnished reputation and lowly status, Rahab decided that she wanted to be a part of this miraculous ride.

Suddenly, the idea of Salmon and his partner showing up at a whore's house didn't seem so far fetched, did it? You see, God was in control all along, guiding these two young men. God knew exactly what was going on in Rahab's heart. On the *outside* it was the home of a whore, but on the *inside* it was a questioning heart looking for answers.

> **Q?**
>
> **What does it take to get you to believe something? Do you need to see it with your eyes? Feel it with your hands? Do you need hundreds of satisfied customers' testimonials? How did you come by your faith in God? Has it become your own?**

Here's the deal ... What's in it for me?

After she'd taken care of the king's men, Rahab went up on the roof to talk with Salmon and his partner. How did she initially convince them to trust her? Did she simply walk over to them and say, "The king's men come to capture you. Follow me or you will be killed." Or: "You are obviously Israelites and should not be here. Follow me and I will help you hide." Or how about this: "Does your God make you wise in discerning the truth? Come I will keep you safe." I like: "You worship The One True God. I believe all I have heard about what He has done for you. Quick, let me show you where to go to stay safe." Whatever Rahab said, the spies trusted her with their lives, believing that she would hide them and keep the king's men from capturing them.

Rahab was true to her word. As night fell and things settled down in the neighborhood, Rahab went up to the roof of her home to … negotiate her terms with the men. Hey, what's wrong with that? God wants us obedient. He doesn't need us to be complacent or careless. God wants seasoned warriors, not namby-pamby doormats. These guys were Israelites, sure, but they were also *men*. Men had gotten Rahab into this predicament and it was only through her own abilities and common sense that she was still alive and kicking. She would be cautious and sit down, stare those men right in the eye and negotiate her terms of agreement. When she was absolutely certain that she could trust the men hiding on her roof as much as she had decided to trust in The One True God, *then* she'd help them escape.

In the safety of the darkness, Rahab, Salmon and Salmon's partner had an opportunity to speak in more detail than before. Rahab set the tone. Maybe, having spent a major part of her life justifying who she was, as opposed to what she was, she knew right where to start. "I know the Lord has given you this land. We are all afraid of you. Everyone is living in terror … For the Lord your God is the supreme God of the heavens above and the earth below." (Joshua 2:9-11, select parts)

> **Leave the broken, irreversible past in God's hands, and step out into the invincible future with Him.**
> Oswald Chambers

Notice she didn't list any excuses. She didn't share with them all the horrible reasons why she was living as a whore. The words "it's not my fault" never left her mouth. Long ago Rahab had learned that excuses were worthless, and wasted valuable time better used to move forward.

She also didn't wallow in self-pity. "I'm just no good to anyone. No one wants me. My past is too tarnished for God to make any positive use of me." It never seemed to occur to her that God would reject her for

His own. All she needed was get the logistics straight on how it was all going to happen.

Rahab didn't ask for leniency either. She didn't shed false tears and remind them that she was a "woman on her own." She didn't remind them that without her help they would be in the king's jail or worse. This woman did not beg or plead. This woman *struck a deal.*

Rahab simply outlined what she'd heard about their exploits, what she believed to be true, and where she stood in regard to it all. In doing so she established the most telling fact about her belief: she *knew* that even though she was a heathen whore, The One True God had the power to make something of quality out of her. Rahab believed that The One True God didn't care about what she was *before*, He only cared about what she was *going to become.*

> **Red,
> the color of blood.
> Blood,
> the price
> necessary for
> redemption.
> Redemption,
> the act of
> rescuing.**
> McG

"Now swear to me by the Lord," Rahab demanded, "that you will be kind to me and my family since I have helped you. Give me some guarantee that when Jericho is conquered, you will let me live, along with my father and mother, my brothers and sisters, and all their families." (Joshua 2:12-13)

Another telling moment in her faith which was much more visible to Salmon and his partner was the phrase "... *when* Jericho is conquered ..." Not *if*. No doubts, no waffling as to which side she wanted to be on, no begging for a few more days or weeks to get her things in order and make sure this was what she wanted to do. Rahab was on board and ready.

The men were convinced. "We offer our own lives as guarantee for your safety. If you don't betray us, we will keep our promise when the Lord gives us the land." (Joshua 2:14)

So the prostitute and the Israelites had convinced on another about their sincerity. Rahab willingly put herself and her family's lives in the hands of these two men whom she had just met, but had judged worthy of her trust. Salmon and his partner saw sincerity, passion, and belief in

Rahab. They willingly obligated themselves to rescue her and her family. Each side committed to a pledge, that only death could break.

Rahab had red cord, strong enough to lower two men from the window of her home outside the walls of Jericho to safety and escape. Hmmm, quite a strong illustration of the biblical theme! The Bible has a "scarlet thread of redemption" from Genesis through to Revelation; a path of blood sacrifices necessary to redeem, save, … rescue. All temple sacrifices that the Israelite nation offered to atone for sins were symbolic representations of the ultimate sacrifice of Christ's death on the cross. From mankind's initial fall in the garden to Christ's crucifixion on the cross, this entire biblical journal account is all about the path that gets each of us to a point, just like Rahab, where we can be rescued from the sinful life we're living in.

Q?

Can you trace the scarlet thread through your own life from start to now?

There was one further stipulation: the spies tell Rahab as they climb out her window, "We can guarantee your safety only if you leave this scarlet rope hanging from the window …" (Joshua 2:17-18)

"I accept your terms," Rahab told them and sent them on their way, leaving the scarlet rope hanging from her window. Rather *obvious* don't you think? *Scarlet*. Bright, like blood. Vividly obvious to anyone who knew what to look for. The only thing guaranteeing Rahab and her family's rescue. "Hey Rahab, why the red rope? Do we get a special deal if we climb in the window as opposed to coming in through your door?" Oh, you get a special deal alright. But just not what you might think!

The apostle Paul will use the same kind of escape – out a window in the wall around the city of Damascenes (although he used a basket, he must not have been as physically fit) in II Corinthians 11:33. Rahab told the two spies to go into the hill country and hide out for three days. Jericho's soldiers searched along the road that led to the Jordan River's crossing without success.

Dr. W. A. Criswell said, "Rahab the harlot is an example of the grace of God at work. Her salvation was not based on her character or merits: she lived in a doomed city, practiced a condemned profession, engaged in subversive activities, and lied about her actions. Nevertheless she ... acted upon faith, and was spared the judgment of God which was executed at the hands of the Israelites."

Grace. Under Pressure. Saved. By Grace. Rahab. Rescued. Redeemed. Saved ...

Hi Mom, Hi Dad ... Wanna come over for dinner?

Quick. Go to your parent's home *today* – immediately - and convince them in any way you can that they (and all your brothers and sisters and their families) must leave their home and their country – in a week to ten days – and move to a foreign land with a different language, completely different customs and a totally different religion. Oh, while you're at it, make sure your family knows that they must completely embrace all aspects of this new country, can only bring a few possessions, and everything and everyone they leave behind will be completely and utterly destroyed. *They will never return.*

Even if you have the best relationship in the world with your family, I would imagine that such an assignment would be rather ... *difficult?* Now imagine being in Rahab's shoes. Remember, relations with the family would have been strained and awkward *at best.* Did they even see or speak with each other? Did the family embrace the custom that once a person was disowned they actually had a funeral and considered the rejected person dead? Had they at some point in the past refused to support or help her when she needed them most?

Somehow, I don't think this scenario would have worked: "These two really nice guys came to my place, Mom and Dad, and they turned out to be spies from the Israelite army! They were *really cute* and said that if I helped them escape they'd rescue us all before they attack and destroy the city. Wasn't that nice of them? Wanna come?" Nor do I think this would have been successful: "Please! You've got to believe me this time! This time I've really changed. *Honest.* These Israelites spies invited me to come along and live with them and I'd really like you to come, too."

Personally, I feel strongly that there must have been some love and affection still existing between Rahab and her family. After all, if she truly hated them she would have been only out to save herself. Why bother with anyone you despised, who had harshly rejected you? I think that perhaps the circumstances that had caused Rahab to become a whore would have been as equally traumatic and hurtful for the family. Her heartache was their heartache. Did Rahab's family still recognize her intrinsic goodness, honesty, and intelligence and, though undoubtedly stunned and terrified, considered no other alternative than to follow their daughter into this uncharted territory?

Maybe the family was just out to save their own necks in any way possible. There could have been no emotional investment involved except panic and self-preservation, prompting a reluctant agreement with Rahab's plan. Perhaps the fearsome reputation of the Israelites was so overwhelming that *anything* would have been preferable to simply waiting in terror for the inevitable attack. "Who cares that we have to throw our lot in with Rahab, at least it will give us a chance to get out of here!"

Lastly, a final outcome could have been that no one believed Rahab and that she left her parent's home discouraged and alone. She would have gone home and made preparations, because with the family or without the family, her decision had been made. Having survived on her own for years, a new beginning was at hand, and Rahab was not going to miss this opportunity. Perhaps the family only changed their tune when the Israelite army crossed the Jordan River and made preparations to attack Jericho. Maybe then, Rahab's family would have had to discuss what 'she who must not be named' had said and offered. And someone would have had to eat his words and show up knocking at her door, hat in hand.

Those Wild and Crazy Israelites ... What's their attack plan?!

The spies' words to Joshua when they returned safely from hiding in the hills near Jericho three days later, were, "The Lord will certainly give us the whole land for all the people in the land are terrified of us." (Joshua 2:24)

The very next day, the entire nation of Israel packed up its tents, gathered up its possessions, and herded all of its livestock across the Jordan River. The Jordan River itself was an excellent initial defense for Jericho, especially when it was swollen with spring rains and winter run-offs. Jericho would have sat smugly and securely behind its formidable walls and waited to laugh and gloat over the impossibility of getting *hundreds of thousands of people* plus all their possessions across a mighty river at flood stage.

The Jordan River's width varies from between 90 to 100 feet and is between three and ten feet in depth. From beginning (at Lake Huleh – called the Sea of Chinnereth back then) to end (the Dead Sea – called the Salt Sea back then), the river drops 1,290 feet, making a swiftly flowing river with over twenty-seven series of rapids. Bridges didn't exist during biblical times, so it was only at the shallow fords that crossings occurred. Possession of these fords was an important military factor, and Jericho would have fiercely defended the locations closest to them.

As a I child, I always was told the story about Moses parting the Red Sea, and how the Israelites passed through on dry land. It wasn't until I was an adult that I found out that God repeated that miracle a second time. The Ark of the Covenant of the Lord was carried by priests to the center point of the crossing and the Jordan River simply "began piling up" (Joshua 3:16) at a town upstream while the rest of the water continued flowing downstream. The Israelites - in the middle of the spring flood season – once again passed through a river *on dry land.*

Can you imagine the pandemonium in Jericho? Already "melting in fear" (Joshua 2:11) simply based on the stories they had heard, *now* much to their horror, the Israelites, along with their God and His miracles, were right in their back yard! And the Jordan River, their first line of defense – which had always worked so well in the past – had *dried up* the moment the Israelites had set their feet in it! "The gates of Jericho were tightly shut because the people were afraid of the Israelites. No one was allowed to go in or out." (Joshua 6:1)

I wonder if *this* was when Rahab's family showed up knocking at her door. Had she officially shut her "business" down? I can't really justify her going on with "business as usual" while she waited for her rescue, can you? Perhaps her father and brothers showed up expecting to blend in with the regular nightly crowd, and were stunned to find an "Out of Business" sign nailed to the front door. Perhaps that when Rahab and her family sat down, hashed things out, and made plans to await rescue? Were they the only family in town with any hope, and not in full panic mode? Had Rahab been able to sell her plan to them early on, and were they all just methodically going through the motions of closing down their current lives?

Whatever the timing of Rahab's family, in the Israelite camp they were in full preparation for battle. Not necessarily doing the things we'd expect in a battle camp, mind you. Oh, they were sharpening their knives, but not for battle. Oh, no. They were making sure every warrior was circumcised. Ouch. I think about the confidence of those Israelites, camped in their enemy's back yard, gearing up for a major battle and having … surgery done on their private parts. Talk about confidence in the Lord!

But the reality was that there wasn't going to be a lot of wall scaling and hand to hand combat. *Sometimes* God had His people fight that way. But not this time. This time, God took a rather unique tact. The siege took seven days. For the first six days, the Israelite priests carried The Ark of the Covenant of the Lord, with armed guards both front and back, and with horns blowing traveled once around the city walls. Then they walked back to camp. No one spoke or made any sound other than the blare of the horns.

Q?

"Talk is cheap. Actions are expensive." How well do your talking and acting match?

The tension inside Jericho must have been astronomical. The fear, worry, stress, and uncertainty must have been almost unbearable psychological warfare. Couple it with the confusion of what exactly the Israelites were doing and … well, I'm glad I wasn't there.

On the seventh day, the Israelite priests led their procession around the walls exactly as they had done the previous six days, only on this last day they walked around seven times. Rahab and her family would have waited tensely in her home, perhaps watching out the window where the scarlet cord still hung. Were they filled with calm? Anxiety? Fear? Doubt? Probably alternating waves of all four.

Standing in the hills were the throngs of Israelites: old men, women, children, and servants, watching the procession around the walls. On the seventh pass, Joshua commanded the people, "Shout! For the Lord has given you the city! The city and everything in it must be completely destroyed as an offering to the Lord. Only Rahab the prostitute and the others in her house will be spared, for she protected our spies. Do not take any of the things set apart for destruction, or you yourselves will be completely destroyed, and you will bring trouble on all Israel. Everything made from silver, gold, bronze, or iron is sacred to the Lord and must be brought into His treasure." (Joshua 6:16-19)

The priests' horns would have been drowned out by the shouts of

> **"May the curse of the Lord fall on anyone who tries to rebuild the city of Jericho."**
> Joshua 6:26a

the Israelites; louder and louder and louder the voices would have become. And then, for those within the city walls, a louder sound would have begun, even more terrifying than the enemy's shouts. It would have been the rumbling and crumbling of the city walls as they began to shake and shudder, crack and collapse. The Israelites spared no one. Every living being was destroyed: men, women, young, old, cattle, sheep, donkeys ... *everything*. (Joshua 6:21)

Except Rahab and her family. "Keep your promise," Joshua said to the two spies, "Go to the prostitute's house and bring her out, along with all her family." (Joshua 6:22) Standing in her home, listening to the horns and then the shouts, feeling the walls crumble all around her home, what did Rahab think? I picture her standing by her window, gripping the scarlet rope - while the family members around her screamed and cried in terror - watching, listening, observing, and *believing* that everything would be okay. When the knock came at her door, she would have rushed to the door and thrown back the bolt to let Salmon and his partner in. She believed in The One True God. She knew He would keep her safe. Didn't everyone else around her see His power and His might? How could anyone *not?*

"So Joshua spared Rahab the prostitute and her relatives who were with her in the house, because she had hidden the spies Joshua sent to Jericho. And she lives among the Israelites to this day." (Joshua 6:25)

The End.

Sigh. I want *details!!* Whoever wrote this part of the journal just doesn't understand romance. Not a bit. Because there *was* a little romance ...

Transformed … How can God change the terrible past?

In those initial days within the Israelite camp, Rahab would have endured significant notoriety. "Did you see the Amorite prostitute yet?" "She and her family are the only survivors! They're camped on the outskirts." "Hey, Mom? Can me and the guys go to the outskirts of camp to try to see the whore?" "She helped Salmon and his partner hide and escape. I heard all about it." "I guess some people will do anything – even betray their own people – just to save their own skins." "Mommy, what's a prostitute?" "I hear she wasn't a temple prostitute. Do you know if she ran her own whorehouse? Can you imagine?" "She acts … haughty." "… cold." " … distant." " … aloof." She would have been whispered about, stared at and avoided. But hey, what else was new? To Rahab it probably almost felt like home.

I'm not one to believe in coincidence. Even if no earthly explanation is available, I believe God was simply causing things to work out just so. Whether God arranged for Rahab to end up living within the tribe of Judah, or Joshua directed that she and her family be incorporated into the nation's largest tribe, or Salmon (as a member of the tribe of Judah) offered to assume responsibility for Rahab and her family's care, we don't know. As the days, weeks, and months rolled on (and the Israelites continued to battle their way through the land of Canaan) Rahab would have been faced with endless challenges.

Did Rahab make a conscious decision to rise above her past, grab hold of the golden opportunity to start anew, and jump right in with both feet? Did she fully immerse herself in the religion, people, and culture so that even the Israelites began to become accustomed to her presence and endless questions? "Rahab was here. She asked me to help her learn to cook properly, according to all our customs." "Rahab helped me all week with the harvesting of the flax. Do you know that she's an

> **And I will give you a new heart with new and right desires, and I will put a new spirit in you.**
> Ezekiel 36:26a

excellent weaver and seamstress? She even knows some wonderful methods for fabric dyeing. She promised to teach me." "Rahab joined us for our Sabbath meal. What a delightful woman she is. We had so much fun talking and laughing!" "Did you know that Rahab spoke with the high priest about what she must do to live among us permanently and become equal before the Lord?" "I believe that Rahab is truly here because she believes in The One True God."

Moses, knowing that God's chosen people were going to live among heathens, and interact with heathens, and probably live, work, and fall in love with heathens, covered rules and regulations for "heathens" thoroughly. Rahab would have made sure to understand the policies regarding herself, and would have been pleased to learn that as long as she followed all the decrees, she was equal in the Lord's sight. "And if any foreigners visit you or live among you and want to present a special gift as a pleasing aroma to the LORD, they must follow these same procedures. Native-born Israelites and foreigners are equal before the LORD and are subject to the same decrees. This is a permanent law for you, to be observed from generation to generation. The same instructions and regulations will apply both to you and to the foreigners living among you." (Numbers 15:14-16)

How *powerful* that promise would have been for Rahab. Not "okay," or "tolerated" but *equal.* Something that had never been possible before would have been attainable in embracing the Israelite customs and The One True God.

I bet Rahab drove everyone crazy asking questions, learning prayers, and listening to any story that would be told. Her enthusiasm would have been contagious. Her sincerity would have been obvious. The old men would have loved her, "Hey Rahab! Come! Sit! I've got another story to tell you!" The old women would have delighted in having someone who wanted to learn all the traditions, recipes, and skills they could impart. "Rahab! Come! We were just getting ready to make soap! We will teach you, and you must show us what you know!"

Did the young women of the tribe envy her freedom and self-confidence? Were Rahab's "escapades" whispered about with awe and titillating fascination? Were they intimidated by her or were they intrigued by her? Did she finally find some friends?

And what about the young men? Surely that would have been the most difficult area. I would suspect that her own wisdom would have kept her away from any situations that would have been or could have been deemed "inappropriate."

The only initially familiar faces would have been those of Salmon and his partner. Did Salmon feel responsible for Rahab? Did he check in on her now and then to see how she was "coming along"? Maybe her name kept coming up in conversations. "Hey, Rahab the whore was here today asking questions." "Salmon! I didn't realize that Rahab was such a good weaver. Why didn't you tell me she kept flax in Jericho?" "Well, Salmon, I'll tell you, *no one* has ever had such drive or enthusiasm to learn. That Rahab is amazing!"

Somehow Salmon began to think of Rahab as more than just an Amorite whore. And somehow Rahab began to think of Salmon as more than just a young Israelite man she had to avoid at all costs. In order to figure out that there even *was* a romance, we are forced to do a little detective work. Rahab is lauded for her faith in both Hebrews (11:31) and James (2:25) but it's her mention in the book of Matthew (1:5) as "the mother of Boaz" that clues us in to the fact that she hooked up with *someone*. Salmon shows up

> **It was by faith that Rahab the prostitute was not destroyed with the people in her city who refused to obey God.**
> Hebrews 11:31b

in the book of Ruth (4:21), I Chronicles (2:11), Matthew (1:5) and Luke (3:32) all in regard to lineage. Guess who was the father of Boaz? You guessed it: Salmon.

What kind of magnificent man was Salmon? How incredible was it that he could look *forward* towards the future that was opening up for Rahab, as opposed to being drawn back to the past reputation that she could never completely escape? He was a man who was trusted by his people. A man who could look beyond what the world saw and see the inside changed heart of Rahab. A man whom God deemed worthy enough to be included in the greatest promise of all. Because not only did Rahab and Salmon find and commit to each other, not only did they have a healthy son, but there was one more wonderful part to this story.

To make a happy ending even better you need to understand that this is the Boaz who is the hero in the book of Ruth. Ruth and Boaz are the couple who give birth to Obed who becomes the grandfather of King David and the great-grandfather of King Solomon. Need more? Well, the Matthew and Luke lineage, in which Rahab and Salmon are listed, is of course the lineage of *Christ*. How cool is that?!

Rahab the whore became Rahab the ancestress of Jesus Christ. Amorite heathen to Israelite matriarch. All she did was believe in The One True God. It was a complete transformation – God style.

For all you Rahabs out there ...

Maybe you don't have prostitution in your background ... But most of us have certain things in our past (public like Rahab's or just our own private disasters) that we'd love to break away from. And while God willingly forgives when we ask and forgets completely, we tend to drag around our rotten past with us like our own personal ball and chain. The distinction between those of us who break away and those of us who don't boils down to our level of belief. Do you believe that God can transform you? Do you honestly believe that there is something in your past bigger and badder than anything that God can deal with? Do you honestly believe that you are the only individual *in the entire existence of mankind* who is exempt from God's promise of a new life? *Don't lie to one another. You're done with that old life. It's like a filthy set of ill-fitting clothes you've stripped off and put in the fire. Now you're dressed in a new wardrobe. Every item of your new way of life is custom-made by the Creator, with His label on it. All the old fashions are now obsolete. Words like Jewish and non-Jewish, religious and irreligious, insider and outsider, uncivilized and uncouth, slave and free, mean nothing. From now on everyone is defined by Christ, everyone is included in Christ.* (Colossians 3:9-11, MSG)

> You are precious to me. You are honored, and I love you.
> Isaiah 43:4b

Grab hold of the opportunity. Embrace the change. Renew your heart.

❖ **Stick and Stones:** We've all heard that saying about sticks and stones breaking bones and names never hurting. *It's a lie.* Sometimes names hurt more than any broken bone we could ever endure. Broken bones *heal* but some names damage us so badly we carry scars for life. Rahab knew all about the hurt of name calling and the power that a label could give. "Worthless whore." "Wrong." "Valueless member of society." "Useless." "I'm done with you." "Rubbish." "Ugly." "Stupid." "Helpless." She knew the power of opinions and the tragedy of life could bring. "I don't believe you." "It's all your fault." "How could you be so stupid and careless?" "I knew you'd mess things up." "Why did I even bother with you?" "You're hopeless." "You'll never amount to anything." "You're not our problem any longer." "Good riddance to bad rubbish." Rahab made a conscious choice to rise above it all. Please note that I didn't say she didn't let it hurt her. She simply refused to let it define how she saw herself. *She never believed what everyone said about her and to her.* And while for a very long time she was a victim of circumstances beyond her control, when the opportunity arose to escape, she never hesitated because *she knew she was worth it,* even though no one else did.

❖ **Present Circumstances:** Rahab's story drives home the point that we are never too low, never in such dire straits that we can't strive to be informed and knowledgeable. When we get to heaven, no excuse is going to dismiss our failure to listen, learn, and believe. Sorry. On this, the Bible is quite clear. Oh, and for those of you who believe but, well,

> **"Believe in the Lord Jesus and you will be saved, along with everyone in your household."**
> Acts 16:31

haven't done much with the information? Sorry, you seem to be in almost as much trouble, if not worse... *So, because you are lukewarm - neither hot nor cold - I am about to spit you out of my mouth.* (Revelation 3:16) This is life and death stuff. You either are or your aren't. You're either with the program or against the effort.

❖ **Earthly Leaders:** The nation of Israel chose an earthly leader who was rooted in the right stuff to obey and follow. While not one biblical leader (besides Christ, of course) was perfect, some did a mighty fine job. Over the course of Israel's history they had good, bad, and downright ugly leaders, and their "spiritual temperature" will reflect their spiritual leadership – or lack of it. What about you? Where do you put your trust? You need a church that is soundly rooted in the Bible, you need a minister who is firmly anchored to Christ and His mission here on earth, and you need to surround yourself with people who are connected with The Truth. Just like Israel, your "spiritual temperature" will reflect your spiritual leadership – or lack of it.

❖ **Be informed:** Do you know what you believe? Can you answer questions about the core tenants of your faith if asked? If you can't, you need to ask questions. If you're confused, you need to keep seeking. If things don't make sense, you must work for clarity. Please don't get me wrong. You don't need to be a biblical Einstein to get into heaven. In fact, Christ told his disciples, *"I'm telling you, once and for all, that unless you return to square one and start over like children, you're not even going to get a look at the kingdom, let alone get in. Whoever becomes simple and elemental again, like this child, will rank high in God's kingdom."* (Matthew 18:3-4 MSG) Have you ever met a child who didn't ask questions or hunger to discover and explore? You need only the basic, core understanding *to get started.* But no one who stays a child all of his or her life is healthy! You need to be a strong, stable, viable Christian with whom others can learn and grow. *It's your job.*

❖ **Our Salvation Should Be Like A Scarlet Rope:** Is your belief as visible to others as Rahab's scarlet rope was hanging out her window? The Truth that we know about and believe in is not meant to be hidden. *You are the light of the world. A city on a hill cannot be hidden. Neither do people light a lamp and put it under a bowl. Instead they put it on its stand, and it gives light to everyone in the house.* (Matthew 5:14) Whoa. How bright are you? Do you fade into the woodwork of the world, or do you stand out like a bright scarlet flag? Our

> Our salvation is a matter of life and death. No thing and no one should stand in the way of it.
> McG

purpose in life is to believe, and then to share what we know with the rest of the world.

❖ **Family:** Rahab's first thought was of her family as she negotiated with Salmon and his partner. "Now swear to me by the Lord that ... you will let me live, along with my father and mother, my brothers and sisters ..." (Joshua 2:12) Good for her. She right away wanted to share what she had discovered, and now believed with all her heart with those she loved and cared about. But what would have happened if her family never came to her and accepted the offer of deliverance? Would Rahab have been better off to stay in Jericho with them and perish? Sometimes family and friends will give you well meaning advice or fail to acknowledge wise information you may wish to share. They'll argue, laugh, and even ridicule your desires to change and improve yourself. In the end, each of us answers for ourselves. Pray. Seek the Lord's guidance. Share what you've taken to heart and believe. *And then stick to the right path God has shown you.*

Homework ... What do you believe?

I take the Bible to heart. I'm not one of those people who believes that you can pick and choose bits and pieces that you like and choose to embrace - it's all or nothing. Over the course of my life God has blessed me with the time and resources to study, learn, and grow in His Word. In addition to being more confident in my faith, I am a better person for it, and a stronger witness because of it. I read the Bible, ask questions from those whom I trust, and enjoy the opportunities when, I have those "A-Ha!" moments of discovery.

> "Anyone who isn't with me opposes me, and anyone who isn't working with me is actually working against me."
> Matthew 12:30

How about you? Where do you stand on the foundations of your faith? *Do you even know them?* On the next few pages are a list of some core aspects of the Christian faith. I tried to pick these that are "across the board" within the majority of the Christian denominations today. (I've not gotten into the areas that have caused the unique distinctions within each.) While I could snow you under with hundreds of Bible verses about each area, I've tried to pick just a few core ones. Read through each verse. Think about your beliefs. Do you embrace what the verses say completely? Or are you "just not sure"? Maybe, you completely disagree. Not only will your *honest* answers (we're not going to publish your responses!) help you outline the strengths and weaknesses of your own personal faith, they will give you a starting point for asking questions, reading and research.

And remember this: doing nothing about your confusion and doubts is doing *something*. It is a conscious decision to live in bewilderment. It is a conscious choice to abandon the truth.

WHAT I BELIEVE ABOUT THE BIBLE

The Bible	❖ **Hebrews 4:12** For the word of God is alive and powerful. It is sharper than the sharpest two-edged sword, cutting between soul and spirit, between joint and marrow. It exposes our innermost thoughts and desires. ❖ **Proverbs 30:5** Every word of God proves true. He is a shield to all who come to him for protection. Do not add to his words, or he may rebuke you and expose you as a liar.	
I Believe this 100 %	**I'm not so sure how I feel about this verse**	**I completely disagree**
Questions, Thoughts, and Issues I have:		

WHAT I BELIEVE ABOUT GOD

God	❖ **Hebrews 4:13** Nothing in all creation is hidden from God. Everything is naked and exposed before His eyes, and He is the one to whom we are accountable. ❖ **I John 4:8** But anyone who does not love does not know God, for God is love.	
I Believe this 100 %	**I'm not so sure how I feel about this verse**	**I completely disagree**
Questions, Thoughts, and Issues I have:		

WHAT I BELIEVE ABOUT JESUS CHRIST

Jesus Christ	❖ **John 14: 6** Jesus told him, "I am the way, the truth, and the life. No one can come to the Father except through me." ❖ **John 1:1-5** In the beginning the Word already existed. The Word was with God, and the Word was God. He existed in the beginning with God. God created everything through Him, and nothing was created except through Him. The Word gave life to everything that was created, and His life brought light to everyone. The light shines in the darkness, and the darkness can never extinguish it. (McG note: Christ = the Word)	
I Believe this 100 %	**I'm not so sure how I feel about this verse**	**I completely disagree**
Questions, Thoughts, and Issues I have:		

WHAT I BELIEVE ABOUT THE HOLY SPIRIT

Holy Spirit	❖ **Galatians 5: 22-23** But the fruit of the Spirit is love, joy, peace, patience, kindness, goodness, faithfulness, gentleness, self-control; against such things there is no law. ❖ **Romans 8:26-27** In the same way the Spirit also helps our weakness; for we do not know how to pray as we should, but the Spirit Himself intercedes for us with groanings too deep for words; and He who searches the hearts knows what the mind of the Spirit is, because He intercedes for the saints according to the will of God.	
I Believe this 100 %	**I'm not so sure how I feel about this verse**	**I completely disagree**
Questions, Thoughts, and Issues I have:		

WHAT I BELIEVE ABOUT SIN

Sin	❖ **Galatians 5:19-21** Now the deeds of the flesh are evident, which are: immorality, impurity, sensuality, idolatry, sorcery, enmities, strife, jealousy, outbursts of anger, disputes, dissensions, factions, envying, drunkenness, carousing, and things like these, of which I forewarn you, just as I have forewarned you, that those who practice such things will not inherit the kingdom of God. ❖ **Romans 2:5-8** But because you are stubborn and refuse to turn from your sin, you are storing up terrible punishment for yourself. For a day of anger is coming, when God's righteous judgment will be revealed. He will judge everyone according to what they have done. He will give eternal life to those who keep on doing good, seeking after the glory and honor and immortality that God offers. But He will pour out His anger and wrath on those who live for themselves, who refuse to obey the truth and instead live lives of wickedness.
I Believe this 100 %	I'm not so sure how I feel about this verse	I completely disagree
Questions, Thoughts, and Issues I have:		

WHAT I BELIEVE ABOUT SALVATION

Salvation	❖ **Romans 3:22-24** We are made right with God by placing our faith in Jesus Christ. And this is true for everyone who believes, no matter who we are. For everyone has sinned; we all fall short of God's glorious standard. Yet God, with undeserved kindness, declares that we are righteous. He did this through Christ Jesus when He freed us from the penalty for our sins. ❖ **Romans 5:8-9** But God showed his great love for us by sending Christ to die for us while we were still sinners. And since we have been made right in God's sight by the blood of Christ, He will certainly save us from God's condemnation.	
I Believe this 100 %	I'm not so sure how I feel about this verse	I completely disagree
Questions, Thoughts, and Issues I have:		

WHAT I BELIEVE ABOUT HEAVEN

Heaven	❖ **Matthew 5:3-12** God blesses those who are poor and realize their need for Him, for the Kingdom of Heaven is theirs. God blesses those who mourn, for they will be comforted. God blesses those who are humble, for they will inherit the whole earth. God blesses those who hunger and thirst for justice, for they will be satisfied. God blesses those who are merciful, for they will be shown mercy. God blesses those whose hearts are pure, for they will see God. God blesses those who work for peace, for they will be called the children of God. God blesses those who are persecuted for doing right, for the Kingdom of Heaven is theirs. God blesses you when people mock you and persecute you and lie about you and say all sorts of evil things against you because you are My followers. Be happy about it! Be very glad! For a great reward awaits you in heaven.		
I Believe this 100 %	**I'm not so sure how I feel about this verse**		**I completely disagree**
Questions, Thoughts, and Issues I have:			

WHAT I BELIEVE ABOUT HUMAN NATURE

Human Nature	❖ **Romans 3: 9b-10** All people, whether Jews or Gentiles, are under the power of sin. As the Scriptures say, "No one is righteous - not even one. ❖ **2 Peter 2:17-19** These men are springs without water and mists driven by a storm. Blackest darkness is reserved for them. For they mouth empty, boastful words and, by appealing to the lustful desires of sinful human nature, they entice people who are just escaping from those who live in error. They promise them freedom, while they themselves are slaves of depravity— for a man is a slave to whatever has mastered him.	
I Believe this 100 %	I'm not so sure how I feel about this verse	I completely disagree
Questions, Thoughts, and Issues I have:		

WHAT I BELIEVE ABOUT CHRIST'S DEATH

AND RESURRECTION

Christ's Death and Resurrection	❖ **I Corinthians 15:3b-4** Christ died for our sins, just as the Scriptures said. He was buried, and He was raised from the dead on the third day, just as the Scriptures said. ❖ **I Corinthians 15:21-22** So you see, just as death came into the world through a man, now the resurrection from the dead has begun through another Man. Just as everyone dies because we all belong to Adam, everyone who belongs to Christ will be given new life.	
I Believe this 100 %	**I'm not so sure how I feel about this verse**	**I completely disagree**
Questions, Thoughts, and Issues I have:		

WHAT I BELIEVE ABOUT PRAYER

Prayer	❖ **Philippians 4:6-7** Don't worry about anything; instead, pray about everything. Tell God what you need, and thank him for all he has done. Then you will experience God's peace, which exceeds anything we can understand. His peace will guard your hearts and minds as you live in Christ Jesus. ❖ **Matthew 21:22** You can pray for anything, and if you have faith, you will receive it.	
I Believe this 100 %	**I'm not so sure how I feel about this verse**	**I completely disagree**
Questions, Thoughts, and Issues I have:		

Now, regardless of how you responded to the previous collection of Bible verses, you must continue to seek, question, learn and grow. Believe it all? Hooray. Chose an in-depth Bible study about one topic that particularly interests you *and do it.*

Puzzled over a few of the verses? Choose one and speak with your pastor, go to the local Bible book store (or try www.cbd.com for a great online Christian book store) or look up verses in the concordance of your Bible (or do a key word search on www.biblegateway.com) and *get reading.*

Absolutely disagree with some of these verses? Again, choose one and speak with your pastor. Ask him or her to recommend some good reading or websites you can visit to do some research on your own. Continue to read your Bible or use www.biblegateway.com to read about your topic of confusion. Are you absolutely certain that your perception or opinion is correct? Try to prove your way of thinking using scriptural references. You may be surprised.

And pray. Always pray for guidance and enlightenment.

Question To Discuss:

Q?

Fill in the blanks:
It was by faith that
_____ **(your name)**
was able to:

_____

_____

_____.

I'll pass on the opportunity to play queen for the day in her palace.

Bathsheba and The Guy Who Didn't Give Her Much Choice

A Heart Of Trust

She married the powerful, handsome, charismatic man named David who was chosen by The One True God to become king over His precious nation of people. Her son, Solomon, went on to bring the nation of Israel to a level of greatness that has *never* been duplicated to this very day. Bathsheba was jaw-droppingly beautiful, astronomically wealthy, and would eventually become the most powerful woman in the kingdom of Israel. Seemed like she had it all, didn't it?

Bathsheba was also a classic example of the saying, "You can't truly understand a person unless you walk a mile in her shoes." Yes, all of this information about Bathsheba was true, and yet when you delve into her life's story, the biblical journal leaves you with a less than a "happily ever after" feeling.

In addition to being beautiful, rich, and powerful, Bathsheba was a victim of circumstances beyond her control and of manipulation by those in authority over her. Eerily silent through most of the biblical account she was a part, she seemed to be little more than a powerless pawn. Up until her life spun out of control, she appeared to be nothing more than an innocent young wife waiting for her husband to come home from war ...

Or not.

You see some people think that she asked for everything she got. Some people believe that Bathsheba was a scheming temptress who lured poor king David down from his lofty spiritual pedestal into adultery and murder. "She should have said no." "She should have resisted." "She asked for it with her exhibitionist behavior." "She was manipulative, trying to gain a better station in life." "The guy couldn't help himself with the way she was behaving." Some people believe Bathsheba played with fire and simply got burned, consequence she rightly deserved.

Bathsheba is one of those Bible stories where two people reading the same passage can arrive at two completely different interpretations. Obviously, based on the way I titled this chapter, I've got my own rather strong opinion about the way things went down.

Was she forced to marry her attacker or was she lucky to snag the king? Was she a poor, innocent widow or a calculating adulteress? Were the consequences of her and David's initial sinful liaison exactly what she deserved, or was she nothing more than the sacrificial lamb?

A majority of her life was lived within the intrigue of the royal palace. How did she manage? How did she survive? You see, that's the whole crux of her story. Because Bathsheba *didn't* manage or survive *on her own*. She learned to trust Someone else to get her through it all ... someone who is available to each and every one of us even today.

First Things First

Scripture references you should check out:	2 Samuel 11:1-12:25, I Kings 1:11-31; 2:13-19; I Chronicles 3:5
Question to ask yourself before you read any further:	Who do you trust implicitly?

What her name means:	"The Seventh Daughter" or "The Daughter of an Oath"
Connections:	Few human beings are worthy of our trust. It is a powerful connection to hold or give trust with another. More often than not, trusting in others leads to disappointment, heartbreak, and even rage. There is only one place to put our wholehearted trust and that is with The One True God. He and He alone is the only one deserving such an honor. In addition, only He is faithful and true; incapable of breaking our confidence.
What the Bible says about trust:	**What Not To Trust In:** Leviticus 19:4, Job 31:24, Isaiah 2:22, I Corinthians 2:5 **What To Trust In:** Psalm 13:5, Psalm 33:4, Psalm 119:138 **Where It Begins:** Psalm 22:9 **Benefits of:** Psalm 25:3, Psalm 26:1, Psalm 34:10, Psalm 112:7, Isaiah 26:3, Isaiah 40:31 **When To Trust:** Psalm 56:3 **How To Trust:** Proverbs 3:5 **How We Show Our Trust:** Isaiah 26:8, **The Promise:** Hebrews 3:14, I Peter 1:9

Questions We'll Never Know The Answers To:

❖ What were the true circumstances of the initial meeting between David and Bathsheba?

❖ What were Bathsheba's thoughts in those early years of her involvement with David?

❖ Did Bathsheba ever come to love David?

Did you know? Interesting Biblical Facts About Bathsheba

❖ **King David:** At this point in his life, David was at the pinnacle of his success. The great prophet Samuel had chosen him above all of his other seven older brothers when he was a mere child to be Israel's next king. (I Samuel 16) As a child he'd slain the giant Goliath (I Samuel 17) and become best friends with King Saul's son, Jonathan. (I Samuel 18:1) As a young adult he became a fearless and victorious warrior, well loved by the Israelite people. The resulting chant of the adoring crowds: "Saul has killed his thousands, and David his ten thousands" (I Samuel 21:11b) caused King Saul to hate David enough to attempt to kill him a number of times. (I Samuel 18:28-29) David dealt with the deaths of both his mentor Samuel (I Samuel 25) and his best friend Jonathan. (I Samuel 31) At the death of King Saul he became king over Judah (the largest tribe) (2 Samuel 2) and finally Israel (the rest of the tribes). (2 Samuel 5) In addition he captured the virtually impregnable city of Jerusalem and made it his capital city – where it will be called The City Of David from then on. (2 Samuel 5) He also married a number of times: King Saul's daughter Michal (I Samuel 18:17-27), Ahinoam of Jezreel, Abigail from Carmel, Maacha daughter of the king of Geshur, Haggith, Abital, and Eglah (I Chronicles 3:1-4) and had many concubines. (Concubines were slaves or mistresses a man was lawfully permitted to have sex with, and by this time in Israel's history something usually only kings were allowed to do.) By the time we take up with King David's journal story, he has numerous sons, at least one daughter worth mentioning, and has had almost too many victories to count. He seems, well, a bit bored with life ...

❖ **Jerusalem:** Jerusalem was an ancient city with a history going back centuries before Abraham. Joshua was never able to conquer this impregnable city (called Jebus because it was held by the Jebusites), although all the land surrounding it was captured and given to the tribe of Judah. With steep ravines on the east, south, and west sides of the city, it was only the northern border that was ever attacked, and which was, consequently, extremely protected. David ingeniously conquered the city by crawling through the sewers with his trusted army (2 Samuel 5:6-10) and established it as the capital city of the nation of Israel. Practically invincible and situated almost directly in the center of the kingdom, bringing the Ark of the Covenant of God to Jerusalem was David's crowning achievement as king. (2 Samuel 6:1-14)

❖ **Uriah the Hittite:** His name means "flame of Jehovah" and although his title indicates he was obviously an "alien" in the Israelite community as Rahab had done, Uriah seemed to have chosen to believe and worship The One True God. He was one of David's mighty soldiers with a strong sense of duty and a commendable loyalty toward his men and his responsibilities.   Hittites had been close associates and trusted companions of David from early on in his military career.

❖ **Ritual Bathing:** There wasn't any indoor plumbing, so bathing was not an every day thing. However, there were stringent requirements dictating *when* and *why* a man or a woman was required to bathe. In reality bathing was rarely done for personal cleanliness but more often for ritual purposes. Leviticus 15 describes the rituals required for a woman who was having or who had finished with her period. There was a time when she was considered "unclean" (seven full days after the bleeding stopped), a requisite sacrifice she was required to make at the end of this time as a sin offering (two turtledoves), and specific requirements to wash her clothes and bathe with water. When our story starts, Bathsheba is bathing in the privacy of her courtyard. (2 Samuel 11:2) Was it a ritual bath from some ceremonial pollution as per Jewish law? Perhaps. However, the definitive answer is impossible to determine.

❖ **The Nation of Israel:** Israel had come a loooong way from just a family with one husband, four wives, twelve wild boys and one daughter. A seasoned warrior nation, they were now a force to be reckoned with. Glorious victories when they were on the right path with God and unbelievable losses when they weren't (the Philistines even captured the Ark of the Covenant of God at one point), their successes or failures were direct reflections of their relationship with The One True God. Having cried out for a king to lead them, the prophet Samuel had, at God's direction, anointed the handsome and charismatic King Saul. King Saul was an object lesson in "looking good on the outside but not on the inside." He died a horrible death, nailed to the wall of an enemy city beside his son and heir Jonathan (David's best friend). (I Samuel 31) By the time David assumed the kingship of the nation, the Israelites were very much like any successful, powerful nation: overconfident in their abilities and careless with their spiritual condition. (Sounds a bit like the USA to me …)

The Core Story

Once Upon a Time ... Why is David home at the palace?

Our story begins with, "The following spring, the time of year when kings go to war, David sent Joab and the Israelite army to destroy the Ammonites ... but David stayed behind in Jerusalem." (2 Samuel 11:1) Already we're forced to read between the lines. Why is David home and not with his army during the time of year *when kings go to war?* I picture David slumped down on the throne, crown askew, bored look on his face, waving his arm in dismissal to his general and saying with a sigh, "You go, Joab. Fighting's no fun anymore. I'm bored with it all. I'll stay here at the palace and hang out. Let me know when the victory is at hand." Joab was a brutal fighting machine. He'd get the job done and David knew it. Why bother tagging along?

"Late one afternoon, David got out of bed after taking a nap and went for a stroll on the roof of the palace ..." (2 Samuel 11:2) Does this man sound bored? Maybe even depressed? Laying around until all hours of the afternoon and then wandering around on the roof with nothing to do but stare glumly over his city and think of better times, David sounds aimless.

(Now, take a moment and think. What do little boys do when they are bored with nothing to do? How about teenage boys who are aimless and unsupervised? Isn't that just trouble waiting to happen?)

Now how about bored, all-powerful kings who've done just about everything there is to do and been astronomically successful? Killed giants? Yup, did that. Conquered impregnable cities in a scene out of a Mission Impossible movie? Yup, did that, too. Achieved nationwide popularity and acclaim? Check. Became so feared and respected by his enemies that fighting them is no longer an adrenaline-rush challenge but just a necessary duty? Yeah that, too.

Padding around early evening with nothing interesting to do, King David wandered up to the roof of his palace and looked out over his city. "He noticed a woman of unusual beauty taking a bath." (2 Samuel 11:2b) Uh, oh. Can you hear the warning sirens going off? David stood there and did something he'd probably never done before ... (Who would have

198

thought that was possible after all he had accomplished, huh?) David became a voyeur. Watching a woman, who just happened to be exquisitely beautiful, take a private bath on the courtyard roof of her home was probably one of the most exciting things David had done in a long time. And when her bath was over, King David wanted more ...

Who could she be? David immediately sent someone to find out who this bathing beauty was. Did he take the messenger up to the roof and point the house out? Did he describe how she looked? Did David impress upon this messenger to hurry with the information he sought? Was it the first time in a while that the king had shown interest and enthusiasm in anything?

David was told, "She is Bathsheba, the daughter of Eliam (Ammiah) and the wife of Uriah the Hittite." (2 Samuel 11:4) For us it may appear to be just a brief bit of information, but for David it spoke volumes. Being the daughter of Eliam established Bathsheba as an Israelite woman. Not heathen, not slave, but one of God's chosen race: special, separate, and protected. In addition, she was the daughter of one of David's trusted men, with a family history that was dedicated and loyal to not only The One True God but King David himself. *And let's not ignore that* she was a *wife*, and not just any man's wife, but the wife of Uriah the Hittite. Another one of David's most trusted soldiers whom David would have also known.

Wow. Talk about big black arrows that said, "NO. STAY AWAY DAVID. THIS WOMAN IS NOT AVAILABLE."

Now King David was God's chosen man. The one whom God had selected, guided, protected, and championed so that his life until this point had been an impressive collection of miraculous successes. David and The One True God had a relationship rooted in trust, belief, and prayerful communication. David would have listened to this obvious "No-no" message, right? Well, you see, David didn't actually *talk* to God about Bathsheba. Maybe at this point in his life, David had become distant and wasn't talking to God much at all. Had David become overconfident and complacent in his faith? Perhaps David's boredom and aimlessness were all part of a bigger, more insidious picture. After all this time and experience, had David drifted from God?

Based on what King David did next, we can only assume one answer. "Then David sent messengers to get her…" (NIV/NLT/MSG) or, "David sent messengers and took her…" (ASV/KJV) (2 Samuel 11:4a) This doesn't sound like a polite invitation to come and have a tour of the palace. Actually, there seems to be no request at all. Sounds quite a bit forceful to me. What do you think?

Temptation … Is it ever a good thing?

I don't know about you, but I'd find it pretty difficult to have a casual conversation with someone I'd just watched in an intimate bath. Somehow, David managed.

What was going through Bathsheba's mind in those initial moments of her arrival? As her husband was away *fighting for the king*, was the town all abuzz that the king was still home at the palace? How

> **You can't claim to be good if you've never been tempted to be bad.**
> **You can't claim to be faithful, if you've never had the opportunity to be unfaithful.**
> Rick Warren

surprising would it have been to have a messenger appear at her home, informing her that they were there to take her to the king? Were her first thoughts of her husband? Was she worried that Uriah had been wounded? Killed? Was she nervous, frightened, or excited? Did she have time to comb her hair and put on a clean dress? Was there a moment of panic as she worried about the proper etiquette required in meeting, greeting, and speaking with a king? Did it ever cross her mind to try to decline the summons? "Please tell the king, 'No,' as I'm busy cleaning my home." Or, "Please tell the king it would be improper for me to meet with him without my husband. Can I have a rain check?"

Actually, could you ever really tell a king no?

Handsome, powerful, rich, confident, and charming, David would have turned on the magnetism. What a delightful reprieve to the neverending boredom of his life. Would Bathsheba have been relieved that the visit was so relaxed, and grateful that the king had been so gracious and friendly? Was she offered wine and food by David as any good host would? Was this beautiful young woman captivated by King David? Did she wish that Uriah was … as handsome … as attentive … as talkative? Did she wonder what it would be like *if only* … ? Did she encourage this dangerous attention from the king?

I can just imagine David's thoughts as the visit progressed, trying to justify where his lust was encouraging him to go. He was the king of Israel, was he not? Didn't he deserve some happiness? Hadn't he given his whole life to securing power and might to the nation? This gorgeous woman was here smiling, laughing, and conversing with him. Surely she had to realize the affect she was having on him? Perhaps she had been aware of him the afternoon of the bath? Had the show been just for him all along? Was Bathsheba as lonely as he was? Perhaps Uriah was a poor husband. Maybe she was an unhappy wife. Could she be as captivated with him as he was with her?

Q?

What are some ways that people without faith deal with difficult times? How do these contrast with the ways of faith?

"And when she came to the palace, he slept with her." (2 Samuel 11:4) Sigh. Oh, boy … maybe they didn't even have time for wine, cheese and conversation after all.

Okay, the Bible doesn't use the word "rape," it says he "slept with" Bathsheba. And there are times when the Bible does use the term. Jacob's daughter Dinah is raped in Genesis 34:2 and King David's son Amnon raped his half-sister Tamar (don't confuse her with Judah's Tamar that we've already talked about) in 2 Samuel 13. It is because of this discrepancy that different interpretations of the story happen. Could David possibly be the innocent victim and she the scheming temptress? Did David fall right into Bathsheba's cunning trap? I have to say that I find such a scenario very hard to believe.

As rape has a more violent connotation, perhaps "coerced" would be more accurate. Maybe David tried to kid himself when he initially sent for Bathsheba. "I just want to make sure she has everything she needs since her husband is away and she is all alone. I sent my men to bring her over because I certainly couldn't go there myself – it wouldn't have been proper." Maybe Bathsheba was complimented and awed at all the kingly attention. "He is so nice! He's been so kind and polite, inquiring about how I am doing with Uriah away at war." When David made his initial moves towards romance was Bathsheba so flattered that she didn't know what to say? "I was completely stunned when the king took my hand and told me I was the most beautiful woman he'd ever seen. I just didn't know what to say or think ..." Did it ever cross David's mind that Bathsheba would have been unwilling? "The smile Bathsheba gave me when I complimented her beauty told me that no one had ever appreciated her as much as I was about to."

I can just imagine the thoughts afterwards. Once the dust settled. Or the hormones calmed down.

David: "She had every opportunity to say no, but she never said a thing."

Bathsheba: "He began to kiss me and I was so shocked that I was speechless."

David: "When I took her hand and led her to the bed she never hesitated."

Bathsheba: "When he took me to bed I knew then that I should have said something sooner ... But what could I have done? Was this my fault?"

David: "I never forced her. I was tender and loving the whole time."

Bathsheba: "We never spoke once he began to kiss me. What could I do?! I was afraid to anger the king!"

David: "Hey, she came when I summoned her, didn't she?"

Bathsheba: "I never should have gone to the palace, but what could I have done once the king sent his men to take me to him?"

David: "I'm the king. I've never had to force a woman in my life. Ask all my wives and concubines."

Bathsheba: "I'm only a woman. What could I say or do once the king made it clear what he wished to do with me?"

After it all went down and she'd gone home (which Bathsheba did, immediately) did King David stare at himself in the mirror and think, "Whoa, I never thought *that* was going to happen!" Did Bathsheba go home and think, "What will I tell Uriah?" In just one verse, II Samuel 11:4 Bathsheba is summoned, slept with, and sent home. What's that David Bowie song say? *Wham, bam, thank-you, ma'am!*

And it gets even worse … Now what?

For a few weeks things are silent in the Bible. Did both David and Bathsheba try to forget that anything had happened? Did David slip back into his bored, depressed slump and did Bathsheba attempt to resume her role as a young woman waiting for her husband to return from war? Maybe.

But for Bathsheba it very shortly became apparent that nothing was ever going to be the same again. For, you see, she was pregnant. And given that her husband had been away at war, and continued to be away, a pregnancy could only mean one thing: adultery. Adultery was not a sin to be taken lightly. As it was one of the Ten Commandments, Moses had made sure that there were no gray areas regarding its severity and its consequences: "If a man commits adultery with his neighbor's wife, both the man and the woman who have committed adultery must be put to death." (Leviticus 20:10) Remember Judah's fury when he found out his widowed daughter-in-law was pregnant? I think he expressed his anger and outrange by demanding, "Take her out and burn her."

Q?

Why does it seem harder to stay close to God during the bright, happy times of our lives than the dark, difficult times?

Bathsheba, in a very short span of time, would have faced similar righteous fury. Because of the customs of the day regarding ritualistic sacrifices after her monthly periods (Leviticus 15:28-29), soon everyone would be aware of her indiscretion. "How dare she! While her husband is away fighting for our rights and freedom!" "Some faithful Israelite she is!" "Quick! Tell the priest! Something must be done immediately." Did Bathsheba fear for David's safety as well, or did she think no one would believe her should she name him as the child's father? With no other options, Bathsheba sent a message to King David informing him that she was pregnant with his child. (2 Samuel 11:5)

Well, this was a fine mess he'd gotten himself in, now wasn't it? Good Jewish girl, both father and husband loyal military men, guilty of adultery with the prescribed punishment being death for both of them. What to do ... What to do ...

David the strategist, who had successfully invaded and conquered the mighty city of Jerusalem, swung into action. Contacting his senior general Joab, David instructed his man to send Uriah the Hittite home. Maybe the problem would work itself out ...

David greeted his returning soldier, Uriah, and made polite small talk inquiring about Joab, the army, and the battle in general. Then, once they'd covered all of the necessary niceties, David said to Uriah, "Go on home and relax." (*Enjoy your wife, Uriah. Make sure you sleep with her and cover up our big, bad mistake. Get me out of this mess I've gotten myself in to.* ST) David even sent a gift to Uriah after he left the palace. (2 Samuel 11:7-8) What a nice guy that king was, huh?

"There," David must have thought with great relief and, I'm sure, a touch of smugness, "that should take care of the problem."

No such luck. You see, Uriah didn't go home. Found sleeping at the palace entrance with some of the king's other servants, I can only begin to imagine David's impatience as he waited for Uriah to appear before him once again. "What's the matter with you?" David asked Uriah. "Why didn't you go home last night after being away for so long?" (*Why didn't you go home and sleep with your wife like you were supposed to?* ST) (2 Samuel 11:10)

For Uriah, the reason was simple. "The Ark [of the Covenant of God] and the armies of Israel and Judah are living in tents, and Joab and his officers are camping in the open fields. How could I go home to wine and dine and sleep with my wife? I swear that I will never be guilty of acting like that." (2 Samuel 11:11)

> True character is determined by what we do when no one is looking.
> Martin Luther King

What must David have felt at that moment? Hearing those loyal words from this honorable man? Was he despairing that this problem was obviously not going to be solved simply? Was he guilty for the deception he had perpetrated on this faithful soldier of his army and his God? Was he reaching a level of desperation that perhaps he'd never experienced before?

"Well, stay here tonight," David told Uriah, "and tomorrow you may return to the army." So Uriah did as the king advised, and that evening David invited him to dinner and got him drunk. But even in an inebriated state, David couldn't get Uriah to go home to his wife. Just like the other night, Uriah instead slept at the palace entrance. (2 Samuel 11:12-13)

Did David sleep that night? I imagine him watching Bathsheba and Uriah's house from the roof of the palace, willing the drunken soldier to stumble on home and do what David so desperately needed him to do.

And what about Bathsheba? Was she aware that her husband was home from the front lines and at the palace with the king? Was she overcome with indecision and guilt? Was she as terrified of Uriah coming home as she was of him not? Perhaps, scheming temptress that she was, she simply sat home eating bon-bons, confident that her king and lover would solve this whole annoying complication one way or the other.

While the Bible is silent about Bathsheba, when dawn came David the strategist was recorded as having a new foolproof plan to solve this problem: Plan B.

Once more Uriah was summoned into David's presence and given a letter to be delivered to David's general, Joab. In it, David had written these instructions to Joab, "Station Uriah on the front lines where the battle is fiercest. Then pull back so that he will be killed." (2 Samuel

Q?

Often our faults are glaringly obvious like David's. Yet, it is the hidden ones that can be the most dangerous, because we can keep them hidden from all but God. Are you honest in your confessional prayers?

11:15) Can you feel a bit of God's disappointment and sorrow? Joab, obedient military man that he was, did exactly as instructed.

When David heard of Uriah's death, he informed the messenger, "Tell Joab not to be discouraged. The sword kills one as well as the other! Fight harder next time and conquer the city!" (2 Samuel 11:25)

So, Uriah was murdered. Bathsheba was now a widow. Problem just about solved.

Two Wrongs ... Is there anything right about this?

The journal account says that Bathsheba mourned for her husband. (2 Samuel 11:26) And while I suppose she would have mourned for him as was the custom whether she cared for him or not, I firmly believe that the Bible would have made plain the fact that she did it "without feeling" or "lacking in emotion" or even "with a gladness of heart, because now she was free to continue on with the king." Did she ever know the complete details of Uriah's death and David's complicity in it? The journal account does not say. Did she and David drink a glass of wine in celebration of the solution of the problem? Could she really have denied the coincidence of it all?

The Bible says absolutely nothing about Bathsheba's motives. As she has done all along, she is exemplary in doing all that is expected, required, or asked of her. Studying just her behaviors recorded in the Bible, it would be difficult to make a case against her and accuse her of culpability. "When the period of mourning was over, David sent for her and brought her to the palace, and she became one of his wives." (2 Samuel 11:27)

Now you may say that if she was a gold digger, she got exactly what she wanted in the end, didn't she? And again, the Bible is silent on what emotions Bathsheba had about becoming the newest queen. *Never* do we hear whether she is happy, sad, lost, excited, lonely, frightened, or satisfied. And while the Bible rarely gives us the level of details we crave, the Bible never minces words on pointing out evil behavior. Is Bathsheba the only exception to this rule?

But we do hear about someone else's opinion about the whole situation. Someone who's been left out of David's strategies and planning regarding this situation all along: The One True God. And the opinion that is expressed is damning. "But the thing that David had done was evil in the sight of the LORD." (2 Samuel 11:27b, ASV) Hmmm, I notice only one person that God was displeased with. For me, this one verse pointed the finger squarely where all the blame needed to be. If Bathsheba was the one who started this whole thing with her "exhibitionist behavior," why wasn't she proclaimed evil as well? Certainly Eve was given equal time when God passed out His reprimands in the Garden. If she was guilty, how come Bathsheba got away with it? Would this be fair? *Can* God be unfair?

Consequences … Can it get any worse?

Perhaps you've not sexually accosted your neighbor and arranged for your neighbor's spouse to be murdered to cover up things, but have you ever *kind of* been in David's shoes? Maybe you made a poor choice and then, when things started to become hot and bothered, made additional poor choices to try to keep things under wraps? And things just kept getting worse and worse … and worse.

The time came and Bathsheba gave birth to a son. Now, David has had *months* to get all this straightened out with God, hadn't he? But no, seems as if he was just enjoying the new little queen, thinking that the whole messy business had been effectively covered up. Sigh.

Once we're told that Bathsheba gave birth to a son, *then* we're told that 'the Lord was very displeased with what David had done.' Seems as if David's time had just run out.

"So the Lord sent Nathan the prophet to tell David a story." (2 Samuel 12:1) Huh? The guy's running around accosting women and murdering their husbands and he gets a *story*? Ah, but what a story. It's all about a poor man who is so poor he can only afford one little lamb. The man loved and valued this little lamb so much that he raised it with his children, let it eat and drink from his own dishes, and "cuddled it in his arms like a baby daughter." (2 Samuel 12:3) When the rich neighbor next door had company, rather than choose a lamb from his own extensive flocks to serve as a meal, he took the poor man's lamb, killed it, and served it to his company.

Now why did God choose to confront David about his sin in this manner? Why didn't God just have Nathan walk up to him and say, "Okay, David. Here's the deal. *We know everything.*" I wondered about this and finally decided that right up until the very last moment, God gave David a chance to come clean. Upon hearing the story, David could have been struck with the unbelievable similarities between this story and what he had done to Uriah. He could have then, before Nathan and God, confessed his horrible guilt and requested forgiveness. He could have, but, unfortunately, he didn't. In fact, he didn't even seem to notice any resemblance. King David, upon hearing the story, was furious. Unaware that he was the rich man in the story and that both Nathan and God are fully aware of his heinous actions, David was cleverly put in the situation of pronouncing his own punishment. "As surely as the Lord lives," David vowed, "any man who would do such a thing deserves to die!" (2 Samuel 12:5)

Q?

David was a man after God's own heart. That's a fact. So, what qualities did he have that we should embrace whole-heartedly?

Talk about putting your foot in your mouth.

Only death seems to be a little bit too quick and easy. Nathan, never one to mince words (prophets almost always had thick skins and big mouths!), said to David, "You are that man! The Lord, the God of Israel, says, 'I anointed you king of Israel and saved you from the power of Saul. I gave you his house and his wives and the kingdoms of Israel and Judah. And if that had not been enough, I would have given you much, much more. Why, then, have you despised the word of the Lord and done this horrible deed? For you have murdered Uriah and stolen his wife. From this time on, the sword will be a constant threat to your family, because you have despised me by taking Uriah's wife to be your own. Because of what you have done, I the Lord, will cause your own household to rebel against you. I will give your wives to another man, and he will go to bed with them in public view. You did it secretly, but I will do this to you openly in the sight of all Israel.'" (2 Samuel 12:7-12)

Ouch!!

I do not believe for a minute that this is a "curse" that God put on David, but rather a foretelling of events that would come about as a result of David's ghastly decisions. In future years, David's son, Amnon, raped his half sister, Tamar. One of David's other son's, Absalom, avenged this rape by murdering Amnon. (2 Samuel 13) Absalom eventually went against his father, trying to take away his kingdom (and, in the process, stealing away – and sleeping with - David's concubines), only to be brutally murdered by David's commander, Joab. (2 Samuel 15-18) David lost the respect of his people (2 Samuel 16), his commander Joab (2 Samuel 19), and at the time of his death left his court in turmoil. (I Kings 1)

So pleasing to God in the earlier part of his career, David illustrated just how far it was possible to fall from God's grace. And unfortunately, God wasn't done with the punishments. *After* David confessed his sin, and *after* Nathan confirmed that the Lord had indeed forgiven David, it was *then* revealed that there was an additional consequence as a result of all this sin. Nathan told David, "You have given the enemies of the Lord great opportunity to despise and blaspheme Him, so your child will die." (2 Samuel 12:14)

Feel the full weight of your sin responsibility, David. You've damaged your reputation, God's and Bathsheba's. You've murdered a loyal servant of the Lord and … well, now you also must bear the weight of the responsibility of your son's death, too. Who knew, David, when months ago in your boredom as you gazed in awestruck wonder at that beautiful woman bathing on her roof, that it would be one of the defining moments of your life *and you would fail so miserably?* Eve has a thing or two discuss with you about temptation and wanting and … well, enough said.

The baby boy became deathly ill immediately after Nathan returned home and David begged God to spare the child's life. For seven days he went without food, lying on the bare ground in prayer and supplication to God. Fearful of how David would react when the child finally did die, the advisors were stunned when, at the discovery of the child's death, the king resumed his normal routine. "I fasted and wept while the child was alive, for I said, 'Perhaps the Lord will be gracious

> A broken and repentant heart, O God, you will not despise.
> Psalm 51:17b

to me and let the child live.' But why should I fast when he is dead? Can I bring him back again? I will go to him one day, but he cannot return to me." (2 Samuel 12:22-23)

I'm guessing you're not too impressed with David so far in this story … What we must remember, though, is that he was called "the man after God's own heart." (I Samuel 13:13-14) Pretty amazing, huh? What could David have possibly done to make himself so precious to God? (Or maybe you should be asking: What do I need to do to make sure I'm in that same category, too?) I believe David's greatest and noblest trait was his ability to repent. And not one of us is perfect, it's another quality we should earnestly try to acquire.

Repent means "to feel remorse, contrition, or self-reproach for what one has done or failed to do ... to feel such regret for past conduct as to change one's mind regarding it ... to make a change." (www.freeonlinedictionary.com) It's a little bit more than saying you're sorry and then going out and doing the same darn thing all over again, isn't it? Psalm 51 was written by David after he was confronted by Nathan for his sin with Bathsheba. He writes, *"Purify me from my sins, and I will be clean; wash me, and I will be whiter than snow ... Create in me a clean heart, O God. Renew a right spirit within me."* (Psalm 51:7, 10) When you read the entire Psalm there is no doubt that David *got it.* He realized the enormity of his sin, his culpability, and the severe ramifications that were going happen for the rest of his life.

> **So we're not giving up. How could we! Even though on the outside it often looks like things are falling apart on us, on the inside, where God is making new life, not a day goes by without His unfolding grace.**
> 2 Corinthians 4:16 MSG

I feel compelled to point out – again in defense of Bathsheba and those who claim her to be the evil seductress - that in Nathan's story she was *an innocent lamb.* I would assume that the grief she felt over the death of her child would have been astronomical. The Bible says that David "comforted Bathsheba, his wife, and slept with her. She became pregnant and gave birth to a son ..." (2 Samuel 12:24) Was it David's physical presence that comforted her, or was it the pregnancy? We have no way of knowing.

How much do you think Bathsheba knew? Throughout much of this story, it seems that Bathsheba had little choice and little say in the course of her life. Would full knowledge have helped or hindered her to cope? Perhaps God sheltered her, and aside from David's all consuming infatuation with her, she knew little of the intrigue that swirled around her. Perhaps she was able to thank God for His faithfulness in providing for her after her first husband's death, and delight and wonder at the gift of her second son's birth and healthy, long life. Maybe that's all she knew of the whole ugly story ...

Or was it only upon the death of her child that Bathsheba was forced to face what responsibility she bore in this sordid relationship? Maybe David's grief over Nathan's condemnation and the subsequent death of his son was something Bathsheba witnessed first hand? Did David's genuine confession to God extend to Bathsheba as well? Was his repentant example something that she could not discount but chose to emulate?

Think about it. If you were Bathsheba, with absolutely no chance of changing the path of your life (you are now the newest queen of Israel) would you want to know *everything*? To what extent would she have been able to compartmentalize her relationship with David? Did she feel real love or merely possessiveness from him? Was he a supportive husband or a kingly conqueror? Did David share with her his confession of guilt to Nathan and ask her forgiveness as well? Would she have been able to forgive him if he did? Did she ever learn the true story of Uriah's death and David's involvement? Did she ever know the true reason behind the death of their child? Would she have been better off knowing or not knowing all these things?

It is reassuring to me to know that God in His perfect wisdom would have taken care of all these difficult questions, as, I am certain, He does with us in our own lives. Sometimes, ignorance *is* bliss.

Solomon ... A mother's pride and joy?

The second son born to David and Bathsheba was named Solomon. The journal entry states clearly, "The Lord loved the child and sent word through Nathan the prophet that his name should be Jedidiah – "beloved of the Lord" – because the Lord loved him." (2 Samuel 12:25) Specially named by God and loved by Him. Surely that would have brought Bathsheba great joy; her worth, determined by both her husband (a king) and her son (specially loved by God), would have elevated her to the epitome of social status.

Bathsheba just about faded completely into the background for the remainder of David's rule over Israel. At the end of his life, David lay in bed old and cold with nothing but a beautiful virgin named Abishag to nurse him and keep him warm and well cared for. (I Kings 1:1-4) Around him his numerous wives and their respective sons began to scramble to position themselves to take over David's kingdom.

Absalom, one of David's favored sons, had already failed and died in an earlier attempt to take the kingdom from his father. Now, it had become a waiting game, for it was obvious the king didn't have too much time left. The poor guy, he was not even able to have sexual relations with the beautiful Abishag! (I Kings 1:4b)

"Queen Mothers" or mothers of the king were fantastically powerful. In a society where women had no real identity except that which they drew from the men in their life, the status of being "Queen Mother" was as close to manly power as was possible. "Though women ... were not allowed to own property, queen mothers could possess real estate and were even able to buy land to supplement their holdings. The queen mother also owned her own storage facilities ... These properties seem to have been managed for the queen mother by administrative personnel under her authority ... The queen mother counted among her household a chief administrative official, a chief counselor, and several ... officials of high rank." (Ackerman)

So, as a woman could never aspire to be *king*, the next best thing would have been to be the *mother of a King!* It was actually better than being queen! Does that put the atmosphere of David's harem with his numerous wives (at least eight, plus all those concubines) and their little princes in perspective for you? Can you imagine the intrigue and divisions that permeated the entire palace as David lay with the beautiful Abishag close to the end of his life?

David's wife Haggith rushes to the head of the pack and has her son Adonijah claim the throne. (I Kings 1:5) Imagine it as a line being drawn in the harem's battle sand. It was not until Nathan the prophet (yeah, he was still around and just as feisty as ever) caught wind of this behind the throne scrambling that Bathsheba came back on the scene.

Nathan went to Bathsheba and said, "Did you realize that Haggith's son, Adonijah, has made himself king, and that our lord David doesn't even know about it? If you want to save your own life and the life of your son Solomon, follow my counsel ..." (I Kings 1:11-12)

Please note that Bathsheba was *not* the impetus behind all of this. Another wife had pushed another son onto the throne and Nathan had had to seek Bathsheba out to inform her. If Bathsheba had been a scheming individual (from the moment of her exhibitionist bath on her roof those many years ago) *what* exactly was she waiting for? Because, amazingly, there was something that apparently the other wives and princes either didn't know or chose to ignore: God has already chosen Solomon to be the next king. David had already told Solomon, "The Lord said to me, 'You will have a son who will experience peace and rest. I will give him peace with his enemies in all the surrounding lands. His name will be Solomon and I will give peace and quiet to Israel during his reign. He is the one who will build a Temple to honor my name. He will be my son, and I will be his father. And I will establish the throne of his kingdom over Israel forever.'" (1 Chronicles 22:8-10) Nathan knew this, we can assume Bathsheba knew this … but David had not officially declared this to the kingdom.

What was Bathsheba waiting for? Was she being patient? Was Bathsheba, after all these years in the palace, completely clueless of the palace intrigue? Perhaps she'd lost the will to fight to get to the top? I suppose, based on your belief of her initial motives, there could have been many scenarios. What I have trouble rationalizing is that *if* she was a gold digging schemer, why would she be sitting idly by doing *nothing* at such a key time? Was she waiting for God's timing and wisdom? Maybe she was unconcerned with the intrigue swirling around her, confident that the Lord would see everything according to His purpose? Did she, after all these years, know that there was nothing *she* could do to control the way her life would go, but that *everything* rested on God's design?

To her credit, when Nathan approached Bathsheba and told her what she must do, she immediately took action. She went to David, informed him of the situation, reminded him of his promise, and pleaded her case. David, old but still true to his word, had Solomon crowned as king. (I Kings 1:15-30)

Who placed the crown on this new king's head? You need to look in Song of Solomon 3:11. "Go out to look upon King Solomon, O young women of Jerusalem. See the crown with which his mother crowned him …"

Respectful, obedient, polite, patient, faithful ... Rather notable qualities when you think about it: I see no evidence when we read the Scriptures that she was the calculating seductress that some Bible commentators have made her out to be. Repeatedly, even in the most difficult of situations, she comes across blameless. I believe that God sheltered her, cared for her, and rewarded her for the belief and trust she placed in Him. Nathan, God's prophet, likens her to an innocent lamb. In a world filled with murder, intrigue, and countless other dangers, Bathsheba seemed to pass through relatively intact.

Her son, Solomon, was beloved of the Lord to such an extent that God offered him *anything*, all Solomon had to do was ask. When Solomon requested wisdom, he pleased God so that God rewarded him with everything else imaginable as well. (I Kings 3:3-14) It was only in Solomon's later life ... when he acquired *seven hundred wives and three hundred concubines* ... that he began to slip down the slippery slope his father had ... and became distant from God.

Solomon was known for being the wisest man who had ever lived. The book of Proverbs is loaded with his insightful observations (there are some portions that are written by others as well). The last chapter of the book lists the qualities of a "Wife of Noble Character." Some traditions attribute the woman who inspired this section to Bathsheba, and that Solomon wrote it to honor her. (Richards) *"Who can find a virtuous and capable wife? She is worth more than precious rubies. Her husband can trust her, and she will greatly enrich his life. She will not hinder him but help him all her life ..."* (Proverbs 31:10-12)

Bathsheba lived a life that was almost completely out of her control. She found little assistance from the culture of the times or in the men who 'loved' her. Her only rock, her only salvation was The One True God. Did she embrace Him and remain steadfastly committed to Him throughout her life? I would like to believe that Bathsheba hooked up with the only One worthy ... The One True God.

For all you Bathshebas out there …

Have you ever felt powerless? Abused? In the dark? It is *you* whom God can use to His greatest glory. Stop trying to swim upstream and climb into God's boat and just flow with His current. *None* of us can control our lives, although some of us foolishly think we can steer a tiny bit. Jobs are lost, disasters happen, and health fails. We find ourselves stunned and confused. We cry, "How did this happen? How could this be my life?"

When we put our trust in The One True God we hook up with the mightiest of powers, the greatest of resources. Though we might regularly not understand the *why,* we should always understand the *Who.*

> **When you really trust someone, you have to be okay with not understanding some things.**
> Real Live Preacher

Faith and trust go hand in hand. They grow together and they fade away together, too. It is a conscious choice. It is believing without always seeing. Oswald Chambers said, "Faith never knows where it is being led, but it loves and knows the One who is leading."

Do you trust? Do you have faith? Do you believe? You. Must. Make. A. Decision. Now. No decision *is* a decision. There is no more time to think. Why not step out on faith? Besides your eternal life, what have you got to lose?

❖ **Signs:** Watch for the signs that God gives to guide you. They are more obvious than you may wish to admit. Let part of your faith and trust be wrapped up in the belief that everything that happens in your life is by God's design. Car breaks down? Hmmm, what does God want me to do with this time while I wait for the tow-truck? Don't get the promotion you so desperately wanted? Hmmm, what good does God want for me right here in this

> **Why should I ask of Him that He would change for me the course of things? I who ought to love, above all, the order established by His wisdom and maintained by His Providence, shall I wish that order to be dissolved on my account?**
> Rousseau

215

place? Win the lottery? Hmmm, what would God want me to do with this windfall? Get the picture?

❖ **Boredom:** Be cautious with yourself and your decisions when you are bored, unhappy, or not focused completely on God. That's a prime time opportunity for temptation, and temptation is usually a big, red flag full of trouble. Prayer during these times surrounds you and opens channels for God to speak to you, guide you, and offer you solutions to what you're struggling with. Don't knock it … have you tried it?

❖ **Fairness:** Even when you are truly repentant, you still have to deal with the consequences of your sin. *God is fair.* He's loving, perfect, and determined for you to grow wise and wonderful. That rarely means the easy way out, and you should stop resenting Him when things don't work out the way *you* think they should. God knows best. God knows all. God knows where He wants you to head. God knows what you struggle with. Stop arguing like a spoiled child and get with the program.

> **Trust in the Lord always, for the Lord God is the eternal Rock.**
> Isaiah 26:4

❖ **Trust:** Mother Teresa said, "*I know God will not give me anything I can't handle. I just wish He didn't trust me so much.*" How much does God trust you? Are you worthy of big things, or only barely able to handle tiny things? Are there parts of your life that God has placed within your reach that you have not taken control of? Is He waiting for you to step up to the plate on something … so He can trust you with more?

❖ **On Forgiveness:** God gives us time to right our wrongs, but He doesn't give us forever. The next time something bad happens in your life that is a direct result of a poor decision you made, take two minutes (once the weeping, wailing, and gnashing of teeth stops) and think about *how much time you had* to fix things before God might have had to step in. We make conscious wrong choices all the time, and He lets us. Then He lets us exist in our joy or our misery awhile. *Then* He steps in and readjusts things to be headed in the direction He needs everything to go. And He gives us another chance … *But those who trust in the Lord will find new strength. They will soar high on wings like eagles. They will run and not grow weary. They will walk and not faint.* (Isaiah 40:31)

❖ **Answers**: Did Bathsheba ask heartfelt questions of God as she mourned her dead husband Uriah? *Why* God? *How* God? Questions that, perhaps for her own peace of mind, He never answered? God must surely do that for us, too. Sometimes we aren't meant to understand the whys and hows of things because God knows that the knowing might be more painful to us in the end. Next time an unhappy circumstance occurs in your life, rather than asking why and how, thank God. For His faithful presence. For His sparing you from a situation that may have been far worse. For His continued guidance in your life despite your constant attempts to go in the wrong direction. For His refusal to give up on you. For His commitment to only wanting the very best for you.

❖ **Being Thankful**: I hate to tell you this, but we're supposed to be thankful *in all situations*, not just the good times. I Thessalonians 5:18 clearly states, *Be thankful in all circumstances, for this is God's will for you who belong to Christ Jesus.* Being thankful during the rough spots of your life implicitly shows that you have placed your life in God's hands and you believe, *regardless how things appear,* that God is fully and completely in control. It releases you from the pressing responsibility we feel that we've got to do something to save/resolve/fix this disaster that has all appearances of destroying us. Try it next time things start to fall apart. Gasp out a, "Thanks for this car accident, God!" or "Thanks that I've lost my wallet, Lord!" It gets easier. As you do it more often and *regularly* you will be stunned at the number of times you think, "Oh, *that's* why that needed to happen …" And yes, I speak from experience (and a lot of God's patience and grace).

Homework … How impossible is this?

Homework this time is different. I'm going to ask you to do something difficult … maybe even impossible. *But,* I am going to lead by example. I'm going to ask you to do some retrospection into your past. Difficult retrospection. I want you to think back on a time that was perhaps the most hard, frightening, embarrassing, awful time of your life.

> **I will not fail you or abandon you.**
> Joshua 1:5b

217

Something that has shaped you and your life and brought you (whether you like it or not) to this exact place in time. I want you to try, maybe for the very first time, to think of your hard times in a new and more positive light … if possible. The belief/trust/faith that God is with you through *all times* - both good and bad - and that He can make *all things* work together for good (Romans 8:28) is something we must *live*.

Could it be possible for you to see anything positive in this time from your past? Is it possible for you to begin to view this moment in your past from tragedy to triumph? I pray it to be so…

A Dark Time: My younger sister Faith suffered from a congenital illness named Cystic Fibrosis. My parents endured the brutal pain of watching their child fade away before their eyes. Throughout my sister's entire life, my parents remained committed Christians, drawing strength and comfort in The One True God's love, comfort, and steadfastness. Yes, they prayed for healing. Yes, they prayed for a miracle. And yes, Faith died when she was eleven and I was fifteen.

The Questions: Go ahead. Ask. *How could God let such a thing happen? How can any goodness come from this?* Faith wanted to be a missionary. *Why? How?* Many people did ask those questions. Furthermore, when my other sister, Amy, battled cancer almost twenty years later people asked us, *Hasn't your family paid its dues? How could God do this to your family again?* There are no real answers for those questions …

Choices: There were so many directions my parents could have taken before, during, and after Faith's death. (And even Amy's subsequent battle with cancer.) They could have allowed anger, hatred, and bitterness to fill their existence, and I imagine there are many people who would have understood why this godly couple would have become distanced from church, religion, and biblical things after they buried their child and faced life without her.

But they didn't. My parents set a powerful example to me, my sister Amy, family, friends, and acquaintances, by continuing to praise God for His love and faithfulness, even though they had no answers to the why questions they most assuredly asked, even though their lives were forever altered … with the absence of their daughter.

Mom went on to lead a Bible study out of her home and spoke numerous times to groups on "Surviving the Death of Your Child." I remember times when she was specifically called upon to try to comfort other women who were dealing with the same terrible situation.

I grew up with parents who focused, trusted, and believed in The One True God, regardless of what life threw at them.

Life Goes On: Now, fast-forward twenty years. I was married to a lovely man and had made my parents grandparents twice over. (My sister Amy, at this point in her life was still single and has not yet been diagnosed with cancer.) Mom's in the "mature Christian stage," (but still learning and growing!) while I was in the "young adult Christian stage" and became the paid children's minister at our local church: running vacation Bible school, nursery, children's worship, junior church, and chairing the preschool committee at church. I was just about as busy as I could manage! But with all that I had going on in my life, I still had a strong desire to start a women's Bible study and decided to listen to God's still small voice. Soon up to ten women were enthusiastically showing up at my door once a week.

There was a woman named Linda at our church who was both a deacon and a founding member. While my husband, David, attended regularly with me, he had not made a profession of faith and been baptized. Linda took the time one night to sit down with him and answer his many questions and doubts about this whole born-again Christian business. (Sometimes it just can't come from the wife, you know?) Patient and eloquent, Linda had just the right style to not only keep David's attention, but cause him to believe, trust, and commit. We delighted in David's baptism at age thirty-four.

Linda offered to come and give her testimony at my Bible study. With great enthusiasm and diligence, my small group of women (my mom included) had become enthralled with Ann Spangler and Jean Syswerda's excellent book *Women of the Bible,* and were working through it.

Linda came and spoke about the "defining moments" in her life; of the times when God spoke to her, and she listened, and of the times she didn't. For her, the turning point in her life was when she attended a luncheon to hear a woman speak of God's graciousness, love and compassion, sharing a particularly dark time in her life. The Bible passage the woman shared with the group was of the Shunnamite woman from 2 Kings 4 and 8 who had suffered the death of her precious child and yet still answered, "It is well" when asked how she was. This speaker pointed out to her audience that while the Shunnamite woman's *life* was in shambles, her *soul* was well and firmly still focused on The One True God – exactly where it should have been.

Linda shared with us that as a nurse, she regularly saw tremendous pain and suffering. One particular family had always stood out in her mind because it had had to deal with the ultimate of tragedies. Linda talked about the strong witness this couple had broadcast throughout the grief and pain of dealing with their young daughter's numerous hospitalizations and eventual death. Linda had always remembered the couple. What an astonishing coincidence it was for Linda to sit at that luncheon that day and listen to the very same woman share her story! For Linda it was a defining moment when God spoke to her and she could no longer ignore Him. This woman's testimony of faith and commitment to God *at all times* and *through all things* made Linda desire that same spiritual relationship. Linda and her husband were instrumental in starting the church David and I were attending, she'd guided my husband towards making a profession of faith and choosing to be baptized, and through her continuing nursing career had had numerous opportunities to witness and counsel to others.

As she spoke to our Bible study group, Linda turned to my mother and said, "Did I remember your talk correctly, Marylynn?" It was then that we all realized that the woman speaker at the luncheon and the woman at the hospital with the child who had died had been my very own mother.

Goodness out of sorrow. *"To all who mourn in Israel, He will give a crown of beauty for ashes, a joyous blessing instead of mourning, festive praise instead of despair."* (Isaiah 61:3a) Beauty for ashes. Festive praise instead of despair. It is right there for us to grab a hold of …

Reality: Mom and Dad could have abandoned the godly life route and taken a completely different path. But their faith remained strong, allowing them to find joy amidst the sorrow, beauty in the ashes, and praise instead of despair. How many lives has Linda touched over the course of her life, helping to establish a church and witnessing to others? This aspect of the story – the Linda aspect, we'll call it – is only one of many pieces of a huge puzzle that radiates out of the center of my parents' dark time when they lost a child to illness.

And before you ask, *No,* God didn't cause my sister Faith to die so this could happen. This world is not the perfect place that Eve and Adam once enjoyed. People get cancer and brain tumors. Women struggle with infertility and miscarriages. Children are abused and neglected because of their parents' personal demons. There are all manners of things that are horribly imperfect. Rather, God can change despair into praise and darkness into light. My parents' faith was strong enough to survive the death of their child, and rather than letting it be a defining moment of failure for them, it became a defining moment of victory. Not only will we see Faith again in heaven, but there will be many more of us there as a result of the path my parents chose to take.

Your Turn: Can you do that with something in your past? Perhaps you cannot. Maybe, instead, you can make a conscious choice to strive for that in the future? I pray you can. Take a moment to prayerfully think of a time in your life that was life-altering with its pain or despair. Can you see any goodness that has come out of that time?

You will keep in perfect peace all who trust in you, all whose thoughts are fixed on you! (Isaiah 26:3) This verse has to refer to the difficult times. Why would God promise you peace in the already peaceful times?

Question To Discuss:

Q?

Why is childlike trust in God sometimes the best weapon for us against the dark times of life?

With where her life's story was headed, she sure needed all the help she could get.

Mary and The Perfect One

A Heart of Obedience

The world saw an unmarried, poor, teenage girl. The biblical journal does not speak of her giftedness, beauty, or any remarkable talents. A young woman whose sanity was questioned, for wasn't she inclined to hallucinations and an extraordinary imagination? Yet she was given the distinction of being "most blessed among women." (Luke 1:28) Just what exactly was the big draw, anyway?

> **Mary kept all these things in her heart and thought about them often.**
> Luke 2:19

God saw a young woman with a faithful heart who believed immediately what she was told by the angel Gabriel: she was going to give birth to the Messiah. "I am the Lord's servant. May everything you have said about me come true." (Luke 1:38)

God saw a young woman with the self-confidence to withstand the doubts and whispers that would surround her all the days of her life: "She's the one that *had* to get married, you know."

God saw a young woman with the strength to survive the difficulties and momentous sorrows that were in store for her: "Standing near the cross [was] Jesus' mother … When Jesus saw his mother standing there … he said to her, 'Dear woman, here is your son.'" (John 19:25-26)

Q?

Are there any qualities, any promises, any guarantees that God has given to us that you find unsuitable or substandard?

God saw a young woman with a heart for God who would be able to *instruct the Son of God* through childhood to adulthood: "… his parents took him to Jerusalem to present him to the Lord." (Luke 2:22b)

God saw a young woman with a patient heart who would be able to wait to bask in the joy surely to come in the future.

The important quality about Mary was her heart. *It was right.* It was perfectly aligned in the direction it was supposed to be, and consequently, God was able to use Mary in the most spectacular fashion. Mary had no doubt, no insecurity, no worrying about a multitude of "what-ifs," no questioning, and no hesitancy. Mary's answer, when she was told that her whole life was going to immediately be turned upside down for the glory of God was effectively, "Great! Thanks so much for believing in me. When do we get started? What do I need to do first?" Mary did think of all the things that the world saw with Gabriel's pronouncement. No, Mary looked at what was in the center of her heart and simply smiled because she'd been found worthy of the task.

Which begs the question: what does God see in you?

First Things First

Scripture references you should check out:	Luke 1:26-56, Luke 2, Matthew 1-2,
Question to ask yourself before you read any further:	Is there anyone you would obey without question? Or are you a law unto yourself?

What the word means:	"Obey" means to carry out or fulfill the command, order, or instruction of. To abide by, take orders, heed, listen to, or act in accordance with someone's rules … There seems to be little wiggle room when it comes to this word's definition.
Connections:	Parents expect it, employers expect it, and to a lesser extent close friends and spouses expect it: obedience. Our entire lives are balanced on the knife-edge of whether we do or we don't. Are your loyalties so divided that you don't know which way to turn when you are faced with the numerous challenges life throws at you? Perhaps, you need to organize, prioritize, and decide who is the top authority in your life.
What the Bible says about obedience:	**How we learn it:** Hebrews 5:8 **Final authority**: Acts 5:29 **Benefits of:** Acts 5:32, I john 3:24 **What's right and what's not:** Romans 2:13 **Our sinful nature:** Romans 8:7 **What it shows:** I John 2:5

Questions We'll Never Know The Answers To:

❖ What heights of joy and success could we have reached had we been perfectly obedient, faithful, trusting, and committed to Christ right from the start?

❖ From the moment of the angel Gabriel's pronouncement, how much did Mary know about her future? Was she, like many of the expectant Jews, anticipating a triumphant, avenging, kingly Messiah, or was she given an intrinsic understanding of how different the real picture was going to be?

Did you know? Interesting Biblical Facts About Women

❖ **Jesus:** Do not ever let anyone tell you that Jesus wished women to be subjugated or treated inferior to men. Throughout His ministry on earth He repeatedly defied all cultural mores that forced women into an inferior role. "Jesus did not perceive women primarily in terms of their sex, age or marital status; He seems to have considered them in terms of their relationship (or lack of one) to God.".(Hurley)

> The most striking thing about the role of women in the life and teaching of Jesus is the simple fact that they are there.
> James Hurley

❖ **Firsts With Jesus and Women:** Take a look at all of these firsts with Jesus and those to whom He ministered:

- *First Person To Know That He Was Coming:* Mary (Luke 1:30-32)
- *First Person To Profess Faith In Him:* Elizabeth (Luke 1:42-43)
- *First Person To Proclaim Him To The World:* Anna (Luke 2:36-38)
- *Longest Recorded Conversation Between Jesus And A Person:* The Woman of Samaria (John 4:1-42)
- *First Person To Whom Jesus Reveals His True Identity As The Messiah:* The Woman of Samaria (John 4:1-42)
- *First Person To Anoint Christ:* The Sinful Woman (Luke 7:36-50)
- *First Person To Be Healed Through Touching Christ:* The Woman With The Issue of Blood (Matt 9:20-22, Mark 5:25-34, Luke 8:43-48)
- *Earthly Home/Place of Rest For The Adult Jesus:* Martha of Bethany's home (Luke 10:38-42)
- *First Person To Express Knowledge/Sorrow Of Jesus' Impending Death:* Mary of Bethany (Mark 14:7-8)
- *Only Person About Whom Christ Pronounced Immortal Fame Because Of A Specific Deed:* Mary of Bethany and her anointing of Christ (Mark 14:3-9)
- *People Who Financially Supported Jesus During His Ministry:* Joanna, the wife of Chuza, Susanna, "and many others" (Luke 8:3)
- *Person Mentioned Most Often In New Testament Scriptures, Besides Twelve Disciples:* Mary Magdalene
- *Witnesses To Christ's Death/Present At The Crucifixion:* Mary (Mother of Jesus), Mary Magdalene, Salome (Zebedee's wife and the mother of James and John), Mary (The wife of Clopas and mother of James the younger and Joseph), John the disciple (John 19:25)
- *Only Person At Every Scene Related To Jesus' Crucifixion And Resurrection:* Mary Magdalene

- *First Person To Whom The Risen Jesus Christ Appeared:* Mary Magdalene (Mark 16:9, John 20:11-18))
- *First People To Know Of The Resurrection:* Mary Magdalene, Joanna, and Mary the mother of James (Luke 24:1-10)
- *First Human Heralds Of The Resurrection:* Mary Magdalene, Joanna, and Mary the mother of James (Luke 24:1-10)
- *First Person To Be Told By Christ To Herald the Resurrection:* Mary Magdalene (John 20:17)

❖ **Culture of the Times Regarding Women:** The world Jesus entered was prevailingly male-oriented and male-dominated. For the most part, men dominated all power structures: civil, economic, military, religious. (Stagg) "Jesus' honor and respect was ... extended to all women - an attitude largely unexpected and unknown in his culture and time. Jesus, unlike the men of his generation and culture, taught that women were equal to men in the sight of God. Women could receive God's forgiveness and grace. Women, as well as men, could be among Christ's personal followers. Women could be full participants in the kingdom of God ... These were revolutionary ideas. Many of his contemporaries, including his disciples, were shocked." (Graham) A woman during biblical times:

> **"It seems to us that a true following of Jesus Christ compels us to recognize the full personhood of woman."**
> Stagg

- Was listed as part of a man's possessions.
- Gained respect and influence upon the birth of her first child, especially if it was a boy. Status was earned, not something already there by virtue of her personhood.
- Were required to be virgins prior to marriage. Failure to prove such could result in death by stoning. (Deuteronomy 22:21)
- Could be divorced by a man, but could not divorce. (Deuteronomy 24:1)
- Could be sold by her father as a slave, (Ex. 21:7) and unlike male slaves was not to be released after six years.
- Could not be priests, menstruation being the apparent reason for exclusion.

- Had jobs which included: grinding flour, baking bread, washing clothes, cooking food, nursing her child, making ready her husband's bed, and working in wool. She was always to be busy.
- Was not to be instructed in the Law and was excluded from the heart of religious practices.
- Was not allowed to bear witness.
- Could offer no sacrifices.
- Could not have "serious conversations" with a man.
- Was to be veiled (unless she was a virgin or a widow).
- Was betrothal on average at age 12.
- Was not to be spoken to in public.

The Core Story

Mary … What was so special about that girl?

There's not much to tell about Mary that we haven't already heard. We're not sure of her looks, her talents, or even her age when she came on the scene. She seemed to have absolutely no political clout, no agenda for social change, and had no dreams of fame and fortune. She seemed, well, remarkably average. Someone you probably wouldn't even notice in a crowd.

For those of us with the benefit of the complete biblical account, the style of Jesus' arrival and the personality He exhibited over the course of His life isn't really that much of a surprise. Why, from the very beginning, God consistently broke every earthbound rule of "what was right," "what was expected," and "what had to be." Eve had learned of His stunning level of forgiveness, Sarah had learned of His uniquely unpredictable time clock, Tamar had learned of His determination to follow through on His covenant at all costs, Leah had learned of His unfailing love and devotion, Rahab had learned of His dismissal of all things forgiven, and Bathsheba had learned of His wisdom and grace. By the time Jesus arrived, born to

> **Mary … did you know that your baby boy has walked where angels trod?**
> Mark Lowry

the young teenage girl named Mary in an animal stall on a bed of hay, it was all just par for the course. What the world expected was not what God planned ... *nor would it ever be.* Those faithful Jews waiting for the chosen Messiah, a victorious king who was going to vanquish their enemies and reclaim the might and power they knew under King Solomon, were confused to say the least, when Jesus finally showed up on the scene.

Did Mary ever impress you as the type of woman who *expected* to be chosen to give birth to the Messiah? "This was no surprise to me," Mary murmured to herself, "haven't I always been pure, faithful, and committed to God? Surely I've been just the woman God has been waiting for all these many generations!" Do you think she walked around proud and full of herself once the angel Gabriel had delivered his spectacular announcement? "Mary said that the angel Gabriel visited her last week and that he said that she was blessed above all women!" Maybe during Jesus' upbringing she had to repeatedly remind Joseph, "Dear, remember God chose *me* not you. I think I'd better teach him this concept of rabbinical law."

Q?

Which would have been easier to bear for Mary: knowing the future or not knowing?

Actually, when Gabriel called her most blessed of all women and told her what was going to happen the recorded response was this: "Mary said: 'With all my heart I praise the Lord, and I am glad because of God my Savior. He cares for me, his humble servant. From now on, all people will say God has blessed me. God All-Powerful has done great things for me, and his name is holy. He always shows mercy to everyone who worships him. The Lord has used his powerful arm to scatter those who are proud. He drags strong rulers from their thrones and puts humble people in places of power. God gives the hungry good things to eat, and sends the rich away with nothing. He helps his servant Israel and is always merciful to his people. The Lord made this promise to our ancestors, to Abraham and his family forever!'" (Luke 1:46-55 CEV) She didn't sound like a young woman full of pride and grandiose expectations, does she?

Here's another thought: could Mary have said no? "Gee, thanks Gabriel, but I think I'll pass on this opportunity." Has God not consistently operated within our privilege of free will? Would Mary, of all people, not have been given such a choice? Of course Mary could have said no. *We do it all the time*, why couldn't Mary? Even if Mary did not understand the full magnitude of the path of her life, the simple facts of conceiving a child outside of marriage and 'betraying' her fiancé would have been a steep price. From the moment she bowed her head in obedience, Mary knew that things were not going to be easy.

Mary was a regular girl who married a regular "Joe." They lived in a regular small town, dealt with regular small town issues and stresses, and had every expectation of living a regular life. Except that's not what God saw when He looked at her. God saw an obedient heart. *God saw greatness.*

Quality, not Quantity ... What really counts?

God saw an obedience in Mary that was so special it distinguished her from every other young woman. Because of that obedience, God chose her to be the mother of His Son. Mary, so average in the world's eyes, had a faith that made her exceptional in God's view.

Young chronologically, she was the poster girl for the verse in I Timothy 4:12: *Don't let anyone think less of you because you are young. Be an example to all believers in what you say, in the way you live, in your love, your faith, and your purity.* "I am the Lord's servant." (Luke 1:38) 'My soul praises the Lord." (Luke 1:46) "The Mighty One is holy and He has done great things for me." (Luke 1:49)

Q?
What would Mary say to us regarding the death of her son on the cross?

Was part of her powerful faith wrapped up in innocent, simple belief? She probably had never sat and debated Mosaic Law with the Pharisees. She'd never argued the perceived inconsistencies between God's love versus God's wrath. Her faith was rooted in uncomplicated trust in God and His promises – nothing more and nothing less. Jesus himself admonished us to become "like little children." *So anyone who becomes as humble as this little child is the greatest in the Kingdom of Heaven.* (Matthew 18:4) It seems to me that Mary's greatness was rooted in her basic understanding of her role was in God's plan ... *in whatever He called her to do.*

You know that expression "God never gives you more than He knows you can handle"? What does that say about what God expected of Mary? Herbert Lockyer said, "If Calvary was our Lord's crown of sorrow, it was likewise Mary's, yet how courageous she was. Others might *sit* and watch the suffering Christ, or smite their breasts and cry, but 'Mary *stood* by the cross.' (John 19:25) No Spartan mother ever displayed such fortitude as Mary manifested at the cross." Today, many revere Mary. Some religions have elevated her to such a vaulted status that they direct prayers to her and

> **If you love me, obey my commandments.**
> John 14:15

believe that she is an intercessor between God and us. What is absolutely important for us to remember is that *Mary was just like us.* She was *not* picked because she was already exceptional. She was chosen because she was simply obedient to God's call and direction, which in turn elevated her above all others. The level of greatness she achieved, not by the world's standards but by God's, was her choice. Her *only* crowning victory was her obedient faith through all things – good and bad. You must never forget that.

God never sends us off into this big world all by ourselves. He *equips us,* giving us talents or people or circumstances that shore us up when things threaten to slip off into the dark void. When Mary came on the scene, she was just a young engaged woman going through the motions of her life, until the angel Gabriel showed up and spun everything into a new direction. But, God had already placed things in Mary's life to help support her. What were they?

Most important would have been the people who surrounded Mary. We know nothing of Mary's parents. There are no names given and no conversations recorded. I suppose it was possible that they were no longer alive when Mary came on the scene. We can *infer* some things though. Someone had taken the time to give Mary a solid knowledge of her God, her people, and her people's history. She evidences that in her song recorded in Luke 1:46-55 speaking of God, His mercy, His deeds, and His history. Eloquent and humble, Mary had to have learned this *somewhere.* Is it too far fetched to imply that her knowledge could have been from parents who set a faithful example? It certainly wasn't at school, since girls were rarely formally educated.

If not from her parents, Mary would have learned from her relatives Elizabeth and Zechariah, who are specifically mentioned in the biblical journal. Parents of the great John The Baptist, "both of them were upright in the sight of God, observing all the Lord's commandments and regulations blamelessly." (Luke 1:6) Wow, how's that for an endorsement? How many couples *in the entire Bible* hold up to *that* description? Elizabeth, described as being "filled with the Holy Spirit" (Luke 1:41) also bares the marvelous distinction of being the first biblically recorded person to profess faith in Mary's unborn child. It is to Elizabeth that Mary goes upon discovering God's new course for her life. Obviously, Elizabeth is a source of comfort and support for young Mary. I'm inclined to say *good choice, too.*

And we must never forget Mary's fiancé, Joseph. Do you know that there is not one biblically recorded word from him? If the saying "Talk is cheap, actions are expensive" is true, then Joseph was absolutely priceless. Described as a "good man" in Matthew 1:19, his brief appearance in the account of Christ's birth shows a tender, spiritual, prayerful, patient, obedient, and faithful man. The angel of the Lord appeared to Joseph not once but twice in dreams comforting, reassuring, instructing, and

> **[Joseph] serves for all times as an example of godly wisdom and tender consideration for others.**
> Lockyer

foretelling. Joseph, the man who never spoke a word in the Scriptures, managed to leave an inspiring example of a godly man.

Strong in her heart, confident in her faith, surrounded by positive, sound people … young, ordinary Mary suddenly seems about ten feet tall, doesn't she? Her choice to be the *mother of the Son of God* seems to be … *perfect.*

Jesus … What was it about that guy?

Jesus, the Carpenter of Nazareth: Mary's baby, Joseph's stepson, John the Baptist's cousin … The first thirty years of his life are pretty much a mystery. In Luke chapters 1 and 2 and Matthew chapters 1 and 2 we hear of his birth and brief snippets of his early years: his circumcision at eight days old, his family's flight to Egypt when he's about three, his return to settle in Nazareth after Herod's death, and the visit to Jerusalem and the temple at age twelve. Yet from age twelve until he begins his ministry at about thirty we hear only silence.

Joseph is never mentioned after the temple visit. Conventional wisdom is that Mary became a widow and Jesus, being the eldest child, would have shouldered the responsibility to care and provide for her. Mary and Jesus would have become constants in each other's lives: by God's choice and by society's dictates. As he hung on the cross, Jesus saw his mother standing beside the disciple John and said to her, "Dear woman, here is your son." He then spoke to John and instructed him, "Here is your mother." The biblical journal tells us "from then on this disciple took her into his home." (John 19:26) Jesus was a faithful, loving, and caring son who provided for Mary's uncertain future at the very moment of his death.

I got a kick out of the way one author described Jesus: he was a man who "wandered the hills with a group of men, was unable to hold down a full-time job, never found a woman to marry, and ended up at parties with drunks and prostitutes." (Valcarcel). I'll add to that: dirt poor, of questionable lineage, and reviled by most of the religious leaders of his time. For the Jews who were waiting for the avenging messiah to guide them back to a level of greatness such as the time with David and Solomon, this lowly, soft-spoken carpenter was a far cry from the Messiah they expected.

Jesus was a maverick. He liked to "go against the flow" or "be independent in his thoughts and actions." (www.freeonlinedictionary.com) He was *in* this world but not *of* this world. He absolutely did not care what others thought of him and what the rules of society were. The ultimate free spirit throughout his ministry, He lived His life within His own parameters and answered to no one but His Heavenly Father. He sought those who possessed hearts that were inclined to listen, learn, believe, accept, and obey.

Sounds like Mary's son through and through, doesn't he? Who else but Mary could have understand, loved, supported and encouraged a son such as Jesus? She was an unmarried woman who had become pregnant before she lost her virginity. She was a married woman who would never be able to satisfy society's standards for how she *should have* done things. Mary understood the commitment involved when God specifically called a person: as a result of her heart of obedience she had witnessed things that no one before or since could imagine.

If ever someone faced opposition and hatred, Christ did. Just like Mary, his earthly life was ripe with reasons to hesitate, quit, hide, or run in the opposite direction. But He forged ahead and completed the difficult task assigned to Him because of His great love for us.

Jesus did not care about race, religion, social status, sex, physical capabilities, or even age. He dismissed anyone who told Him He couldn't, shouldn't, wouldn't, and mustn't. He said clearly and unequivocally that, *"Humanly speaking, it is impossible. But with God everything is possible."* (Matthew 19:26) That's pretty clear isn't it? He was talking *miracles,* unexplained occurrences, events that appeared inexplicable by the laws of nature. He was saying it won't make sense to your brain or the world in general, but it still will happen.

Jesus was the human, visible, earthly version of what God had been demonstrating throughout the Old Testament. God's message, as was Jesus', is *stop listening to the world, stop judging yourself by the world's standards, stop restricting yourself based on your human level of understanding, and step out on faith and believe what I've been saying all along:* I want you to be Mine.

Q?

What are the roadblocks that keep others from committing, trusting, and believing with child-like abandon?

Satan … What's he up to now?

When we think about the Christmas story, we think of Mary and Joseph in the stable, angels dancing across the sky, shepherds quaking in fear and then kneeling in wonder … but we rarely think of Satan, do we? And yet, at the moment of Jesus' birth in Bethlehem, the battle gloves were thrown down in challenge. Here then was going to be the final showdown. While Jesus went through his earthly life of growing up into adulthood, Satan was no doubt scrambling to spin the final webs of confrontation and deceit.

God tried setting down boundaries in The Garden. "Don't touch or eat this." We blew that. (Let's cut Adam and Eve a break and assume some of the responsibility. Do you really think you would have done a better job?)

> ## Q?
> In what areas of your life are you the easiest in which Satan is able to tempt, weaken, cause doubt, lose confidence, and become impatient? How is recognizing these areas helpful to you?

Then God tried setting down rules and commandments to give us an opportunity to achieve goodness and purity all on our own. (Hey, we weren't willing to follow His garden rules because we obviously thought we knew better. God gave us a chance to prove our ability … or inability.) We know how successful we've all been with the Ten Commandments.

God made a promise to Eve in The Garden, and reaffirmed that same promise repeatedly over the following centuries. Jesus spent approximately thirty-three years here on earth living an exemplary life and then, obediently, followed through with The One True God's design: leaving the last and final opportunity for us to get back on the right track.

Or, in other words, give us one more opportunity to fix our hearts.

Do you think, on the day after Christ's crucifixion and death as the disciples hid in the upper room, devastated and afraid, that Satan was doing the victory dance? If Satan had known all along that Jesus was going to be triumphant over death, would Satan *have even bothered?* If Satan had suspected the planned resurrection in three days, wouldn't he have tried something else to ensure his ultimate success? Wasn't Christ's resurrection and subsequent ministry *after* His earthly demise that much more powerful because of the course of events - from crucified criminal to miraculously resurrected Lord? I believe that at the moment of Christ's death on the cross Satan thought he had won the fight.

> **At the cross, did Mary feel that all she had gone through had been in vain? Or, had she understood all along the cost of obedience and the worth of sacrifice for Who you love?**
> McG

Talk about underestimating your enemy.

Could it be that the reason for all of Jesus' parables and sometimes cryptic comments was so that Satan would not have been any more wise than the disciples? Could it be that the disciples, with their right hearts, understood *even more* than Satan? *And we know that the Son of God has come, and he has given us understanding so that we can know the true God.* (I John 5:20a)

Whoa. That's an incredible concept. Could it be that Satan's deceptions and lies are the extent of his power?

If Satan ran around in a big red suit with a pointed tail and a pitchfork he'd be so easy to recognize and avoid, wouldn't he? But he's the great deceiver. He watches and learns. He's smart, calculating, and driven. He's got a pretty good handle on the human nature and he's got a personal file on each one of us to add in specific details. He's a master at blurring boundaries, compromising values, and graying out the distinctive lines of right and wrong. Depending upon the strength of our hearts, we either are easy, moderate or difficult prey.

Q?

If you could ask God ONE question, what would it be? If God could ask you one question, what do you think it would be?

Whatever you do, don't underestimate *your* enemy.

How do you qualify? Do you fill your heart with godly thoughts, surround your life with godly people, and reinforce your personal boundaries with daily prayer and devotions? Is Satan likely to pass you by because you're too difficult to tempt and trick, or does he love to stop and visit you for a simple conquest? While friends and family can surround you with prayer and words of wisdom, what you have at the center of your heart determines your final status.

Are you His or are you his? There is no middle ground. You are either with one or the other. Please understand this: Satan doesn't need you to be evil personified, he is completely victorious if he just keeps you from not doing the job that God wants you to do.

You could read the Bible from cover to cover and would not find a single individual who started out strong, powerful, and confident and *succeeded* in a life pleasing to God. What you *would* find consistently is the "underdog" succeeding against impossible odds. I love how Rick Warren said it in his book *A Purpose Driven Life*, "Abraham was old, Jacob was insecure, Leah was unattractive, Joseph was abused, Moses stuttered, Gideon was poor, Samson was codependent, Rahab was immoral, David had an affair and all kinds of family problems, Elijah was suicidal, Jeremiah was depressed, Jonah was reluctant, Naomi was a widow, John the Baptist was eccentric to say the least, Peter was impulsive and hot-tempered, Martha worried a lot, the Samaritan woman had several failed marriages, Zacchaeus was unpopular, Thomas had doubts, Paul had poor health, and Timothy was timid. What excuse have you been using?"

What *is* your excuse for not stepping up to your godly responsibilities? I guarantee that any reason you come up with is already illustrated and blasted to pieces in the Bible. The only thing that is stopping you from being a productive, viable member of Christ's team here on earth is yourself. He needs you right now, exactly where you are in your life. You are there by His design and grace. He's letting you make all the decisions, because that's what a loving parent does, but He's ever hopeful that at some point that you'll turn to Him and ask for some advice and guidance. He desires a personal relationship with you so that He can begin to use you for His glory and goodness. He wants to take complete possession of your heart *right now*.

Why waste any more valuable time? All he needs is a personal invitation from you to enter your heart, take control and get started.

New Testament Women and Us ... Are we really that different?

Just as the Old Testament was filled with women like us, so is the New Testament. However, the New Testament women had additional struggles. They had to battle discrimination, the power of old traditions that simply wouldn't die, the hesitancy to forge new paths, and the ever present group of people waiting to point a finger in smug criticism. Given the commission by Christ to go out and preach the Gospel, the astonishing reality is that WE are the New Testament women! Shake hands with Mary Magdalene, who struggles even today with a reputation of having been a whore, when in reality she was cured of demon possession. (Luke 8:2) Give a smile to Priscilla who was a victim of prejudice, which forced her from home because of her faith. (Acts 18:2) Bless Joanna who while she lived in the most evil of places – Herod's palace – managed to support Jesus' ministry with her own funds. (Luke 8:3) Be in awe of the widow who was so destitute that she had only two pennies to give in offering at the temple. (Mark 12:42) Each of these women overcame momentous obstacles to make God smile. These women are our sisters in Christ.

If it hasn't already sunk in yet, then let me say it one more time: God needs *nothing* but a right heart to accomplish *everything* that needs to be done. Earthbound barriers, physical restrictions, and cultural obstacles are completely useless against the God who created the universe. The single restricting barrier is YOU.

> **Happily ever after was never part of your life's story … Obediently ever after is.**
> McG

There is another quality that is readily available to each one of us: the ability to be chosen for great things. To be called for a mighty purpose. Used for an eternal example. Every one of us has the potential for this distinguished service.

Or not.

I can hear you saying, "I don't want to!" "I don't want to be an example!" Yeah, me too. I really don't think that *any* of the women we've read about so far would have chosen the difficult path she lived had she been given the opportunity. Have you ever heard anyone wish, "Oh, I'd like the opportunity to experience the untimely death of my spouse so that I can set a wonderful example for all those who get to watch." *Yeah, sure.*

The point is that when hard times happen they give us the opportunity to grow: in relationship with God, in personal strength, and in influence. If we succeed in the "test," we move to a higher level. If we fail, we are given another opportunity. *That is the purpose of our lives:* to please God, to glorify God, to worship God, and to obey God. Sorry, if you thought it was gaining the most fame, money, or toys … it's time you knew the truth.

For all of you Marys out there ...

So your faith is nothing like Mary's, you're surrounded by people nothing like Joseph and Elizabeth, and Satan stops by your place so often you feel like he's got your phone number on speed dial. What's a girl to do?

Just as God put things in place for Mary before the angel Gabriel made his announcement, He has done the same for you. What and whom do you have on your side? What precious things are in your life that others cannot claim? Remember, Mary didn't have *a lot* of things on her side, but what she did have was priceless. *May He equip you with all you need for doing His will. May He produce in you, through the power of Jesus Christ, every good thing that is pleasing to Him.*

> **You should be known for the beauty that comes from within, the unfading beauty of a gentle and quiet spirit, which is so precious to God.**
> I Peter 3:4

(Hebrews 13:21)

Don't do *anything more* until you begin to pray. Your prayers may be casual, even tentative at first, but you *must* begin. Praying for the right thing can be tricky. Think of it this way: if we don't know the whole picture and God does, how can we presume to ask Him to do specific things in regard to our lives? Seeking *God's will* as you pray is almost as critical as the action of praying. I try, no matter how desperate I may be, always to preface each prayerful request with, "If it is Your will, Lord ..." and then make my requests. I pray all the time for "big, black arrows and no gray areas," because I'm rather dense and preoccupied as I make my way through life and may miss God's subtle little signs or not hear His still, small voice. So just spray paint a big black arrow, Lord, and I'll follow. "I'll go anywhere You want me to go, Lord. Just make the way clear."

And remember, God says "No" as well as "Yes." Big plan not work out that you were counting on? Try viewing that as God saying, "The plan was not worthy to pursue." The 'perfect man' suddenly confesses he's been embezzling his company for years, but would you keep his secret? Try realizing that God thinks he's not as perfect as you think he is. Traffic so bad you're going to miss your flight? Try believing that if God wants you on that plane, a little bit of traffic is going to stop you. Here are some other prayer request suggestions.

Prayer Requests Regarding Youself In General:

❖ Pray for a heart that's focused on God.

❖ Pray for personal strength in being committed to God and all of His Promises.

❖ Pray for the ability to hear God's still small voice when He gives you His guidance regarding your relationships. (And remember, God says, "No," as well as "Yes". We often tend to only want to hear the affirmative answers.)

❖ Pray that you *will listen* and *obey* God's still small voice if and when you do hear it. (That's definitely the hardest part.)

❖ Pray for a strong sense of self and the ability to recognize and appreciate all your God-given talents and abilities. (In Other Words: Be strong. Don't settle. Appreciate the unique person that you are.)

> **Prayer is a subversive act performed in a world that constantly calls faith into question.**
> Philip Yancey

❖ Pray that God will surround you with solid, dependable, faithful friends.

❖ Pray for godly influences from friends, family, and acquaintances.

❖ Pray for a discerning spirit: that means you can pick out the good and avoid the bad.

Prayer Requests Regarding Past Relationships:

❖ Pray that you will learn from past relationship mistakes so that you won't repeat the lessons.

❖ Pray for the ability to objectively see both the good and the bad you must take responsibility for.

❖ Pray for the ability to *let go* of feelings and emotions that will hinder your progress.

❖ Pray for forgiveness for the times when you fell short of the standard God requires.

Prayer Requests Regarding Future Relationships:

❖ Pray for someone who will love you as much as you love them.

❖ Pray for Big Black Arrows that lead you in the right direction.

❖ Pray to be surrounded by others who will champion all the good qualities you have and compliment those areas in where you are weakest.

❖ Pray for a strong conviction that there is a perfect person out there for you that the Lord will send to you at The Perfect Time.

❖ Pray that you will be patient as you wait for The Perfect Person, using your time wisely to make yourself stronger and more faithful towards God's will.

❖ Pray for the Lord to send you opportunities to meet people He wants you to meet, befriend, and become involved with.

❖ Pray that the Lord will surround you with people intelligent in His wisdom.

Prayer Requests Regarding Your Current Relationships:

❖ Pray that the Lord will give you wisdom in words and deeds.

❖ Pray that your commitment to the Lord and the person He wants you to be will be pleasingly evident to all who know you.

❖ Pray that your partner will seek to be as close relationed to the Lord as you are.

❖ Pray that you will have a deep insight into your partner's moods and actions that will lead to understanding.

❖ Pray for opportunities to communicate with your partner.

❖ Pray for positive changes in you that will enrich and enhance your relationships.

❖ Pray that you learn from past mistakes and have the wisdom and insight to forge ahead positively.

❖ Pray for the ability to forgive and forget.

❖ Pray for the opportunity to learn something new about your partner.

❖ Pray for renewal in your love.

Homework ... What are your top five prayer requests?

Take a few minutes to list the top five things you would like to prayerfully request of God *if it is His will.* What five key changes in your life would improve your life so that you could become closer to and more productive for The One True God? (When you think about your requests this way, it's hard to ask for a brand new Ferrari, isn't it?)

Please Lord, if it is Your will, I ask for the following five things.

#1	
#2	
#3	
#4	
#5	

Question To Discuss:

Q?

How was your performance during your defining
moments of life?
Are you an example of success?

Wherever your treasure is, there the desires of your heart will also be.
Matthew 6:21

The Heart Of The Matter

A Heart Committed To God

Every relationship in your life, past, present, and future, is directly related to the state of your heart. The state of your heart is the very essence of who you are as an individual. Who you are as an individual is matchless, one of a kind. The unique person that you are is precisely designed and carefully and specifically created by God. God does not make mistakes.

> The human heart feels things the eyes cannot see, and knows what the mind cannot understand.
> Robert Valett

Hmmm. Where have you heard that before?

Exactly the person you are *today* is exactly the person God needs and can use to His greater glory. He doesn't need us to be perfect. He simply needs us to be willing and obedient.

The Bible is full of women just like you. Women who had stunning successes and unbelievable failures. Women who got the job done … regardless. Women who never thought they were good enough, strong

enough, talented enough, or smart enough, but in reality were *just perfect.*
Women who were unloved and unappreciated by their husbands but found
to be *priceless* by the One Who Mattered Most. Women who were
depressed, anxious, and unhappy, and yet still found the strength to look
and step *forward.* Women who had such huge
skeletons in their closets that it should have
completely consumed them, but instead were
able to *rise above it all.* Women who had
wishes that never came true and dreams that
ceased to exist, but found hope that was
incomparable to anything on this earth.
Women who made such poor choices that
their lives were permanently and irrevocably

> The best and most
> beautiful things in
> the world cannot
> be seen or even
> touched - they
> must be felt with
> the heart.
> Helen Keller

altered, and yet still counted themselves in the end as successes. Women
who got fed up with waiting, wanting, and never getting, but who never
stopped believing, trusting, or hoping. Women who were powerless and
unable to control the direction of their lives, yet came to understand where
True Authority and Power lay. Women whom the world abused, rejected,
and considered absolutely worthless, and yet God considered them *priceless.*
Women whom God chose not because of their beauty, might, wisdom, or
skill but because of their *hearts.*

God chooses people who listen, obey, believe, trust, and have the
courage to step out on faith. *In fact,* God seems to regularly delight in
choosing The Least Likely Candidates for every job: a woman like Eve
who made The Biggest Of All Mistakes to produce His ultimate Victor
Jesus Christ: a barren woman like Sarah to be the mother of His chosen
race, a whore like Rahab to be His heroine, a worthless, rejected widow like
Tamar to make the choice His chosen man wouldn't make, an unloved wife
like Leah to carry on His privileged line, a victim of abuse and murder like
Bathsheba to be His champion, and a young, poor unmarried girl to be the
mother of His Son ...

God's still operating in the same contradictory style. His goal is to
be the center of your life – the desire of your heart – and in doing so to
turn your failures and disappointments into His victories and His successes.

Are you ready? Willing? Able? Are you listening? Seeking? Obeying? Are you believing? Faithful? Trusting?

It all starts with the condition of your heart …

First Things First

Scripture references you should check out:	Psalm 37:5-6
Question to ask yourself before you read any further:	To whom or what are you committed?
What the word means:	"Commit" means to bind or obligate, to consign for future use, to place officially in custody, to entrust … which leads to a … "Covenant" which is a binding agreement, a law, a promise …
Connections:	What or whom are you committed to in your life? Whom or what have you bound your life to? Is it your job? Your family? Your hobby? Your friends? Does The One True God fit into your picture as an afterthought or as the title page?
What the Bible says about commitment (and covenants):	**God's:** Psalm 105:8 **Our's:** I Timothy 3:9 **Communion:** I Corinthians 11:24b-26 **Jesus':** Romans 11:27 **Benefits:** Psalm 25:10 **Caution:** Psalm 74:20 **Guarantees:** Psalm 111:9

Questions You Must Work To Know The Answers To:

I asked you these questions at the beginning of this book. Now I'll ask them again. The issue isn't really if you *can* answer them. The issue is *are you brave enough* to honestly admit the answers.

❖ Can you pinpoint a moment in your life, upon making a decision to commit to Christ, that you felt new?

❖ Who is the ultimate authority in your life? Whom would you risk your life with and for?

245

❖ What are your strengths?

❖ What are your weaknesses?

❖ What are your interests, God-given talents and abilities?

❖ What is more important to you: God's will or your will?

❖ Are good things really worth the wait?

❖ Are many of the difficulties in your life end results of choices you wish you hadn't made in the first place?

The Core Point

Over the course of our lives we hook up with a lot of people: family, friends, colleagues, and lovers. Each and every one of them influences us as we grow and mature. We allow ourselves to be influenced by these relationships and in some cases we become completely consumed. We learn about love, hate, sorrow, joy, deception, trust, jealousy, and forgiveness.

How we deal with the people and circumstances of our lives depends on who we are at our core, our center, our *heart*. Each of these women we have read about: Eve, Sarah, Tamar, Leah, Rahab, Bathsheba and Mary were examples of women who, although not perfect, were pleasing to God. They went about their daily lives with their various trials and tribulations, and they chose to allow God to be the primary person they hooked up with. In doing so, they did not guarantee themselves a happily ever after life, but they did guarantee themselves a life filled with godly purpose, design and triumph.

> **I am not complaining about having too little. I have learned to be satisfied with whatever I have.**
> Philippians 4:11 CEV

Is there anyone you know other than God who you would feel secure in trusting *everything* to? Everything including your past secrets, your future dreams, your most important hopes, your darkest failures, your most precious loves, and your deepest worries?

Do you feel so much more powerful or more knowledgeable than God so that you feel secure making decisions on your own rather than with His guidance?

Can you honestly say that your performance thus far in this "test of life" has been so stellar that you feel there is no room for improvement?

Are you so strong and so self-confident as you need to be, so that there is nothing in your life you fear or you believe you cannot handle?

Are you content with your life and the way it is unfolding, secure in the knowledge that it cannot be any better?

Do you have no curiosity regarding the ultimate destinies that God has for you and those you love?

I have recounted to you over these few hundred pages, sometimes with tongue-in-cheek sarcasm and humor, the ups and downs of seven biblical women. How would your story look in print? Would people smile, roll their eyes and yet, in the end, feel uplifted and inspired by your triumphs? Or, unfortunately, is your story the kind that others must learn from by examining all your mistakes and missed opportunities? You are in either one category or the other.

Q?
What justification do committed Christians give for believing and trusting in The One True God?

The precious gift of free will given to Adam and Eve in The Garden, is still with us today. With belief in Christ at the center of our hearts, our free will is guided toward choices that lead toward perfection in knowing God, patience in all our life experiences, self-confidence when faced with evil temptation and doubt, strength when we face trials and tribulations, trust in the wisdom of the choices we make, and obedience to the One Who Knows Best.

Can you imagine living a life any better than that?

For all of you out there ...

This book has been a labor of love for me.

Without God, I am a shy, introverted, insecure woman who feels that she's never pretty enough, smart enough, clever enough, or strong enough to be much good to anyone. Without God I would have gotten pregnant before I made it out of high school, been divorced more than once, and become a bitter, reclusive woman.

With God, I have learned to battle my personal demons. I still quake with fear before I do something public like speaking before the church, conducting a training session for my peers, or presenting my written works to curious strangers. But I do it because I know, without a shadow of a doubt, that once I get up there, magic happens with my words and thoughts and I become this coherent, intelligent woman. With God, I had the wisdom to say no to the wrong men and yes to my wonderful husband David allowing me to be part of a relationship that has made me effective in my gifts and even successful in spite of my weaknesses. With God, I enjoyed a successful career in teaching despite conventional wisdom and advice that told me to try another career with more opportunities and better pay. I believe I make a difference in this world that pleases God when I use my talent of teaching. Now I soldier on with wonder and awe in this writing career as I obediently follow God's big black arrows. I feel God's hand on the small of my back when I hesitate, I delight in the warmth of His smile when I get things right now and then, and I run and hide with Him in prayer when it seems the world is winning.

I. Am. Never. Alone.

With God, I am a capable, outspoken, confident woman who feels she's been blessed with God's grace and strengthened by God's guidance.

Much of my strong faith is rooted in personal Bible study, and much of my personal Bible study has been spent studying the men and women of the Bible. I have learned more about my faith and my God through the biblical men and women who have gone before me than any other way. These men and women with their successes and failures, triumphs and disasters, joys and sorrows speak to me, a flawed Christian woman who still regularly doubts herself and her abilities. *How* could God really want *me*? *What* could He possibly accomplish with *me* when there are so many other more imminently qualified people available? *Why* does He love *me* when all I ever seem to do is get it wrong, mess things up, and miss the key point?

In studying these people, I began to delight in their flaws because it made their victories so much more spectacular. Somewhere along the line I began to realize that my imperfect, bumbling self was *exactly* what God was probably looking for. Let's face it: God will *really shine* if He can make a success out of me!

Please, please, *please* the next time you think "I can't," or "I never," or "It's impossible for me," ... instead of letting those thoughts draw you down into the pit of unaccomplishment, take a minute. Say a quiet prayer for strength and confidence and then let yourself ... smile a bit. Look up to your Lord, take a deep breath in preparation, and say, "I'm game if You are!"

Hook up with The One who really counts and all the rest will fall into place. I guarantee it.

Homework ... What's your story?

Imaging I'm writing *your* story for this book ... except, it's not done. I've told all about your good points and have had grand fun outlining all of your bad. I've come up with impressive quotes that pinpoint sensitive areas and found some Bible verses that really hit the center of things. But how will your story end? How will your story be the success God wants it to be? Perhaps this very second is a defining moment for you. What will your chapter title be? What kind of heart will you leave the world remembering? Who will you hook up with in the end?

Question To Think About:

Q?

Which of the women we
have discussed
impressed you the most?
Why?

A PERFECT HEART

LOVES: Matthew 22:37

Love the Lord your God with all your heart and with all your soul and with all your mind.

LEARNS: Colossians 2:17

Let your roots grow down into him, and let your lives be built on him. Then your faith will grow strong in the truth you were taught, and you will overflow with thankfulness.

PRAYS: Jeremiah 33:3b (MSG)

Call to me and I will answer you. I'll tell you marvelous and wondrous things that you could never figure out on your own.'

OBEYS: I John 2:5

But those who obey God's word truly show how completely they love him. That is how we know we are living in him.

BELIEVES: Acts 16:31a

Believe in the Lord Jesus and you will be saved.

RECEIVES: Revelation 3:20

Listen! I am standing and knocking at your door. If you hear my voice and open the door, I will come in and we will eat together.

TELLS: Mark 16:15

Go into all the world and preach the good news to all creation.

TREASURES: Matthew 6:20-21

Store your treasures in heaven, where moths and rust cannot destroy, and thieves do not break in and steal. Wherever your treasure is, there the desires of your heart will also be.

Bibliography

WEBSITES

www.despair.com

www.biblegateway.com

www.reallivepreacher.com

www.associatedcontent.com

www.wikipedia.com

www.thefreedictionary.com

www.bibleinfo.com

www.religionfacts.com

www.carm.com (Christian Apologetics & Research Ministry)

www.wcg.org

QUOTED PEOPLE

Oswald Chambers

Robert Valett

Blaise Pascal

C. S. Lewis

Mahatma Gandhi

Rick Warren

Catherine Cameron, 1965

Ovid 34 B.C.

Gustavus F. Swift, 1839-1903

John Ortberg

Reverend Doctor Todd Buurstra

Eleanor Roosevelt

Ralph Waldo Emerson

Reverend Billy Graham

William James

Dr. W. A. Criswell

Alice Walker

Rousseau

Philip Yancey

Tertullian (155-220 A.D.)

Martin Luther King

Helen Keller

James Hurley

Marylynn Oudheusden

Herbert Oudheusden

BIBLE TRANSLATIONS

MSG: *The Message*, By Eugene H. Peterson, Copyright 2002, Navpress

NLT: *New Living Translation Life Application Study Bible*, By Tyndale Charitable Trust, Copyright 2004, Tyndale House Publishers

NIV: *New International Version*, By International Bible Society, Copyright 1973, 1978, 1984

NKJV: *The New King James Version*, By Thomas Nelson, Inc., Copyright 1982

ASV: *The American Standard Version*, The Lockman Foundation, Zondervan Publishers, Copyright 1995

KJV: *The King James Version*, Public Domain, Zondervan Publishers

CEV: *Contemporary English Version*, American Bible Society, Copyright 1995

ST: Sue Translation – Please Pardon My Irreverence!!! ☺

SONGS

ARTIST: 10 CC, SONG TITLE: *The Things We Do for Love* ALBUM: Alive

ARTIST: Michael Card, SONG TITLE: *They Called Him Laughter* ALBUM: The Beginning

ARTIST: Carly Simon, SONG TITLE: *You're So Vain* COPYRIGHT: 1972 by Quackenbush Music, Ltd.

ARTIST: Willie Nelson, SONG TITLE: *On The Road Again* ALBUM: On The Road Again

ARTIST: Nicole Nordeman, SONG TITLE: *Brave* ALBUM: Brave

ARTIST: Margaret Becker, et. al., SONG TITLE: *Jesus Draw Me Ever Nearer* ALBUM: New Irish Hymns COPYRIGHT: 2002 by Thankyou Music

ARTIST: Billy Joe Shaver, SONG TITLE: *I'm Just An Old Chunk Of Coal* ALBUM: I'm Just An Old Chunk Of Coal COPYRIGHT: Koch Records, 1998

ARTIST: Mark Lowry & Buddy Greene, SONG TITLE: *Mary, Did You Know?* COPYRIGHT: 1984

PUBLISHED REFERENCES

Amendment V (the Fifth Amendment) of the United States Constitution, which is part of the Bill of Rights. Adopted on September 17, 1787 by the Consitutional Convention in Philadelphia, Pennsylvania.

Susan Ackerman, *Warrior, Dancer, Seductress, Queen*, Doubleday, New York, 1998, ISBN: 0-385-48424-0

Oswald Chambers, *My Utmost For His Hightest*, Barbour Publishing, Uhrichsville, OH, 1963, ISBN: 1-57748-142-9

Antoine De Saint-Exupery, *The Little Prince*, Harcourt, Brace & World, New York, 1943, ISBN: 0-15-246503-0

Shiela Graham, *Jesus and Women, The Plain Truth*, July 1994, www.wcg.org

James Hurley, *Man and Woman in Biblical Presepective*, Zondervan, 1981

Herbert Lockyer, *All the Men of the Bible*, Lamplighter Books, Zondervan Publishing House, Grand Rapids, Michigan, 1958, ISBN: 0-310-28081-8

Herbert Lockyer, Sr., Editor, *Illustrated Dictionary of the Bible*, Thomas Nelson Publishers, Nashville, 1986, ISBN: 0-7852-1230-2

Victor H. Matthews and Don C. Benjamin, *Social World of Ancient Israel 1250-587 BCE*, Hendrickson Publishers, 1993, MA, ISBN: 0-913573-89-2

John Ortberg, *If You Want To Walk On Water, You've Got To Get Out Of The Boat*, Zondervan Publishers, Willow Creek Resources, Grand Rapids, Michigan, 2001, ISBN: 0-310-22863-8

J.I. Packer, *Illustrated Manners and Customs of the Bible*, M.C. Tenney, Editors, Thomas Nelson Publishers, Nashville, 1980, ISBN: 0-7852-1231-0

Lawrence O. Richards, *The Bible Reader's Companion*, Chariot Victor Publishing, Wheaton Illinois, Cook Communications, 1991, ISBN: 0-89693-039-4

Sue & Larry Richards, *Every Woman in the Bible*, Thomas Nelson Publishers, Nashville, TN, 1999, ISBN: 0-7852-1441-0

Larry Richards, *Every Man in the Bible*, Thomas Nelson Publishers, Nashville, TN, 1999, ISBN: 0-7852-1439-9

Hershel Shanks, Editor, *Ancient Israel*, Biblical Archaeology Society, Washington, D.C., 1999, ISBN: 1-880317-54-0

Eveylyn & Frank Stagg, *Women in the World of Jesus*, The Westminster Press, Philadelphia, PA, 1978, ISBN: 0-664-24195-6

Dorothy Valcarcel, *The Man Who Loved Women*, Winepress Publishing, Enumclaw, Washington, 2007, ISBN: 1-57921-878-4

Rick Warren, *A Purpose Driven Life*, By Rick Warren, Zondervan, Grand Rapids, Michigan, 2002, ISBN: 0-310-20571-9

Philip Yancey, *Prayer Does It Make Any Difference*, Zondervan, Grand Rapids, Michigan, ISBN: 978-0-310-27105-5

POEMS

The Deer's Cry, By St. Patrick, c. 390-461 A.D., Lorica of St. Patrick, http://www.maryjones.us/ctexts/lorica-e.html

SCRIPTURE VERSES QUOTED:

THE HEART OF THE MATTER:

- Ezekiel 36:26a
- I Samuel 16:7b
- Amos 4:13b
- 2 Corinthians 5:17

EVE:

- I Corinthians 2:9
- Deuteronomy 32:4
- I John 4:7-8
- Romans 8:28
- Psalm 57:1-3
- Psalm 32:1-3
- Isaiah 43:4
- Philippians 3:12-14
- Revelations 4:1

> **Take the time to underline every one of these verses in your Bible!!**
> McG

SARAH:

- Isaiah 41:8
- Genesis 15:6
- Psalm 34:8-9
- Hebrews 11:1
- Ecclesiastes 3:1
- Matthew 23:37b
- II Corinthians 10:15b

LEAH:

- Jeremiah 29:11
- Romans 16:19
- Psalm 44:21
- I Corinthians 2:9
- 3 John 1:4
- Proverbs 16:9
- Jeremiah 17:7

TAMAR:

- Exodus 4:22
- Proverbs 4:4-6
- Hebrews 11:1
- Psalm 44:21
- Philippians 4:6-7
- I Corinthians 14:33
- I Peter 1:6-7

RAHAB:

- Leviticus 20:24b
- Hebrews 11:31b
- Colossians 9:3-11
- Isaiah 43:4b
- Matthew 5:14
- Matthew 18:3-4
- Acts 16:31
- Ezekiel 36:26a

> **Take the time to underline every one of these verses in your Bible!!**
> McG

255

- Revelations 3:16
- Matthew 12:30

BATHSHEBA:

- Isaiah 26:4
- Isaiah 40:31
- Psalm 51:17b
- I Thessalonians 5:18
- Isaiah 61:3
- Joshua 1:5b
- Isaiah 26:3
- 2 Corinthians 4:16
- Psalm 51:7-10
- Proverbs 31:10-12

MARY:

- John 14:15
- Matthew 19:26
- I John 5:20a
- I Peter 3:4
- I Timothy 4:12
- Hebrews 13:21

YOU:

Take the time to
underline every
one of these
verses in your
Bible!!
McG

- Matthew 6:21
- Philippians 4:11
- Matthew 22:37
- Colossians 2:17
- Jeremiah 33:3b
- I John 2:5
- Acts 16:31a
- Revelation 3:20
- Mark 16:15
- Matthew 6:20-21

About The Author

Susan McGeown is a wife, mother, daughter, sister, friend, aunt, uncle (don't ask), teacher, author … but, most importantly, a "woman after God's own heart." Living in Bridgewater, New Jersey, with her husband of over fifteen years and their three children, writing stories is just about the best way she can imagine spending her free time. Each of Sue's stories champions those emotions nearest and dearest to her: faith, joy, hope and love.

Philippians 1:20-21

For I fully expect and hope that I will never be ashamed, but that I will continue to be bold for Christ, as I have been in the past. And I trust that my life will bring honor to Christ, whether I live or die. For to me, living means living for Christ, and dying is even better.

www.ingramcontent.com/pod-product-compliance
Lightning Source LLC
Chambersburg PA
CBHW021047090426
42738CB00006B/228